Amatterofdesign™
It's a matter of Editorial Design

Amatterofdesign™
It's a matter of Editorial Design

Published and distributed in Europe
and Latin America by

INDEX BOOK

Index Book S.L.
Consell De Cent 160 Local 3 08015 Barcelona Spain
Phone: +34 93 4545547 / +34 93 4548755 Fax: +34 93 4548438
Email: ib@indexbook.com URL: www.indexbook.com

viction:ary™

Published and distributed for
the rest of the world by viction:workshop

Rm2202 22/Floor Kinsfield Centre
18-20 Shell Street North Point Hong Kong
URL: www.victionary.com Email: we@victionary.com

Edited and produced by viction:workshop

Book design by viction:design workshop
Art direction by Victor Cheung

© 2004 viction:workshop
The copyright on the individual texts and design work is held by the respective designers and contributors.

ISBN 84-89994-99-4

All rights reserved. No part of this publication may be reproduced, stored in retrieval systems or transmitted in any form or by any means, electronic or mechanical, including photocopying, recording or any information storage and retrieval systems, without permission in writing from the copyright owner(s).

The captions and artwork in this book are based on material supplied by the designers whose work is included. While every effort has been made to ensure their accuracy, viction:workshop or Index Book S.L. do not under any circumstances accept any responsibility for any errors or omissions.

Printed and bound in Hong Kong

Contents

Introduction 004
It's all about readership 007
Interview #01 / Deanne Cheuk 008
Interview #02 /
Jop van Bennekom 016
Section one 023
Printed materials made to last 093
Interview #03 / Sagmeister Inc. 094
Interview #04 / Flink 102
Section two 109
Contributors 189
Acknowledgements /
Future Editions 192

Pg.04 / Introduction

Editors and art directors may be constantly waging a war against one another, but they do share a common goal: to present information in the best possible light. Design is not just about making something look pretty, nor is it simply about the measure of usability. Editorial design combines craft and creativity, functioning as the building block upon which an argument is based and a conclusion is drawn.

The symbiotic relationship between editorial and design can be easily illustrated with the coffee table book. To somebody unfamiliar with publishing, the phrase 'coffee table' might seem a strange precursor to the word 'book'. Why don't we have the 'bedroom nightstand book', or the 'kitchen cabinet book'? Or even the 'bathroom shelf book'?

It may be simplistic, but we call a book a coffee table book because it is something that was created to be seen in varied ways, as you would an object lying on a coffee table. We want it to be looked at both closed and open, at rest and flicked through, in passing and in depth. We are referring to a book that is highly functional.

Coffee table books focus mainly on the more attractive subjects of art, photography, architecture, illustration and design. But the fact that a book 'looks good' should not in any way weaken the content of a 'good book.' One must never forget that a concept must first be worth publishing before even thinking about the design. For if it is truly successful, a coffee table book must be capable of serving as a conversational piece. The content must have some validity to the reader, because oftentimes a coffee table book can almost be seen a status symbol. Some of the time mere ownership makes the buyer even feel intelligent or hip.

And so we aim to have the perfect balance of editorial substance and design co-existing within the ideal 'coffee table book.' We have a book that looks the look and talks the talk.

There is an extremely entertaining episode (number 74) of the American sitcom *Seinfeld* where Kramer, a regular fixture in the series, comes up with an idea for the ultimate book: a coffee table book about coffee tables that physically turns into a coffee table! Elaine, another regular character on the show, doesn't think this is such a great idea but her company loves it and some episodes later (number 86), Kramer presents the book on morning television. This concept worked so well as a fictional piece that it is even rumoured there will soon be a *Coffee Table Book* in real life, made of wood and incorporating *Seinfeld* episodes, photographs and memorabilia.

Most books don't have to reach this level of complexity to be something that looks good and is useful. However, some do (and these are much more fun to talk about). A number of ambitious publications have recently been released that challenge the relationship between design and content, by packaging an extraordinary concept with revolutionary execution. Most notably there is *G.O.A.T.: A Tribute to Muhammad Ali* published in 2004 by Taschen (with art direction by Benedikt Taschen and the design agency SenseNet, who are based in Cologne). If you are not familiar with *G.O.A.T,* here are some vital statistics: there are 780 pages and over 3,000 images; the dimensions are 26.5 x 27 inches, not to mention a depth of 10.5 inches. At a retail price of $3,000, this book is for true aficionados only – there were only 10,000 copies printed (1,000 of which are special 'Champs editions' that retail for $7,500).

Another example of the sublime is a book released last year, apparently the largest publication ever produced. The book is entitled *Bhutan: A Visual Odyssey Across the Last Himalayan Kingdom.* This 60 x 44 inch monster, also 6 inches thick, is the brainchild of Michael Hawley and is produced in association with MIT and Friendly Planet. Only 500 copies will ever be printed on demand, with all profits from the $10,000 price tag donated to charity. That is almost $100 a page. While an interesting concept, it is questionable just how many people would welcome an 133-pound book in their own home.

Whether it is the biggest tome on record, or a miniature book that fits into the palm of your hand (as deftly illustrated in the pages that follow), a book can come in all shapes and sizes. But more often than not, publishers and corporate clients face many issues when it comes to producing books. Size is very important, as bookshelves are made to certain specifications and when not lying on coffee tables, a book must fit to be stocked on a shelf. From a retail standpoint, whenever size or weight is a concern, shipping is also an issue. Not to mention binding, paper, colour – the list goes on.

These limitations all contribute to what could easily become the generic formatting of many coffee table books. The same can be said of magazines and other printed publications. After sifting through dozens of magazine racks containing hundreds of titles, you begin to understand the dilemma. So how does something stand out from the crowd without having to become either highly expensive, a large format, or hard to buy? Without having, or being in itself, a gimmick?

This book is the third instalment of Index Book's new Amatterofdesign™ series. In this volume the focus is editorial design, primarily exploring books, magazines and periodical publications. The intent is not to instruct or survey, but to spark the reader's imagination and provide inspiration through numerous real-world design practices and the use of design basics.

Included are contemporary samples of work from Europe, the United States and Asia. On top of covering the celebrated work from some of the most well-known and popular design firms from around the world, the Amatterofdesign™ series also explores the fresh ideas and examples from up-and-coming designers.

Boldly illustrated, the following pages will demonstrate how editorial boundaries are creatively pushed through both subtle and obvious design techniques. In some of these examples, a brief will allow the designer a level of freedom to achieve an extreme product like with the G.O.A.T. and Bhutan projects. In other instances you will be amazed with just how interesting a book can be under restrictive boundaries.

So even if at first glance most books and magazines appear to look the same, you will find that if a talented art director is involved, when you peel off the shrink-wrap you will soon discover just how intelligent and hip a printed publication can be.

It's all about readership

The first section of this book will focus on magazines, periodicals and catalogues. These formats are transient in nature: deadlines need to be hit and shelf lives are short. Usually the editorial content is highly functional and focused to satisfy the reader's needs or consumer's desires. The examples illustrated in the following pages feature some of the more inspiring design treatments in these traditionally market-led mediums.

Pg.8 / Interview #01 / Deanne Cheuk

Interview with Deanne Cheuk

Featured by The Face Magazine as one of the world's top 50 creatives, Deanne Cheuk comes from Perth in Western Australia where she graduated from Curtin University with a Bachelor of Arts Degree in Graphic Design and Photography. The *Canadian National Post* called her 'the fashion world's darling of the moment' while *Flaunt* Magazine also ranked her as 'a leader'. She has art directed 12 magazines including her self published *Mu*. Her clients are as diverse as *Tokion* magazine, Urban Outfitters and Levi's Strauss. She is the brainchild behind the widely acclaimed graphic 'zine *Neomu* which she compiles regularly.

Deanne moved to New York four years ago and has been living and working there since.

TITLE // Neomu
TYPE OF WORK // Book
CLIENT // Neomu
YEAR PRODUCED // --
ART DIRECTION // Deanne Cheuk
DESIGNER // Deanne Cheuk

DESCRIPTION OF WORK //
Deanne Cheuk calls it a 'graphic 'zine of inspiration' and 'the graphical progression' of her *Mu* Magazine. A big part of the idea of *Neomu* is to pass on inspiration from the contributors that are in it to the stores that sell it and then donate the money to the charities that benefit from it.

How did you start doing *Neomu*?

Neomu is something I publish – I call it a 'graphic 'zine of inspiration', others have called it a book or a magazine, but I like to call it a 'zine because I still think of it as this little thing I do when I have time. I started on the first issue in 2000. It came out at the beginning of 2001, it was 128 pages, 11 x 11cm, full colour and I had it printed in Perth with waterless printing. The idea came about after I moved to New York. I had ended my last magazine (*Mu* magazine) after 5 issues, but I still had all my contacts and I still had the publishing urge. I had friends e-mailing me saying 'when are we going to do something else together?' and I just kept thinking about it and decided I wanted to make a 'zine. It was originally going to be colour photocopied and just sent to my friends, but as I started planning, it just kept escalating. So finally I contacted a printer and asked what was the smallest size they could bind with Notch binding. That was how I came up with the size — I thought the size would make it cheaper to print, but it didn't! The concept of having just graphics/illustrations and no words came about because I didn't want to bother with editing stories this time (as I used to with *Mu* magazine). Also I was frustrated with design books being really overpriced for what I thought was just a few pages of good work. I really wanted to make something that was free and inspiring on every single page. I have also referred to *Neomu* as 'the graphical progression of *Mu*', as this was how the idea really came about. Since it came out, there have been many others who that have copied the idea of publishing just graphics/illustrations in the same way. Before *Neomu* came out, there was only *Tank* which published just photos. Now I feel like everyone is doing it or is trying to do it... This makes it harder to do each issue.

Could you describe what *Neomu* is?

With the first issue it was really just the work of friends or friends of friends; by the second issue word had spread about it and I knew maybe half of the contributors. With the latest issue, number 6, I think I only knew one or two of the contributors. It puts me in such a fortunate position – I get to see the work of all these young amazing artists and many of them have never been published before. I feel really lucky that they put the faith in me to 'judge' their work. So basically I put out a call for submissions by email and people send in their work. The last issue was 164 pages, with black-foiled cover, spot UV and varnished paper throughout. It gets picked up all over the place and a lot of the contributing artists have gotten magazine commissions or gallery requests for being in *Neomu*, so it has become almost a sourcebook of sorts which I think is great! I pay for the printing and distribution which I do myself; I send it to the stores for free and they sell it for $1 in that country's currency and I ask them to donate the money to a charity of their choice. A big part of the idea of *Neomu* is to pass on inspiration from the people that are in it to the stores that sell it and then donate the money to the charities that benefit from it.

What is your objective in doing *Neomu* and what do you expect from it?

Just to pass on inspiration. I had this idea a long time ago that I wanted to change the ideas of publishing and profitability. I don't know about the last statement anymore. I thought about that when I was a lot younger. I hadn't really thought of it again until just now actually!

Do you see any difference working as a designer in Australia and the US?

For me, yes. I came to New York thinking my work wasn't good enough, as I had never been recognized for it in Australia. I published my first magazine when I was 22 and yet I never got any press for it in Australia and for three years it was always such a battle. And then I came to New York with a folio full of club flyers I had done and a bunch of magazines and immediately I felt embraced and respected for everything I had done. It really was an incredible contrast!!!

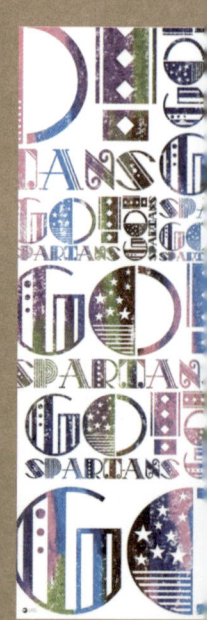

Interview #01 // Deanne Cheuk
Page 10/11

TITLE // Tokion Magazine
TYPE OF WORK // Magazine cover and inside spread
CLIENT // Tokion Magazine
YEAR PRODUCED // 2003/2004
ART DIRECTION // Deanne Cheuk
DESIGNER // Deanne Cheuk
PHOTOGRAPHER // ++++++ Julia Soilis

DESCRIPTION OF WORK //
116 page magazine, 9" x 10.875"
+ issue #39 cover ++ issue #38 cover
+++ issue #36 cover ++++ issue #40 inside spread
+++++ / ++++++ issue #41 inside spread

++++

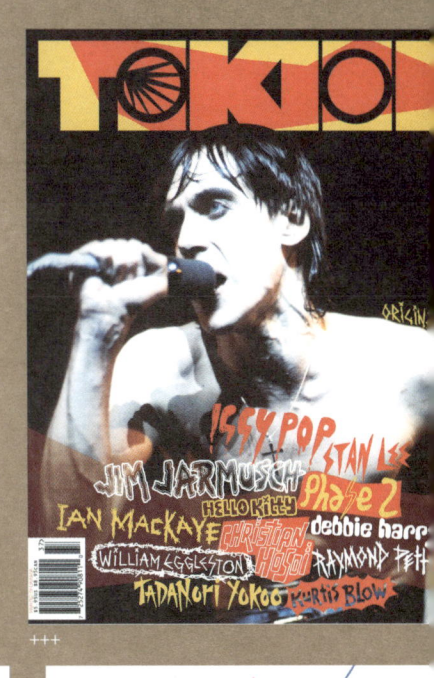

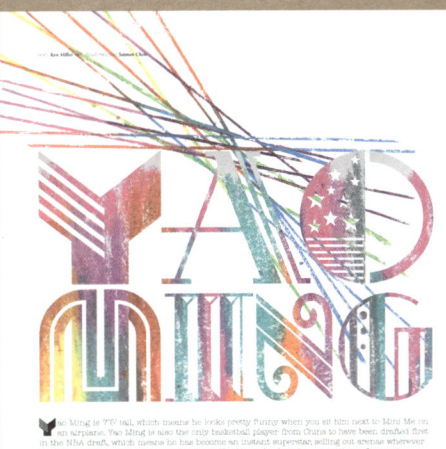

+
++
+++
++++
+++++
++++++

What do you think is the difference between handling magazine and book design?

The differences are probably the deadlines and editorial staff and considerations about the magazine readers and thoughts of not alienating them and all that rubbish. I hate that stuff actually... Though of course it was different when I did my own magazine, as I just did whatever I wanted!

For each magazine, what factors dictate its design decisions?

For all the magazines I have worked on, like *Big*, *Tokion*, *Mu* and *Surf in Rico*, I was allowed to do whatever I wanted, I've always had almost complete freedom in all of my work, so I am quite fortunate in that respect.

I am impressed by the various illustrations and typography in the *Tokion* layouts. How do you come up with the ideas when you start laying out an article?

I wish I knew, maybe I could do it faster then! It's just random, some pages I can do quickly, others I will lay out 10 times and still not be happy and then run out of time and have to use whatever... I place the text and images that I have and the rest comes from there. There is always movement on the pages, as this is something I incorporate into all my work.

Illustration has become an essential part of editorial design. How do you see this trend?

Illustration is something I do as well as art direction – though I only started it 4 years ago, it has definitely changed the way I work in terms of how I would approach a page I was designing or typography or anything. When I mentioned movement before, this came a lot from my illustrations and also from working with a lot of Surf clients when I worked with David Carson on Quiksilver and *Surf in Rico* magazine – the expressiveness and power of a wave and the ocean has been a big influence on my work.

Interview #01 // Deanne Cheuk
Page 12/13

TITLE // Tokion Magazine
TYPE OF WORK // Magazine inside spread
CLIENT // Tokion Magazine
YEAR PRODUCED // 2004
ART DIRECTION // Deanne Cheuk
DESIGNER // Deanne Cheuk
PHOTOGRAPHER // + Magnus Unnar
++ Katsuhide Morimoto

DESCRIPTION OF WORK //
Issue #41, 116 page magazine, 9" x 10.875".

Do you have any favourite artists/designers? What is it that you like about them?

Aquirax Uno, a Japanese artist from the 60's-70's. I was so blown away when I first saw his work and I still am. His use of colours and drawings are incredible. He is an obvious influence to a few well-known illustrators out there and I am amazed that he is never mentioned.

Do you think you have been influenced by him? If not, where comes the strongest influence on you and where do you seek inspiration from?

I was more influenced by the artists who were influenced by him, as I only came across his work really recently. Of course now I love him more! I don't look anywhere for inspiration as it is all around me; I can stare at a piece of string on the ground and get inspiration from that.

Are you satisfied with what you're doing now? What is the greatest satisfaction so far in your career?

Yes I love my work and everything I do. The greatest satisfaction so far is getting some acknowledgement for *Mu* magazine finally. It is great to meet and to hear from people that knew of it and wondered what happened with it!

Do you have any future projects to share with us?

My book, www.MushroomGirlsVirus.com and the clothing line I am spending a lot of time on now www.Liness.net

What kinds of publications do you usually read?

If I have time to read, I'll be engrossed in some crazy Philip K. Dick novel.

Finally, could you recommend some publications to our readers?

Tokion magazine of course, *Giant Robot, Beikoku Ongaku* magazine and *America* magazine, by one of my favourite art directors Graham Roundthwaite.

Photographer: **Magnus Unnar**
Stylist: **Jodie Barnes**
Hair: **Tomo Jidai**
Model: **Ekaterina** @ Idole Paris

love vigilante

halterneck top by **hussein chalayan**

PHOTOGRAPHER: **KATSUHIDE MORIMOTO** @ GUNN'S
STYLIST: **SHUNSUKE OKADA**
HAIR: **TETSU** @ SEAIKA MS OFFICE
MAKE-UP: **RIE SEKINE** @ FEMME
MODELS: **SACHI** & **CAROLINA** @ FEMME
PHOTO RETOUCH: **TAKAO SASAKI** @ CAPSULE WORLD TOKYO

CAROLINA wears jacket by VIVIENNE WESTWOOD GOLD LABEL

URBAN
OUT
FITT
ERS
GIFT 03
URBANOUTFITTERS.COM

URBAN
OUT
FITT
ERS
HOLIDAY 03
URBANOUTFITTERS.COM

URBAN
OUT
FITT
ERS
SPRING 04
URBANOUTFITTERS.COM

URBAN
OUT
FITT
ERS
SPRING 04
URBANOUTFITTERS.COM

Interview #01 // Deanne Cheuk
Page 14/15

TITLE // + Urban Outfitters Holiday 03 Catalog
        ++ Urban Outfitters Spring 04 Catalog
TYPE OF WORK // Catalog
CLIENT // Urban Outfitters
YEAR PRODUCED // + 2003
                ++ 2004
ART DIRECTION // Deanne Cheuk
DESIGNER // Deanne Cheuk
PHOTOGRAPHER // + Tom Betterton
                ++ Coliena Rentmeester

DESCRIPTION OF WORK //
60 page clothing and accessories catalog, 8" x 10.5".

Pg.16 / Interview #02 / Jop van Bennekom

Interview with Jop van Bennekom

Jop van Bennekom is an editor, art director, author, designer and strategist, as well as a publisher. He was born in Scherpenzeel, Netherlands in 1970 and graduated with an M.A. from the Jan van Eyck Academy in Maastricht. After college he started to examine the meaning and possibilities of the media, resulting in the creation of his own magazine titled *RE-* (later on re-named *Re-Magazine*). This experimental journal was established as a personal platform for communication and aimed at redefining the potential role of editorial design. Its appearance has changed many times and since *Re-Magazine* #9 each issue is about 'the life of one person'. The first issue sold only 50 copies, the fourth one jumped to 2,500. The latest issue #11 has already hit 10,000 and is distributed worldwide.

Bennekom has also briefly art directed at *Blvd.* magazine in 1998, but quit shortly afterwards to begin his own publishing. He designed the architecture magazine *Forum*, which won the Rotterdam Design Prize in 2001. That same year he launched his other internationally acclaimed gay magazine *BUTT*.

TITLE // Re-Magazine
  + #5 'Re-Connect'
  ++ #7 'Re-View'
  +++ #6 'The Information Trashcan'
  ++++ #9 'John'
TYPE OF WORK // Magazine
CLIENT // Re-Magazine
YEAR PRODUCED // 2000-2002
ART DIRECTION // Jop van Bennekom
DESIGNER // Jop van Bennekom

DESCRIPTION OF WORK //
Re-Magazine is an intersection of visual culture and editorial experimentation. Each issue is about the life of one person. *Re-magazine* is interested in stories about extreme personalities, people who make a difference.

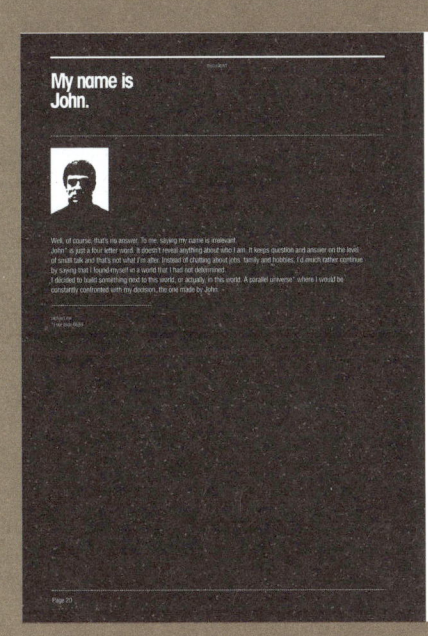

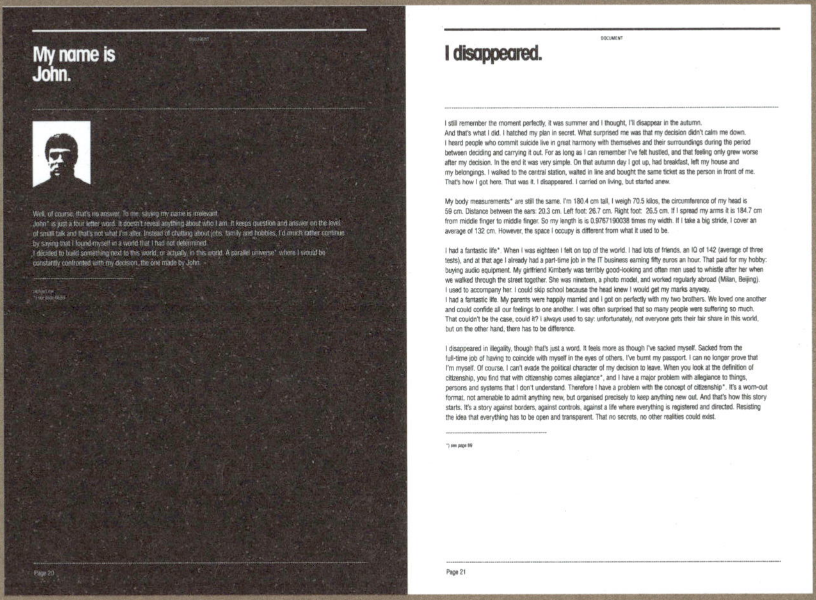

My name is John.

Well, of course, that's no answer. To me, saying my name is irrelevant. 'John' is just a four letter word. It doesn't reveal anything about who I am. It keeps question and answer on the level of small talk and that's not what I'm after. Instead of chatting about jobs, family and hobbies, I'd much rather continue by saying that I found myself in a world that I had not determined. I decided to build something next to this world, or actually, in this world. A parallel universe*, where I would be constantly confronted with my decision, the one made by John.

*see page 66 / I am John

I disappeared.

I still remember the moment perfectly. It was summer and I thought, I'll disappear in the autumn. And that's what I did. I hatched my plan in secret. What surprised me was that my decision didn't calm me down. I heard people who commit suicide live in great harmony with themselves and their surroundings during the period between deciding and carrying it out. For as long as I can remember I've felt hustled, and that feeling only grew worse after my decision. In the end it was very simple. On that autumn day I got up, had breakfast, left my house and my belongings. I walked to the central station, waited in line and bought the same ticket as the person in front of me. That's how I got here. That was it. I disappeared. I carried on living, but started anew.

My body measurements* are still the same. I'm 180.4 cm tall, I weigh 70.5 kilos, the circumference of my head is 59 cm. Distance between the ears: 20.3 cm. Left foot: 26.7 cm. Right foot: 26.5 cm. If I spread my arms it is 184.7 cm from middle finger to middle finger. So my length is is 0.9767190038 times my width. If I take a big stride, I cover an average of 132 cm. However, the space I occupy is different from what it used to be.

I had a fantastic life*. When I was eighteen I felt on top of the world. I had lots of friends, an IQ of 142 (average of three tests), and at that age I already had a part-time job in the IT business earning fifty euros an hour. That paid for my hobby: buying audio equipment. My girlfriend Kimberly was terribly good-looking and often men used to whistle after her when we walked through the street together. She was nineteen, a photo model, and worked regularly abroad (Milan, Beijing). I used to accompany her. I could skip school because the head knew I would get my marks anyway. I had a fantastic life. My parents were happily married and I got on perfectly with my two brothers. We loved one another and could confide all our feelings to one another. I was often surprised that so many people were suffering so much. That couldn't be the case, could it? I always used to say: unfortunately, not everyone gets their fair share in this world, but on the other hand, there has to be difference.

I disappeared in illegality, though that's just a word. It feels more as though I've sacked myself. Sacked from the full-time job of having to coincide with myself in the eyes of others, I've burnt my passport. I can no longer prove that I'm myself. Of course, I can't evade the political character of my decision to leave. When you look at the definition of citizenship, you find that with citizenship comes allegiance*, and I have a major problem with allegiance to things, persons and systems that I don't understand. Therefore I have a problem with the concept of citizenship*. It's a worn-out format, not amenable to admit anything new, but organised precisely to keep anything new out. And that's how this story starts. It's a story against borders, against controls, against a life where everything is registered and directed. Resisting the idea that everything has to be open and transparent. That no secrets, no other realities could exist.

*see page 66

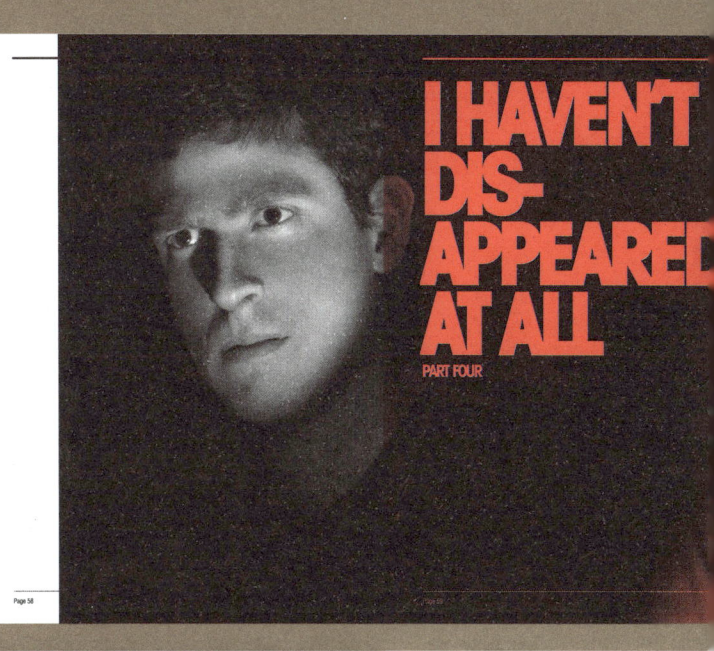

I HAVEN'T DIS-APPEARED AT ALL

PART FOUR

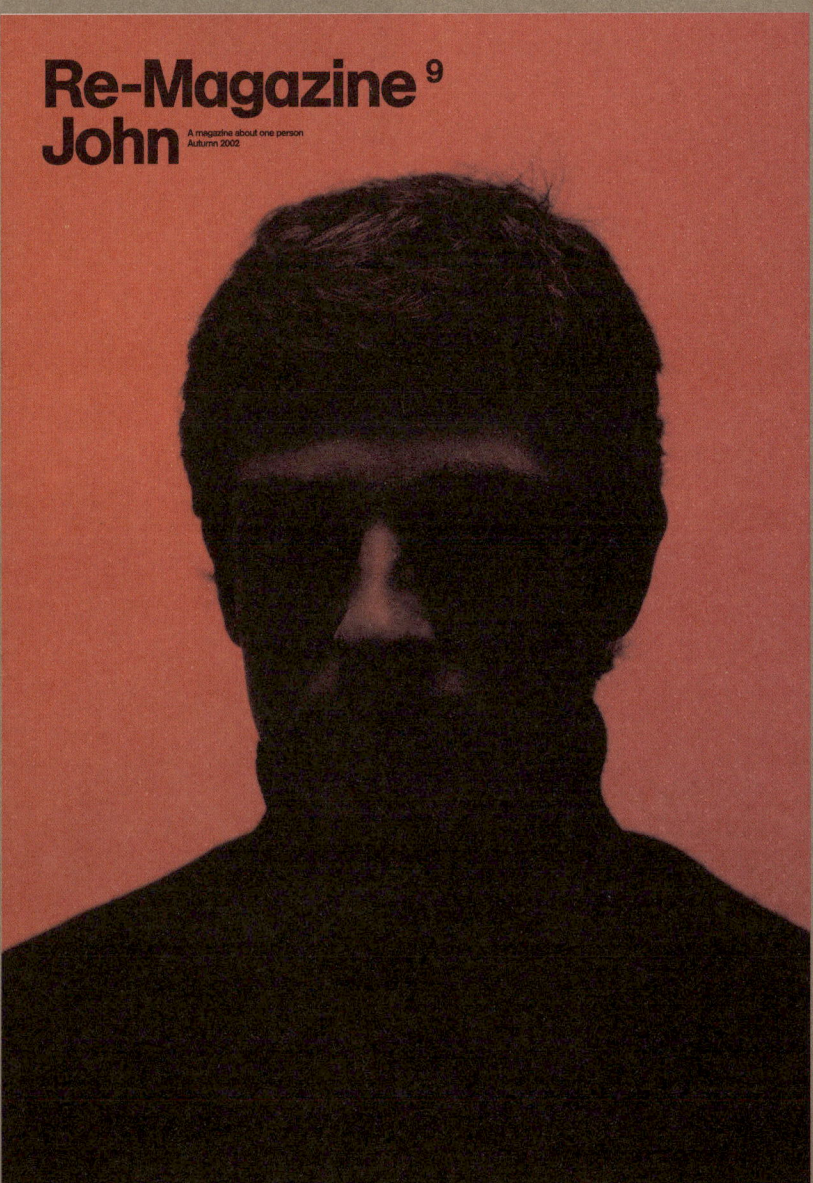

Re-Magazine 9
John

A magazine about one person
Autumn 2002

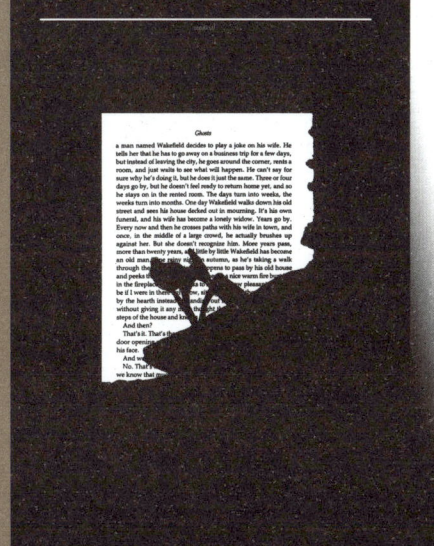

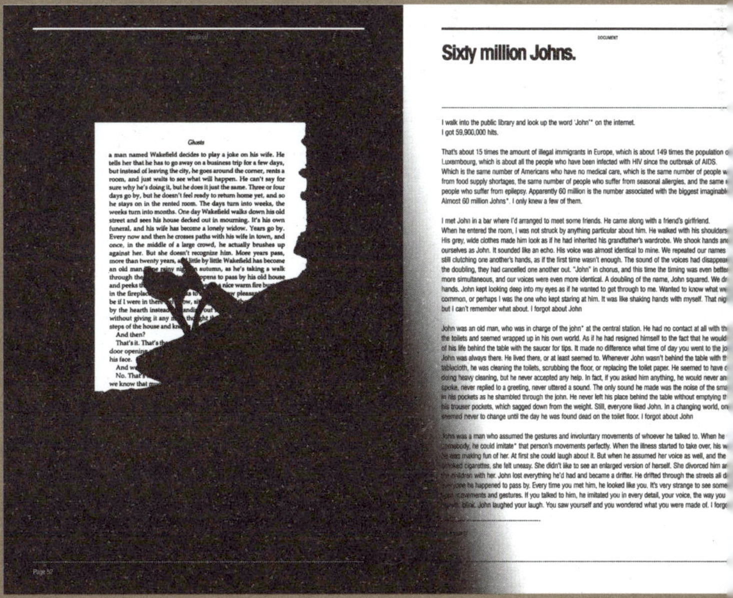

Sixty million Johns.

I walk into the public library and look up the word 'John'* on the internet. I got 59,900,000 hits.

That's about 15 times the amount of illegal immigrants in Europe, which is about 149 times the population of Luxemburg, which is about all the people who have been infected with HIV since the outbreak of AIDS. Which is the same number of Americans who have no medical care, which is the same number of people who suffer from food supply shortages, the same number of people who suffer from seasonal allergies, and the same number of people who suffer from epilepsy. Apparently 60 million is the number associated with the biggest imaginable amount. Almost 60 million 'Johns'. I only knew a few of them.

I met John in a bar where I'd arranged to meet some friends. He came along with a friend's girlfriend. When he entered the room, I was not struck by anything particular about him. He walked with his shoulders up. His grey, wide clothes made him look as if he had inherited his grandfather's wardrobe. We shook hands and introduced ourselves as John. It sounded like an echo. His voice was almost identical to mine. We repeated our names, still clutching one another's hands, as if the first time wasn't enough. The sound of the voices had disappeared by the doubling, they had cancelled one another out. 'John' in chorus, and this time the timing was even better, even more simultaneous, and our voices were even more identical. A doubling of the name, John squared. We shook hands. John kept looking deep into my eyes as if he wanted to get through to me. Wanted to know what we had in common, or perhaps I was the one who kept staring at him. It was like shaking hands with myself. That night I had but I can't remember what about. I forgot about John.

John was an old man, who was in charge of the 'john's at the central station. He had no contact at all with the world outside the toilets and seemed wrapped up in his own world. As if he had resigned himself to the fact that he would spend the rest of his life behind the table with the saucer for 5p. It made no difference what time of day you went to the john. John was always there. He lived there, or at least seemed to. Whenever John wasn't behind the table with the saucer with 50 cents in it, he was cleaning the toilets, scrubbing the floor, or replacing the toilet paper. He seemed to have all the time in the world for doing heavy cleaning, but he never accepted any help. In fact, if you asked him anything, he would never answer you. He never really spoke, never replied to a greeting, never uttered a sound. The only sound he made was the noise of the small change he jingled in his pockets, which sagged down from the weight. Still, everyone liked John. In a changing world, everyone seemed never to change until the day he was found dead on the toilet floor. I forgot about John.

John was a man who assumed the gestures and involuntary movements of whoever he talked to. When he met somebody, he could imitate* that person's movements perfectly. When he assumed her voice as well, and the way she smoked cigarettes. She didn't like to see an enlarged version of herself. She divorced him and John was left a John. When John lost everything he'd had and became a drifter. He drifted through the streets all day and copied whatever happened to pass by. Every time you met him, he looked like you. It's very strange to see someone else's movements and gestures. If you talked to him, he imitated you in every detail, your voice, the way you nodded your elbow... John laughed your laugh. You saw yourself and you wondered what you were made of. I forgot

What prompted you to launch *Re-Magazine*? How did you start it?

I started it when I was studying for my M.A.. I wanted to make a vehicle for a very personal platform of information, whereas the media is generally impersonal. I wanted to make something that I could have direct contact with. I used to call it 'Daily Life magazine'. I interviewed my friends instead of pop stars or models. I would rather make a magazine that is truly about reality.

I also wanted to get out of design, get out of all the forms and all the formal aspects. I really wanted to go into communication, to re-define design by doing everything just by myself: taking the photographs, binding, designing, and editing. I got right into the editorial, from the concept to the very last coma/full stop. Even the very last detail of a magazine is a part of the same story and they should all contribute to each other.

What is the objective of the magazine? What do you expect from it?

To explore the editorial construction itself… What I am looking forward to is examining how design, concepts and stories can come together. And how design can dictate text, the way that the text has to be written. Also the other way round, how written text can influence the way things look. Yes, in a way it is experimental. The appearance of every issue is varied: every time it is another project, so every time it is a big experiment.

But I also like it as a magazine that tells a completely different story. It is there because it wants to communicate something. It is there because I want to make a magazine, not just because I simply want to experiment – it's a part of it.

My other aim is to make something that is interdisciplinary: in-between different disciplines. It's not only bringing this and that together, but also we study. It's storytelling but within the format of a magazine.

How would you describe *Re-Magazine*?

Now I would always describe it as a magazine about one person because ever since *Re-Magazine* #9, each issue is dedicated to the life of one person. The last issue is about Marcel.

If I could go into content, I would always describe it as an intersection between writing, editing and designing. Perhaps the best way to describe *Re-magazine* is to tell what it isn't. It's not an art magazine; not literature; it's not about design, fashion, nor photography. It's not about one discipline, but is in between all of them. It's a project in itself. It's always a project that involves all different fields.

We are very impressed by its interesting topic/personality, which is varied every issue. For example the 'Boring' issue. How did you come up with these ideas? Where was the inspiration from?

Maybe I just like its negativity. I like it when I can put things into the media that normally don't get into the media. I really like to publish the hidden things. I don't want to represent the kind of shiny happy world because it just isn't.

The format of the magazine has been changed quite a lot since its launch. Why? Would it go on changing?

It started as an art school project of three issues. For the first one I did everything myself. The second I asked people to contribute. For the third one I wanted to be more of an art director and editor.

It was executed that way. The first and the second sold only 50 copies. Suddenly the third one sold 2,500, was distributed abroad and all written in English. All this changed the magazine itself.

And yes, each issue looks very different… I think for the reader it's always changing. But for me as a maker I can see the issues are related in many ways, such as the style of writing is consistently very serious as well as very humorous. We like to talk about really trivial information that seems meaningless and then connect them with bigger stories in life. We try to bridge those gaps. And I guess people can see the same hand of the designer. Its style is very, very dry; it almost has no style.

Obviously you can't make the whole magazine on your own. It's too much work. I was searching for how to make it. And I still do. It is reinventing itself every time… and I can ensure you that you'll get another very different *Re-magazine* next time because I'm *working on it* now…

What is the greatest challenge in making such an international magazine?

First is to make it happen, without making any compromises. Every issue is such a struggle, extremely knackering, with no budget… 'Can we actually do it?' is always the question. But then every time you manage.

Interview #02 // Jop van Bennekom
Page 18/19

TITLE // Re-Magazine #4 'Boring!'
TYPE OF WORK // Magazine
CLIENT // Re-Magazine
YEAR PRODUCED // 2000
ART DIRECTION // Jop van Bennekom
DESIGNER // Jop van Bennekom

DESCRIPTION OF WORK //
This issue is an investigation of the actions and non-actions resulting from boredom and nothingness: basically about the inspiring effects of boredom.

RE-

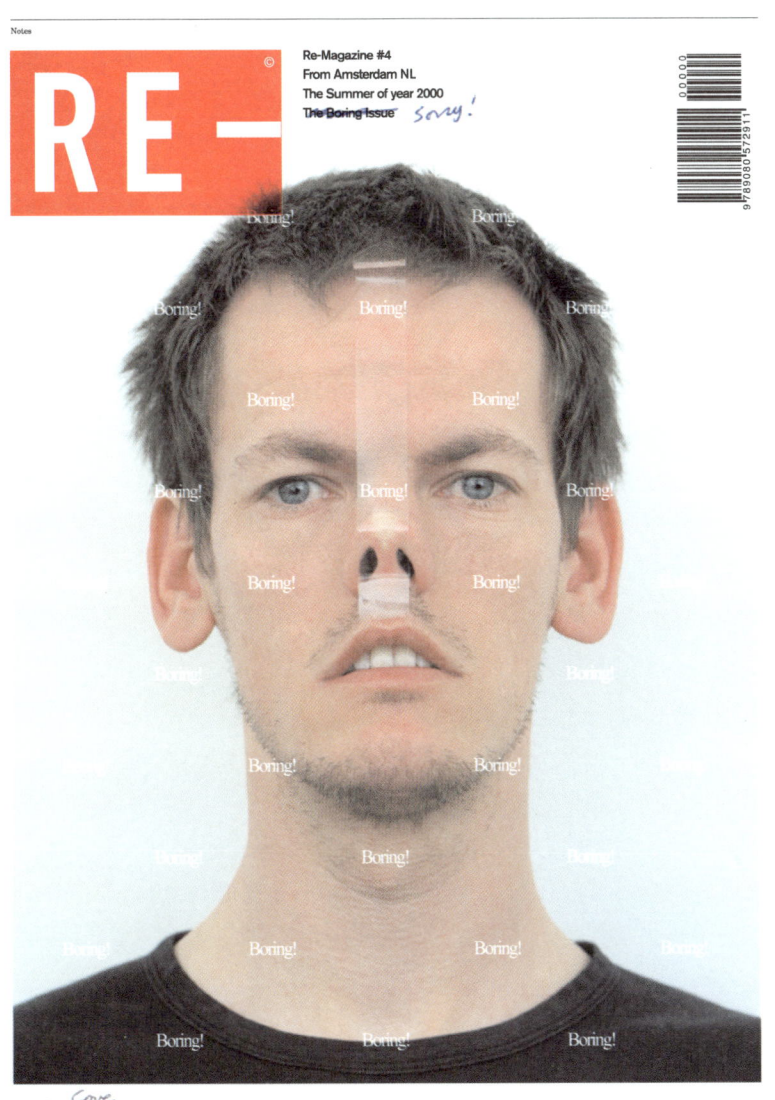

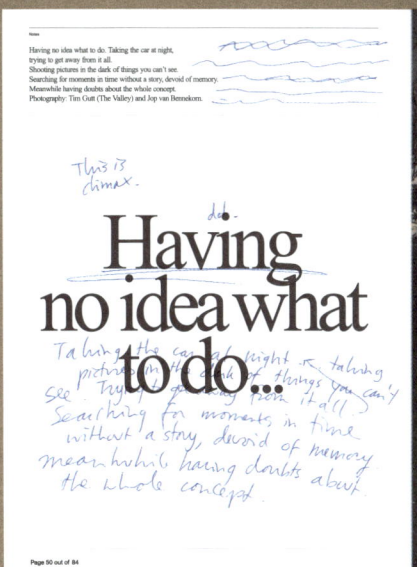

Re-Magazine #4
From Amsterdam NL
The Summer of year 2000
~~The Boring Issue~~ sorry!

Boring! Boring!

Having no idea what to do...

Having no idea what to do. Taking the car at night, trying to get away from it all. Shooting pictures in the dark of things you can't see. Searching for moments in time without a story, devoid of memory. Meanwhile having doubts about the whole concept.
Photography: Tim Gutt (The Valley) and Jop van Bennekom.

FreeStylin'
Looking at forms of boredom. Creating clouds of text.

Freestylin': an analysis by Wilfried Nijhof and Jop van Bennekom.
Photography by Maurice Scheltens.

Dead End

Team Dead End-stickers by Daniel van der Velden and Jop van Bennekom.
Photography by Martine Stig.

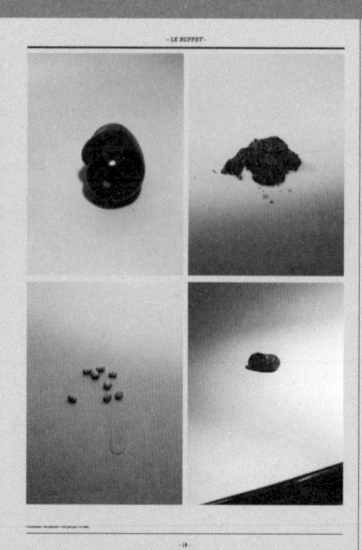

Interview #02 // Jop van Bennekom
Page 20/21

TITLE // Re-Magazine #11 'Marcel'
TYPE OF WORK // Magazine
CLIENT // Re-Magazine
YEAR PRODUCED // 2004
ART DIRECTION // Jop van Bennekom
DESIGNER // Jop van Bennekom

DESCRIPTION OF WORK //
Re-Magazine #11 features Marcel, a 44-year old sales representative from Wavrin, a little village on the outskirts of Lille, France. Over the last ten years Marcel has followed just about every diet imaginable. A year ago he took the radical decision to stop being a victim to all the contradictions about food, choosing to embrace them instead. In *Food Coma* Marcel talks in three monologues about food experiences that commence where diet gurus, chefs-de-cuisine, bulimia patients, slowfood activists, fruitarians and other foodies stop.

MARCEL

NOTES LE BUFFET

MONOLOGUE II
EATING

FOOD COMA

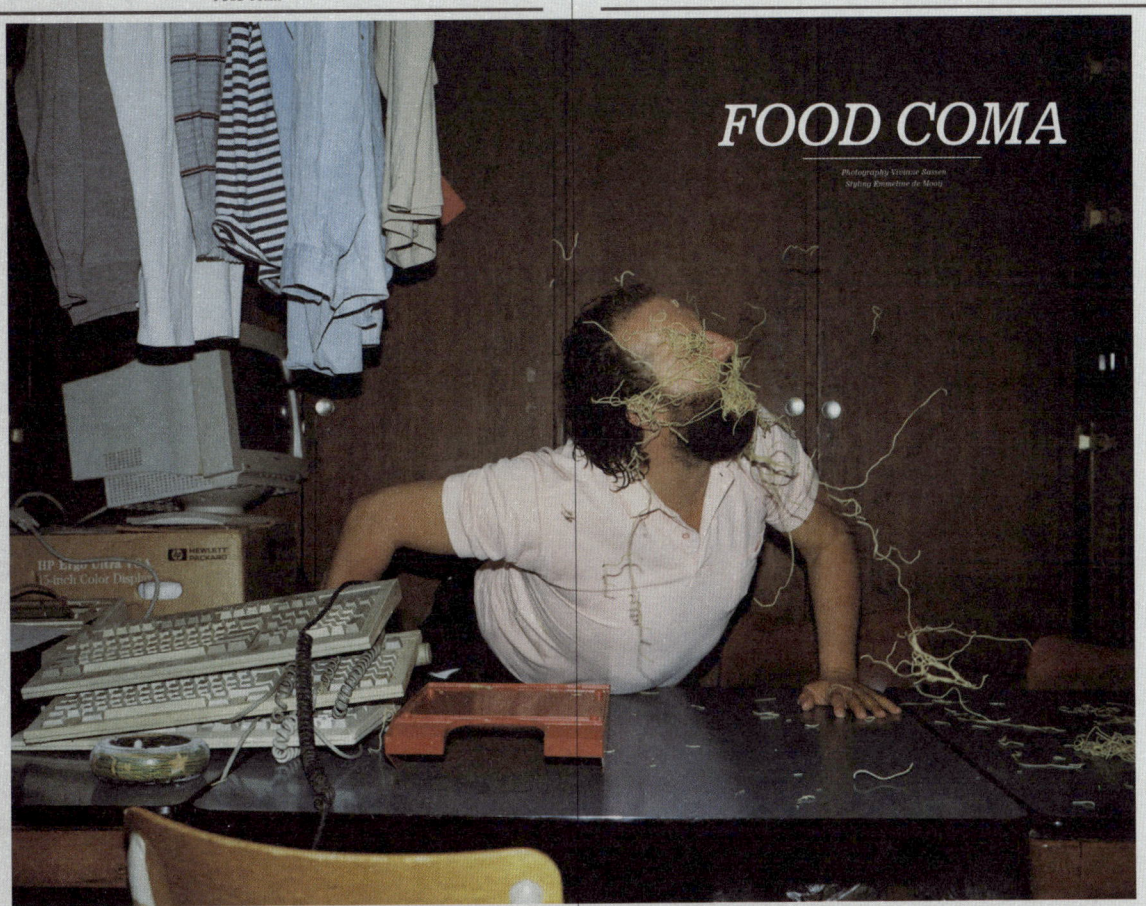

Photography Vicenzo Sassen
Styling Emmeline de Mooij

Another thing is to make it an alternative. We need alternatives, especially when most magazines are so much the same. I want *Re-magazine* to be unusual, so as to make new connections. Rather than introducing what's happening in the city, where the nice bars are, I want a 'story' magazine, which is something nobody does. It can be read like a novel, or a movie… I would like it to be more recognisable. It still is a challenge, because there still are people asking what *Re-magazine* is exactly about. But I've noticed that when you keep on trying, people will pick it up and start to recognize it…

We don't have much advertising and hardly do any marketing, to be honest. Yet a lot of people interview us. I think the press is the best marketing. I think a magazine should be a thing that you pick up yourself. Actually that's how people find us, they read about us in other magazines or books.

Would you share with us your most favourite project/issue? Any unforgettable experiences so far?

I really like the 'Boring' issue and the 'Information Trashcan'.

The 'Boring' issue was such an anti-magazine. The last thing you expect from a magazine is for it to be boring. It was about boredom, but was definitely not boring. I think it's very nicely designed. It was 2000, the time of the economic boom. These dotcom businesses and people lounging with champagne surrounded us. I thought that issue hit the right timing. I like it also because it took a long time before it actually was finished. It came out almost one and a half years after the previous one. Not until then did I get a foundation and a publisher. I had to re-arrange everything to make it happen – flew in and out, had people contributing, arranged financial matters… It kept me busy for nine months putting things together.

The 'Information Trashcan' was an aggressive issue. It was all about embarrassment, lies… all bad things that one carries along. It was one big monologue but made up by four people and written from the first person's point of view, so everything clashed. Everything was not true. I really like it because it was so embarrassingly honest.

Interview #02 // Jop van Bennekom
Page 22-24

TITLE // BUTT Magazine
TYPE OF WORK // Magazine covers + inside spreads
CLIENT // BUTT Magazine
YEAR PRODUCED // 2001-2004
ART DIRECTION // Gert Jonkers and Jop van Bennekom
DESIGNER // Gert Jonkers and Jop van Bennekom

DESCRIPTION OF WORK //
BUTT is a pocket-size, quarterly magazine for and about homosexuals, founded in 2001, published and printed in The Netherlands and available world-wide.

Do you have any favourite designers/artists? What do you like about them?

Yes, say Peter Saville. In the 80's, when I didn't know what design was, I had just started to collect records from the 4AD label and The Smiths. I was into these weird covers that had nothing to do with the music. Then I thought that there might be something I wanted to do.

I just like things that are a little bit subversive. I really like The Smiths and Joy Division, or things that represent alternative but at the same time are so implicit, so well behaved. There is a balance in-between. I like them to be intelligent. There's something exciting to discover instead of everything that's just out there.

How do they influence you? Or what is your strongest influence?

Yes, they influenced me. But it was when I was a kid. At art school I was very much influenced by Karel Martens, who taught me for five years. His work is very simple, typographic and very modernist, as well as very playful. He is extremely honest about his work. I've learnt a lot about how to approach things, how to stick with your own idea and how to make things as simple as possible while not losing the layers within. Also skills. Everything.

Are you happy with what you are doing now? What is the greatest satisfaction in your career so far?

Yes and no. *Re-magazine* is doing well, my other magazine *BUTT* is doing extremely well. It is very nice, very fantastic to realize that you can actually make things happen. And you go through all these phases … You get to a point where you never thought you would be. Because you can imagine yourself somewhere, you know.

Then it goes further and you would never know where exactly it's going. Right now I've got so much attention, but it's a pressure too. I get so many e-mails, interviews, students coming to review things and trips abroad, but I also have to do my own stuff. So it's a lot of work, but still not much money. Things just cancel out.

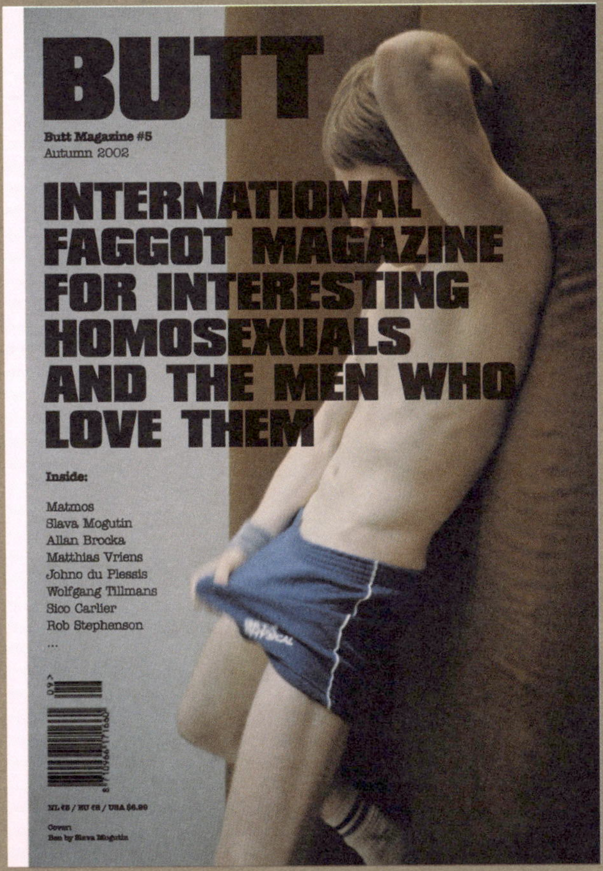
BUTT
Butt Magazine #5
Autumn 2002
INTERNATIONAL FAGGOT MAGAZINE FOR INTERESTING HOMOSEXUALS AND THE MEN WHO LOVE THEM
Inside:
Matmos
Slava Mogutin
Allan Brocka
Matthias Vriens
Johno du Plessis
Wolfgang Tillmans
Sico Carlier
Rob Stephenson
...
NL €5 / EU €8 / USA $6.99
Cover:
Ben by Slava Mogutin

BUTT
Fantastic magazine for homosexuals
BUTT No. 9
Spring 2004
NL €5.00 EU €8.00
USA $8.00
Michael Stipe by Wolfgang Tillmans

BUTT
Butt Number Six
Fagazine
Spring 2003
NL €5 / EU €8 / USA $6.99
Cover:
Heinz Peter Knes
by Heinz Peter Knes

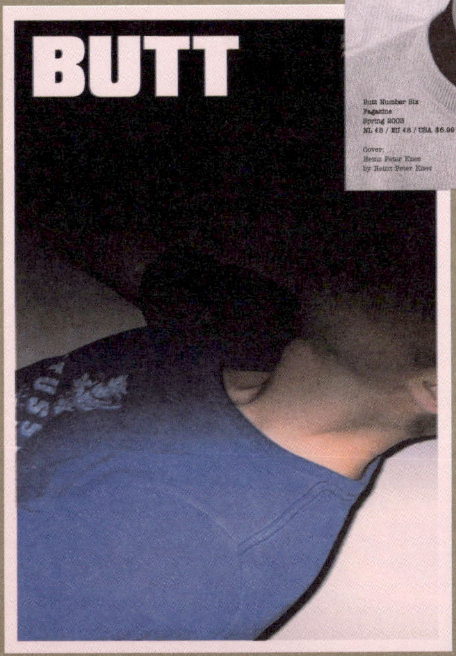
BUTT

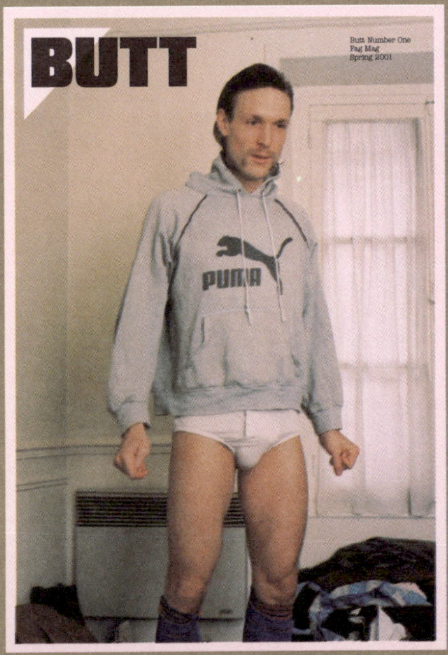
BUTT
Butt Number One
Fag Mag
Spring 2001
PUMA

BUTT
Butt Number Four
Fag Mag
Summer 2002
NL €5 EU €8
USA $6.99

Is there a future project that you would like to share with us?

I'm working on a new menswear magazine. It's called *Fantastic Man*. It will come out at the beginning of 2005, a magazine about menswear and personalities. It's a spin off from *BUTT* – more of a fashion variation and bigger. It goes towards the other end of normal fashion magazines, because I think the current ones are extremely boring and all look alike. I want to do something new and fresh.

What sorts of publications do you usually read?

I do hate a lot of magazines, I mean, there are so many magazines and publications out there, it seems like nothing means anything anymore. But I do like established magazines such as *The New Yorker*, for instance. I also like *Italian Vogue*. Whether I like them or not, I do read *i-D* magazine and *Self-Service*. I also like *O32C*, a very good magazine from Berlin. But to be honest, I'd rather read newspapers. I am more a newspaper person.

Do you have any recommendation for our readers?

I really like *O32C*… I guess people who read this book will know of these magazines already.

You are the editor of *BUTT* magazine, too. How do you see, in terms of editorial design, the difference between the two?

For *Re-magazine*, I always have to re-invent the form, to find a solution and to do the text. Each time I have to look for a way to build an editorial construction that started from one particular concept.

For *BUTT* magazine, it's much more formatted. It's consistently very thin, small and feels intimate. There are always very personal interviews. The challenge for *BUTT* is not about the design, but much more on the editorial side.

I think it is one of the most transparent magazines out there. There's the portrait, then the interview… the simplest thing you can do in journalism. There's no voice from above, just two people talking, like a transcript. No interference. The headline is always on the same page, at the same spot. It's nearly a machine and so the form almost disappears. When you read it, you don't notice it at all. You're really looking at who's saying what now. So the challenge is how much we want to create a very specific selection. That's what we call 'a Butt selection'. We interview very specific people. Each time we try to make it a very good variation, while at the same time be extremely specific. It's a real challenge when you want to do it EVERY TIME.

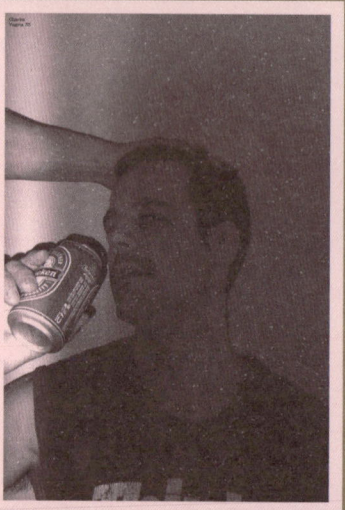

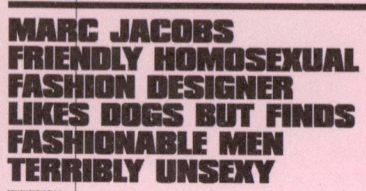

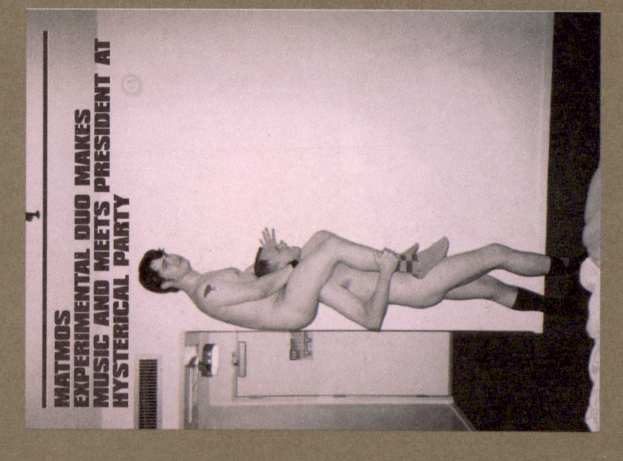

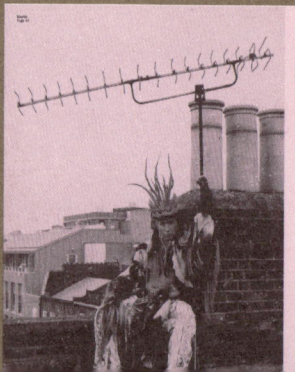

+ Big Active

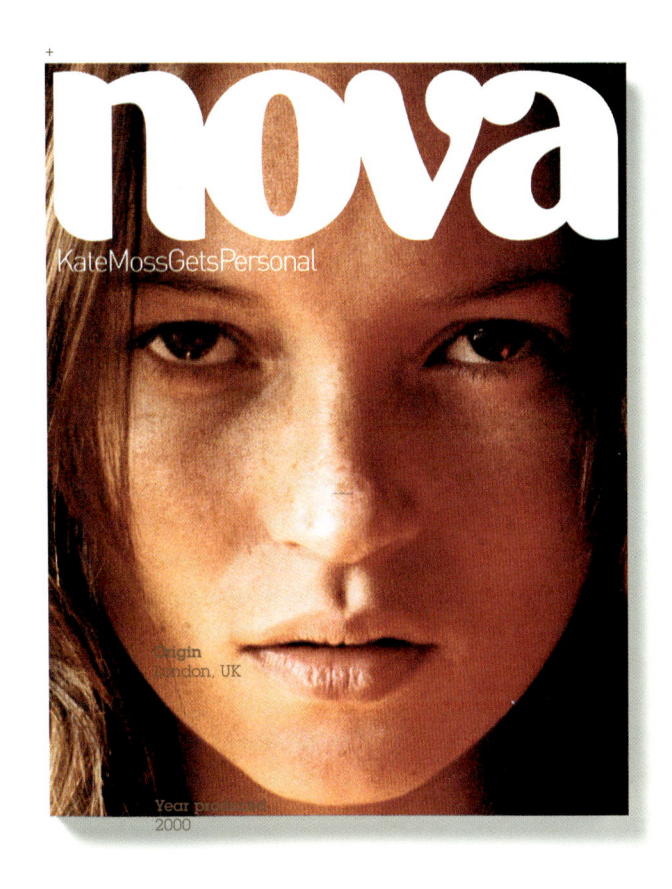

Page
25

Title of work
Nova Magazine

Type of work
Magazine cover

Client
Nova

Art Director
Gerard Saint

Designer
Gerard Saint
+ Juergen Teller
++ Thomas Schenk

Origin
London, UK

Year produced
2000

Description
–

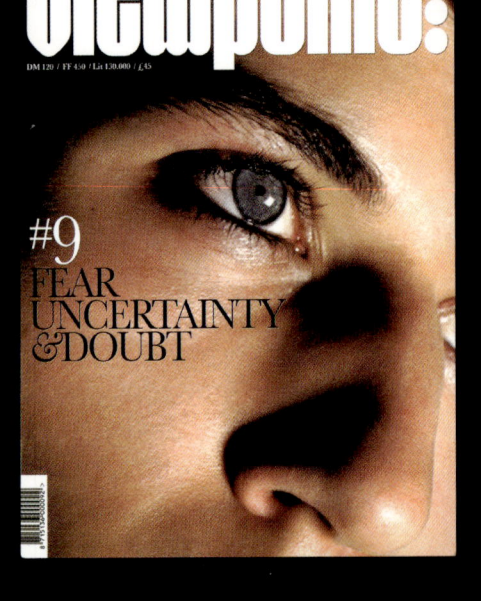

Viewpoint:

#9
FEAR
UNCERTAINTY
& DOUBT

#10
TheStateOfMan

+ Big Active™

KOS OSMOND
London, United Kingdom, Aged 30,
Girlfriend, artist, variable salary
'I seriously get pissed off with the whole
"aspirational" lifestyle advertising lark that
means we have to buy chrome-polished
fondango hub-caps and have a nice looking
supermodel 'bird' to replace the speed stripes,
all encapsulated within a 1970's road-movie
soundtrack. Clothes are an annoyance
because I'm so romantic about them, and
I wish it was the other way around. I like
things to be just right and they never are so
I'm fighting a losing battle.'

Page
26

Client
Viewpoint

Origin
London, UK

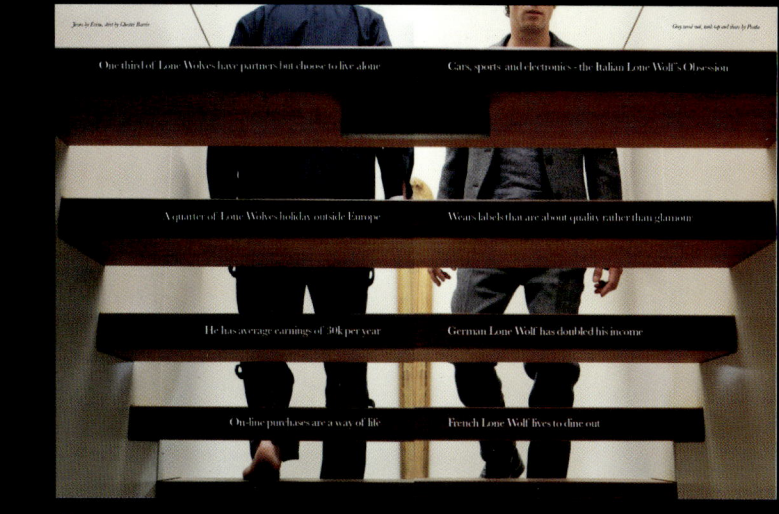

One third of Lone Wolves have partners but choose to live alone   Cars, sports and electronics - the Italian Lone Wolf's Obsession

A quarter of Lone Wolves holiday outside Europe   Wears labels that are about quality rather than glamour

He has average earnings of 50k per year   German Lone Wolf has doubled his income

On-line purchases are a way of life   French Lone Wolf lives to dine out

++

TRANSLATOR

Language barriers no longer exist - it's as simple as using technicwear which enables you to speak. Electroplated panels of fabric developed by artist Isaac Corwin and sound sensors to report Rue Greens, will sense vibrations from the wearbot, and, using Voice Response Translate technology developed by IVT (Integrated Wear Technologies), translate to the desired language it meets up with. The potential for vibration technology is enormous, says Ron Greens: 'Not just with sound, but feelings and emotions also translated into clothing the deeper levels you can get hold of, to people along with verbal contact, the better continuum status can be.' www.iwl.com / www.isaaagwn.com

CONCEPT: Christopher Sandison.sf
IMAGE: Ron Haberknocks.sf.uknus/tnpsttutorem
www.sncx.suppersnwitz.uk

+++

TheInformation

The 'lovemark' as hallmark, the death of the 'Values' Generation, smart cars, net publishing, the lightness principle, the male himbos' wardrobe, solutions for a small country, the beauty register, designer drugs, personality pets, decompression culture, 'experience wells'... It's all here. *Text: Martin Raymond, Justine Harvey & Dene October*

++++

TheHidden

COVERT SCANNING and surveillance technologies are increasingly used by consumer profilers to map the dreams and desires of 21st Century shoppers. But CCTV cameras are only the tip of a fast growing iceberg of psycho-technologies, marketeers, ethnologists, psychologists and retail analysts who are being called on to map and codify the consumer's every move, writes *Dene October*.

The Mall of Louisiana in Baton Rouge is 1.4 million square feet of high tech shopping paradise, so you are hardly surprised as you enter its 6,000-space car park that the $200,000 surveillance equipment immediately picks you out. Neither are you perturbed. After all, tight security means the protection of all property - yours included - while the monitoring of traffic flow means you quickly find your space. As you leave your car, the cameras continue tracking you. They watch over you en route to the elevators, survey you as you enter the trading units, scrutinise your scrutiny of promotional displays and check on you while you make your purchase.

But is all this surveillance really necessary for your shopping convenience? Yes, say the owners, because to keep the customer satisfied you must keep the marketeer informed. Marketing is perhaps the most obvious benefactor of surveillance technologies, originally developed to fight wars and keep a watch on neighbours. Which is why this particular shopping mall, and hundreds more like it across the mid-west, are investing so much money in covert surveillance technologies to help them and their sales teams find out more - about how you shop, where you shop, with whom, and more importantly, why.

Even face recognition technologies from companies like Mikos Bio-tech in Virginia, developed initially to thermographically track our facial gestures (and thus warn police that we are about to commit a crime by reading pre-recognisable facial expressions) are now being used to help predict, assess and analyse the precise moment of purchase. From this technology, retail psychologists and marketeers hope to work with companies to identify the hidden things that bring about sales, and thus create the ultimate 'purchase theatre scenario.'

Market intelligence from credit reference agencies such as Experian, for example, are also being drawn on more and more to create customer purchase maps. Recent data mining work by the marketing department of home entertainment manufacturers Bang and Olufsen (which had previously targeted a professional mid-twenties male on $50,000) learned, to their surprise and profit, that they should, in reality, be targeting a 50+ homeowner earning $100,000!

According to John Parker, author of 'Total Surveillance', Experian boasts 'a database of consumer marketing information on the residents of 98 per cent of US households', while its digital interface tool 'Visitor Insight' can gather instant profiles of customers while they are on-line. For Parker, and civil rights activists worldwide, this represents a serious threat to consumer privacy. Although data surveillance is not an e-commerce invention - Alfred Sloan used it at General Motors back in the 1920s - it is increasingly regarded as an essential e-commerce tool. Even pollsters like Harris have gone the real-time data collection route with their Planet Project poll (see The Information) which interviews 400,000 people from 135 countries worldwide on an ongoing range of lifestyle issues.

Real time data provision means improvement to sales, service and consumer experience. As 'fly-on-the-wall' television demonstrates, spying on customers - online, with cameras, via the mining of existing data depositories - has the edge over formal 'focus group' settings where time is limited and recruitment of members potentially leads to bias. Conventional information gathering strategies may be better signifiers of business integrity, but going through a customer's bins (see Viewpoint 8, 'Special Ops target, consumers'), is likely to generate significantly more useable data (on, deeply personal issues like toiletries) than asking the customer about their spending habits.

'From a research point of view, surveillance TV is fascinating,' says Mark Robinson, marketing director for advertising agency J. Walter Thomson, who has filmed consumer reaction to products and shops. 'We use it as a new business tool

+++++

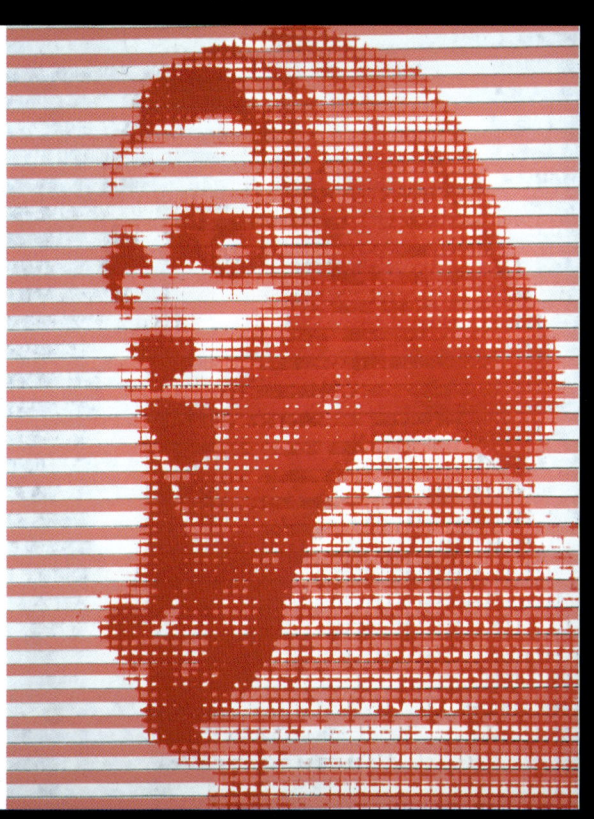

+ So+ba

Page
28

Title of work
Plant Magazine

Type of work
Magazine

Client
So+ba

Art Director
Susanna Baer

Designer
Susanna Baer

PLANT
TOKYO PEOPLE MAGAZINE

東京人のマガジン
Origin
Tokyo, Japan

プラント
1月創刊号

Year produced
2000

Description
Photography
PETER BEARD
Media
GENE KRELL
Architecture
KAZUYO SEIJIMA
Books
KYOICHI TSUZUKI

conflicts and desperation
by Christiane HASENÖDER

SEGMENTS OF CHANGES
Films are for Tada a tool to grow up. Four years ago he finished his first full-length feature film "Pygmy".

Film director **Akio Tada**, 45, is well known to Tokyo's insider art and party scene. His "night-picnic" gatherings in Shibuya are legendary, as is his outspoken criticism of the Japanese society. "We pretend to function like in the world of children's comics," he explains, "where conflicts are taboo!"

論争と絶望

WELL SHAPED:
Akio Tada was practiced with a powerlifters performance group in Yoyogi park in "freedom as alternative society."

happy garden

In today's Japan – since the war, I would say – people have been pretending to live in a kind of happy garden, where nothing bad should happen and everybody is gentle and polite. This was different in the Meiji period, when society was more "grown up." It faced conflicts and did not suppress them, as it is the rule today. Our society lacks reflection, and therefore originality. People don't know why they do things, they just repeat without corresponding what others or generations before them did. Japan's history was chopped up and wiped out several times. Everything had to start at point zero over and over again. But we didn't think how to start, we just adapted what suited us best. We didn't ask any questions like why, how and what for.

Films are a tool for Tada to grow up. Four years ago he finished his first full-length feature film "Pygmy," where he cut up the whole plot and put it back together in a completely different order. This technique frees the sequences from all formalities of a narrative film. The remaining cuts are reduced to a very abstract pattern-structure.

mishima

Only later I found out, that Yukio Mishima too was involved in a similar experiment. The development in the Japanese post-war society was unrealistic and that's probably why he committed suicide in the end. It was in the year of the Japanese Expo, where everybody was excited and expected a bright future. Mishima still carried a dream from the Meiji-area with all its values.

As a child, long before encountering Mishima's work, I felt already desperate and artistic with a desperate aura very appealing to me. But considering that I "like" this desperation I have to conclude that I can't be that desperate. This is what distinguishes me from Mishima. Due to a Dutch group that covered "Nakajima," artistes for a documentary, Tada moved to Amsterdam and stayed for 4 years, experimenting with films and stage. Although he had produced his film "Pygmy" in Japan it was only shown in Europe. He actually doesn't follow the film scene of his home country and lives in Tokyo rather secluded. Quite in contrast to his crowded and popular parties.

tokyo

The problem in Tokyo today is, that everybody is so busy making a living, that there's no time to think about the world anymore.

暴力

幸せの庭

東京 三島

Kyoichi Tsuzuki

this man never rings twice!
by Andrew STURMLAINE

一度あることは二度はない

書店には彼の本が所狭しと並んでいる。アパートを舞台に綴った東京スタイルが、様々なエディターであり、今回たまたま大阪版の取材を担当したかっている。芸術と大阪の若者が同居も、し当異を希望されるなら掃除をしないように。

num: **Bookstores in Japan are stocked with Kyoichi Tsuzuki's colorful apartment-espionage report TOKYO STYLE. The seasoned magazine editor and photographer-by-chance is now working on a Kansai version of his bestseller. People in Kyoto and Osaka get ready! If you want your place to be featured, you'd better not clean up.**

num: **Foreigners love your books. Great souvenirs!**

TSUZUKI: Don't forget, I'm not a professional photographer. I work in an editor for books and magazines. Most of the time I have only a small budget available, which doesn't allow me to hire a professional photographer. That's why I take photos myself.

Ryoji Ikeda's sound creations demand a full body experience deep down to your nervous system. "I want to disappear since public exposure of myself only distracts the audience from my sounds," he explains. At "Watari-um" Plant, Tokyo talked to the 32-year-old artist who's also a member of Dumb Type, the legendary performance group based in Kyoto.

smart sounds from a dumb type
by Christiane Hagenauer

無が紡ぎだすスマートな音

IKEDA: I played guitar as a teenager, studied economics and have even been in a karaoke bar.

num: **Never went to a karaoke bar?**
IKEDA: You know, I don't have so many friends, and the ones I have are like me.

num: **So how did you come upon electronic music?**
IKEDA: I'm basically a lazy person and when I was studying the guitar as a child I quickly hated it. I simply wanted to have more control over the playing and without being handicapped by technique. Soon I also discovered that I needed a certain distance from the "instrument". For a while, about 16 years ago, I was a DJ, in a very abstract and experimental way. My idea has never been to create music or to entertain, but to make people feel and experience sound. I consider a lot of material and data until I reached point zero, I mean, where there's only a sine wave left. But at that stage it came to me that the simpler the sounds, the more sophisticated the ways in which they can be used.

num: **Are you following a scientific method when composing?**
IKEDA: I'm not a mathematician. Intuition plays an important role, but I construct the pieces very precisely - no improvisation or random results. When I do a live performance, everything's already prepared, down to the last detail, and unlike other live performers, the process of being on stage is not that important to me, from the audience perceives and experiences the predetermined outcome of my sounds is all that counts.

num: **There are foreign critics who compare your sound dances with Zen.**
IKEDA: A relationship with Zen does not exist, but my music is very minimal and simple, so people can freely interpret it for themselves. During a performance, the audience should not be bothered by the performer. They should be accepted with themselves only. Sound installations, therefore, serve my purpose much better than live performances, where I have to be present. Ideally, I would like to see my body disappear, which also explains the complete darkness during my solo performance.

With "Dumb Type", though, it's different. We include

The slightly famous **Uchujin (alien),** wears a tight silver body suit and has no place to live. But that's part of his performance, besides engaging in traffic control at the busy Shinjuku east exit crossing. Nearby restaurant owners donate meals. Who knows if they are acting as art enthusiasts or out of pity? And who cares? When traffic lights for cars turn red, Uchujin storms the intersection and runs among pedestrians, kicking the ball in front of him in all directions. People stop, the lights for cars turn green again, Uchujin continues to eat "I have no desire to become famous," he says. "I just want to make people laugh!" When he lives in Shinjuku, he moves on to Shibuya or even Ginza. Coins nightfall, Uchujin finds a place to sleep at a friend's house - when he's lucky and if not, well, street life has always an apartment somewhere for spaced-out aliens under a bridge, stairway or park bench. It comes with the certainty that lights never stay red forever.

red-light district
by Shin IWATA

赤信号区域

One of Japan's most sought-after architects is Kazuyo Sejima, 43. Trial and error are the pillars of her dual world. Welcome

parallel architecture
by Christiane HAGENAUER

パラレル建築へようこそ

もっとも注目されている建築家の一人妹島和世、四十三歳。試行錯誤は彼女の建築哲学の柱である。

1. SEJIMA PROJECT: N-Museum
2. SEJIMA PROJECT: O-Museum
3. SEJIMA PROJECT: Police Box

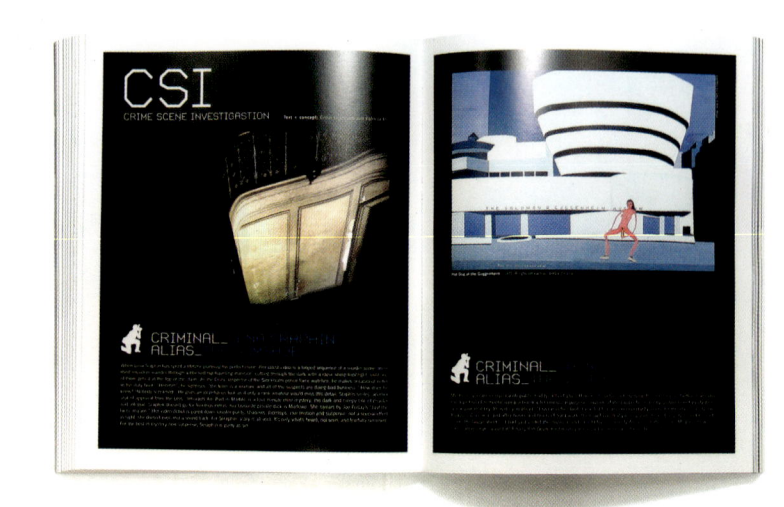

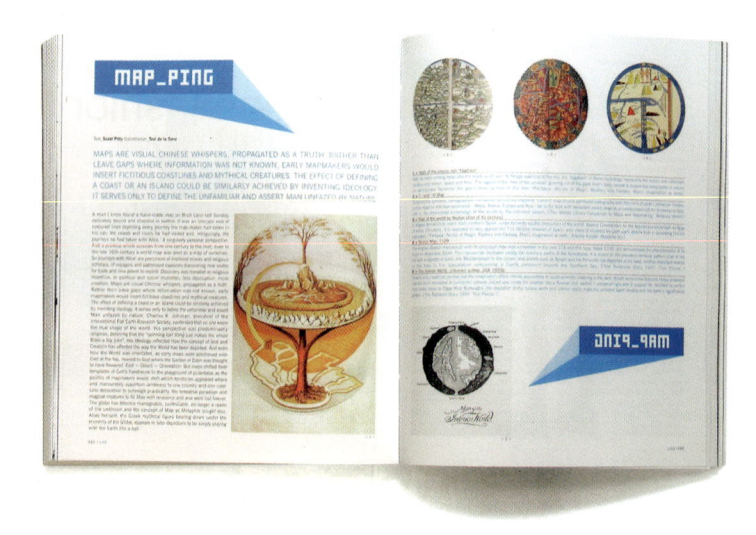

+ Astrid Stavro

Page
30

Client
Pavlova

Title of work
+ Lab 04
++ Lab 05

Art Director
Astrid Stavro, Joana Ramos-Pinto

Type of work
Magazine

Designer
Astrid Stavro, Joana Ramos-Pinto

++

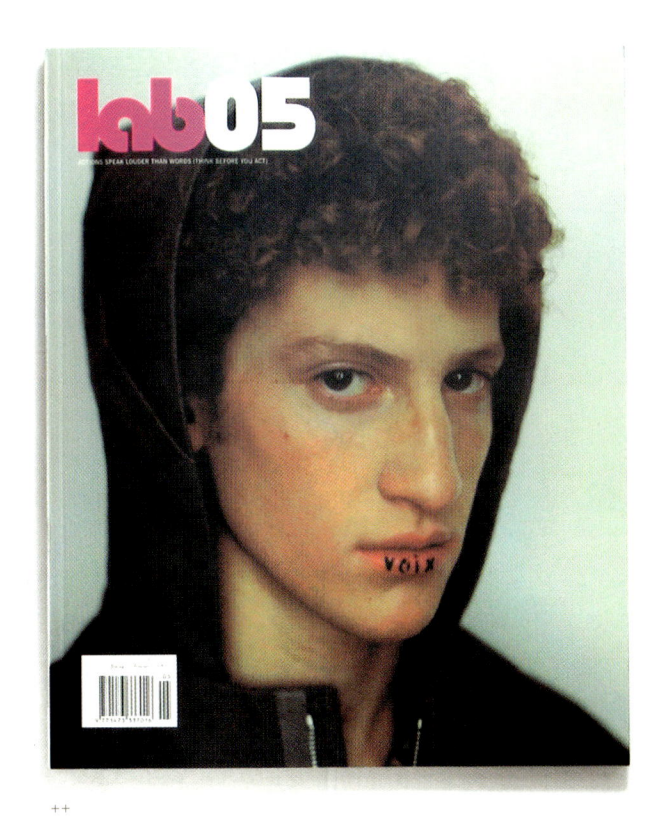

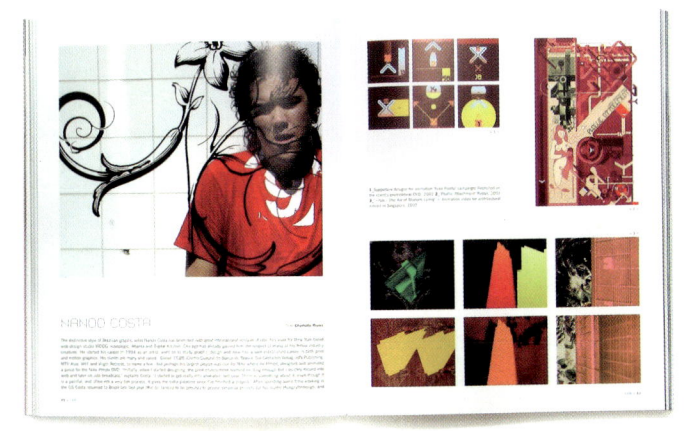

Origin
London, UK

Year produced
2003

Description
Lab is a laboratory of visual and theoretical experimentation that aims to promote and inspire. By combining the directorial and exciting work developed by new and emerging talent, *Lab* stands alone on a meritocracy of design, where what matters is not reputation as much as ability. The layout, typography and grid change with every issue in order to reflect this experimental philosophy.

+ Moiré

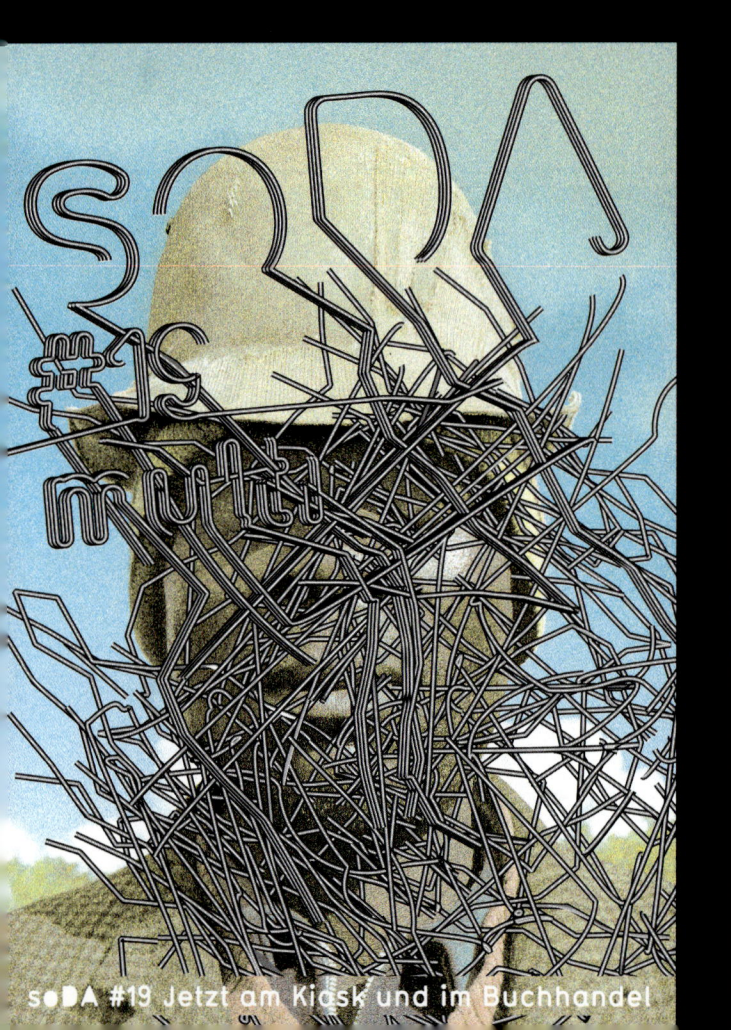

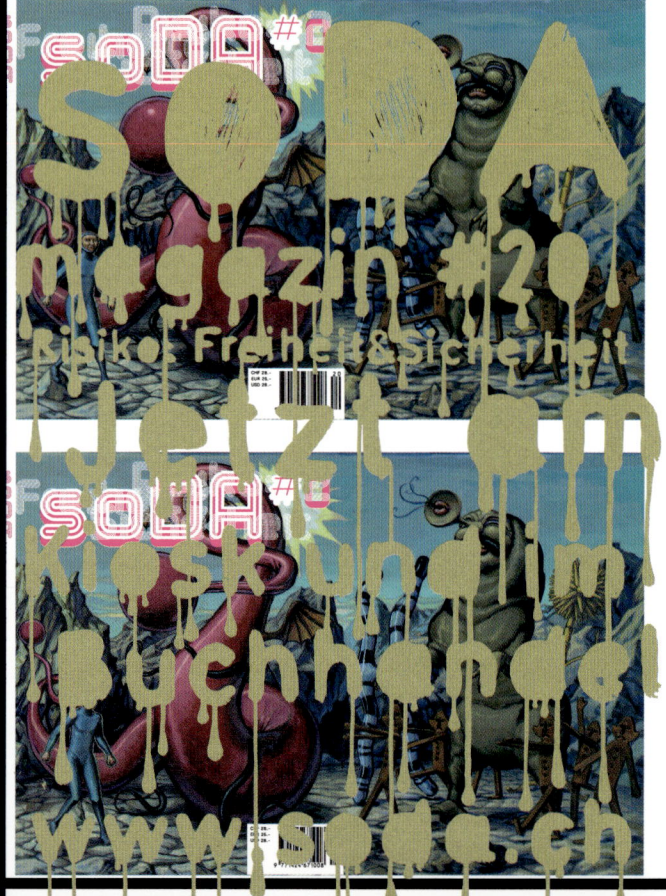

Page
32

Client
soDA Magazine

Title of work
soDA Magazine

Art Director
Marc Kappeler

Type of work
Magazine
+ Cover (Issue# 21)
++/+++ Poster (#19 / #20)
++++ Cover and inside spreads (#18)

Designer
+ Martin Woodtli (magenta)
Happypets (yellow) Norm (
Marc Kappeler (black)
++ Marc Kappeler
Jackie Nickerson (photogr
+++ Marc Kappeler
Chrigel Farner (illustrator)
++++ Marc Kappeler
Benjamin Güdel (illustrator

soDA #19 Jetzt am Kiosk und im Buchhandel

Baisez la police? Nein, danke!

SODA #11

MILLENNIUM STARTER KIT (MSK)

FINDE DEIN RAUMSCHIFF

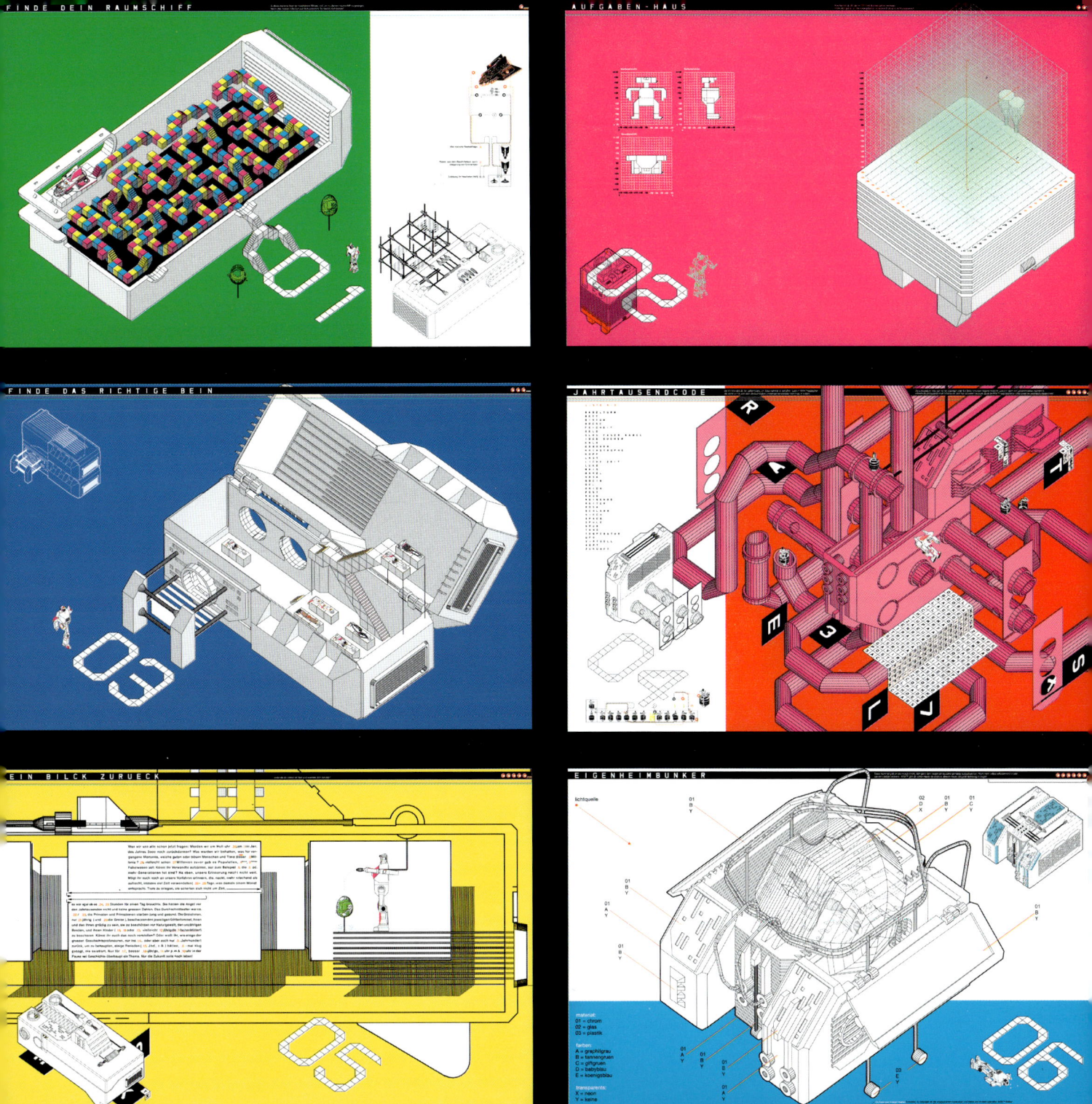

AUFGABEN-HAUS

FINDE DAS RICHTIGE BEIN

JAHRTAUSENDCODE

EIN BILCK ZURUECK

EIGENHEIMBUNKER

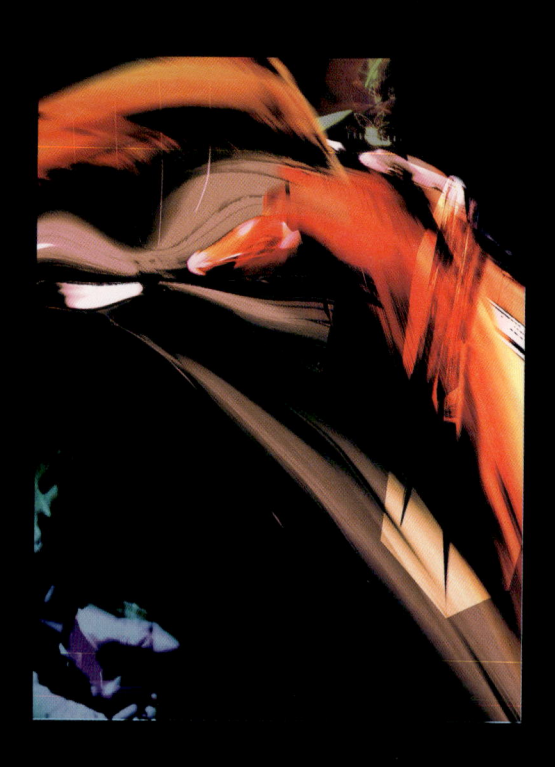

+ CHK Design

Page
36

Title of work
AD Architectural Design Magazine

Type of work
Magazine
+/+++ Cover
++ Inside spreads

Client
John Wiley & Sons, Publisher

Art Director
Christian Küsters

Designer
Christian Küsters

Origin
London, UK

Year produced
2000 - 2003

Description
AD magazine was re-launched with a new look in 2000. The logo was re-drawn based on a square, circle and triangle. Foundry Gridnik became the main headline font. The lgrid system is set up to allow for enough flexibility to respond to the material supplied by a new guest-editor for every issue.

Fashion Art in New York

From the streets of New York's SoHo, all you can (route inside the Yves Saint Laurent Rive Gauche Homme boutique in a gigantic, shiny, red rhinoceros ready to charge customers entering the store – if it is a place. Lettering on the window says it is, as does that on the old-fashioned awning. But you have to climb a short flight of open, steel, industrial stairs before you really see any clothing. The glass front door leads into a gallery for temporary art shows, now completely filled with Xavier Veilhan's big beast.

The exquisitely arranged garments are around the corner in a dematerialised space where scrims veil walls (ined with classical cast-iron columns and loaning screen-hanging racks.

Only a few years ago, the streets of this 19th-century industrial district were lined with real art galleries. Today, most of them have moved a mile or so north to a more barren area in West Chelsea, where warehouses and garages still coexist with the growing art scene – dozens upon dozens of galleries and residential lofts

... Since the Second World War, however, the ... of the international ... ... New York's display magazine. Network house ... ... are of perfumes and the city processed into a ... ... in a town deeply restored ... ... above the skin Floors ...

with bare concrete floors, concrete walls, concrete ceilings, exposed ducts and industrial light fixtures.

It all began in the east of West 22nd Street where New York architect Richard Gluckman, who designed the ro, SoHo store, transformed a 40,000-square-foot warehouse into the Dia Foundation's non-profitmaking exhibition space in 1987, creating a taste for the Minimalist aesthetic he had developed over the years when working with collectors and artists such as Dan Flavin and Donald Judd. The architect went on to design galleries all over New York and museums around the world, and these in turn influenced younger architects who were designing galleries, photography studios, retail stores and

apartments for art collectors, dealers and fashion people. Gluckman, now practising as Gluckman Mayner Architects, has recently done stores for Helmut Lang in SoHo, Gianni Versace in Miami Beach and in, Homme in New York and Paris.

While other New York architects – Deborah Berke, Frank Lupo and Daniel Rowen, David Piskuskas (at 1100 Architect), Michael Gabellini, Rogers Marvel, Tsao & McKown – were developing their own versions of Minimalism in the mid-1990s, Calvin Klein hired John Pawson to design his flagship store on Madison Avenue. At one stroke, the shop established an emerging trend in the city's swankiest shopping street and made the most celebrated retail outlet of the 1990s 12 blocks north (which happened to belong to Klein's main competitor) seem slightly old-fashioned. Of course, the French Renaissance Revival mansion that Ralph Lauren had turned into a $14 million, 28,000-square-foot fantasy (with designer Naomi Leff was supposed to be old-fashioned. It offers shoppers a chance to enter the Gilded Age, wandering from parlours where accessories are strewn across sofas into bedrooms where sweaters are stocked

in closet-like niches, while they suit themselves out in the trappings of lineage. But once Pawson's study in abstraction (complete with Donald Judd furniture) opened, nostalgia suddenly seemed less stylish. The Calvin Klein store, which was perfectly attuned to the plain, structured, monochromatic goods for sale, seemed more classically up-to-date. Its 36-foot-tall windows are set between two-storey Ionic pilasters on the base of a 1927 bank. Inside, Pawson painted everything white, covered the floors with stone from his native Yorkshire, smoothed out all surfaces and built crisp, rectangular niches (with tubular, stainless steel, right-angled racks for clothes) in the three-storey shop to emphasise the 20-foot-high ceilings and large blocks of unobstructed open space.

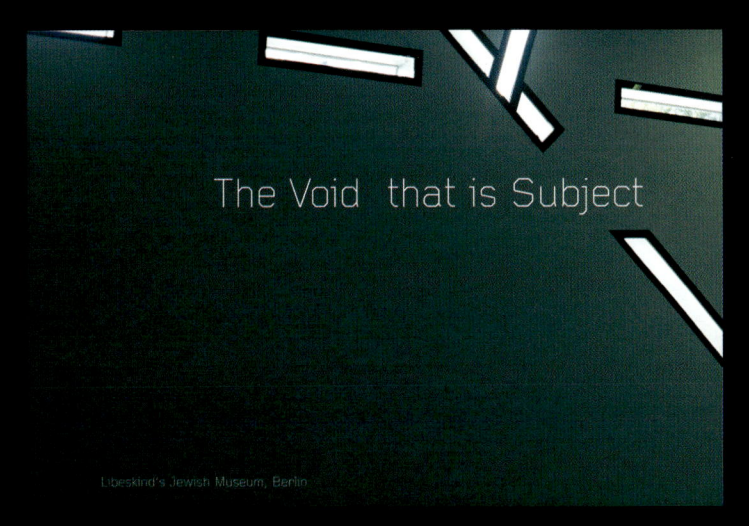

New Realism in Film Architecture

Digital Fiction

The designer of a whole new generation of architectural film sets, Eric Hanson chronicles recent developments in computer-aided design in the cinema and suggests the important new role architects may take in 3-D film design. He shows examples of his work in creating large-scale digital environments for the simulation-ride film *Mars Odyssey* as well as on Luc Besson's *The Fifth Element* and Disney's new *Fantasia 2000*.

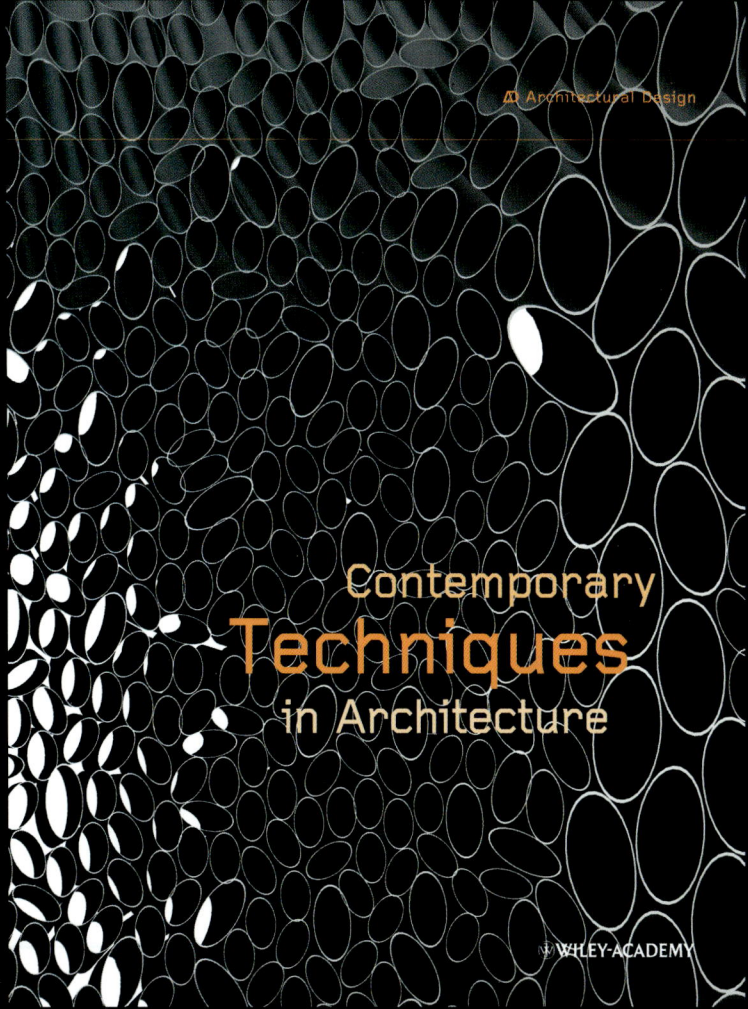

Contemporary Techniques in Architecture

△ Architectural Design

WILEY-ACADEMY

The Void that is Subject

Libeskind's Jewish Museum, Berlin

+ CHK Design

Page
38

Client
Keith Talent Gallery London

Title of work
Miser & Now Magazine, Issue 1

Art Director
Christian Kùsters

Type of work
Magazine

Designer
Christian Kùsters

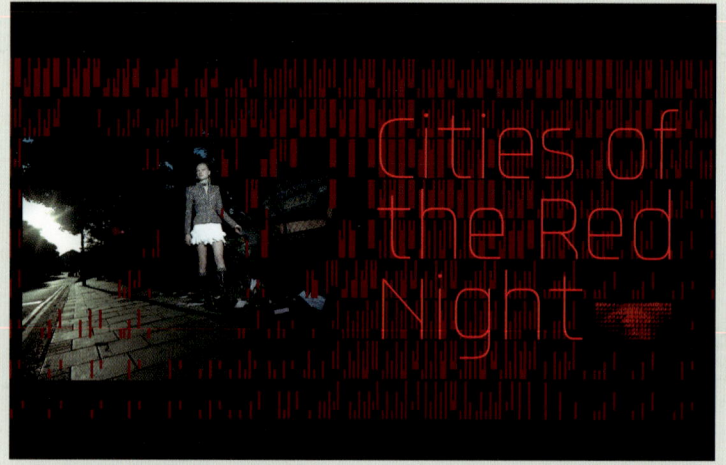

Origin
London, UK

Year produced
2003

Description
The design for the first issue is based on: a) the name of the magazine ('miser' being an old-fashioned word for someone who doesn't like to spend money); and b) the theme for the first issue: collage. The backgrounds of the entire issue are made up of details of international bank notes. These details, chosen for every page, then interact with the art shown.
This also tries to point at a parallel between art and currency and to interpret art as an international currency. The logo was originally drawn on paper and then redrawn by a traditional engraver in Hatton Gardens. It tries to visually refer to the 'Bank of England' lettering on all notes for England and thus emphasise the 'miser' reference. The actual copper template was then scanned and used for the cover.

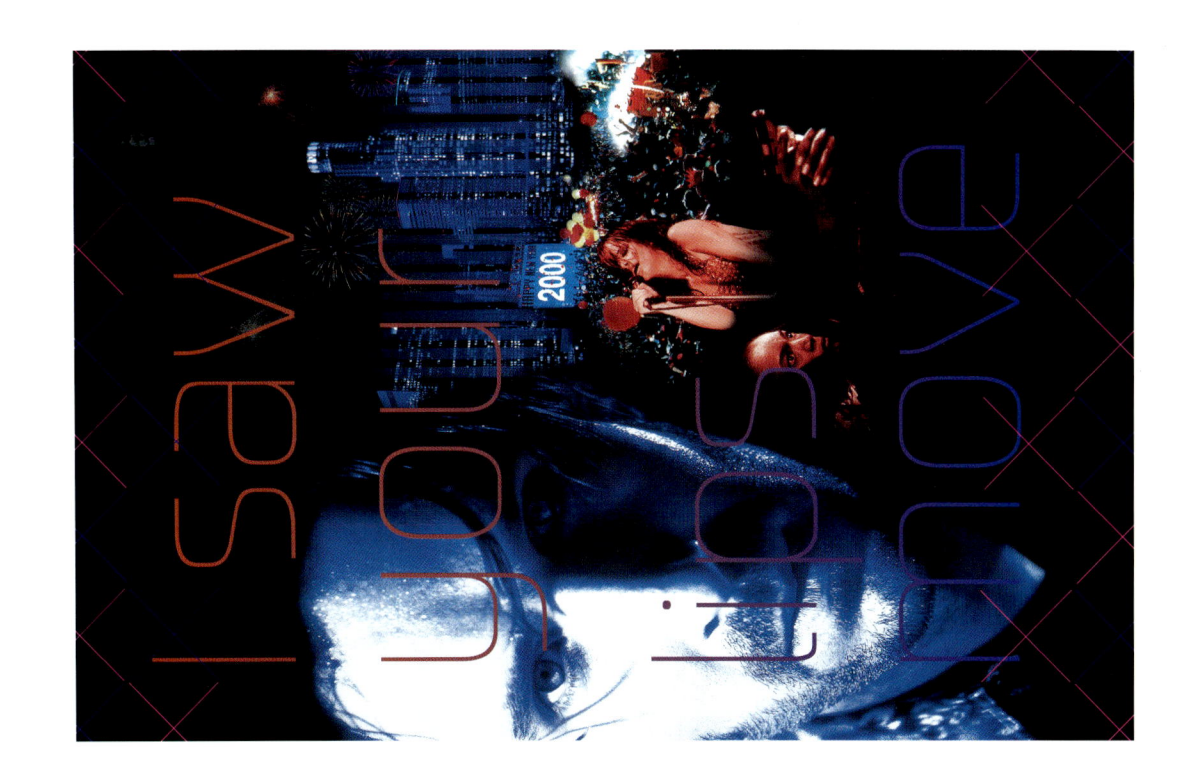

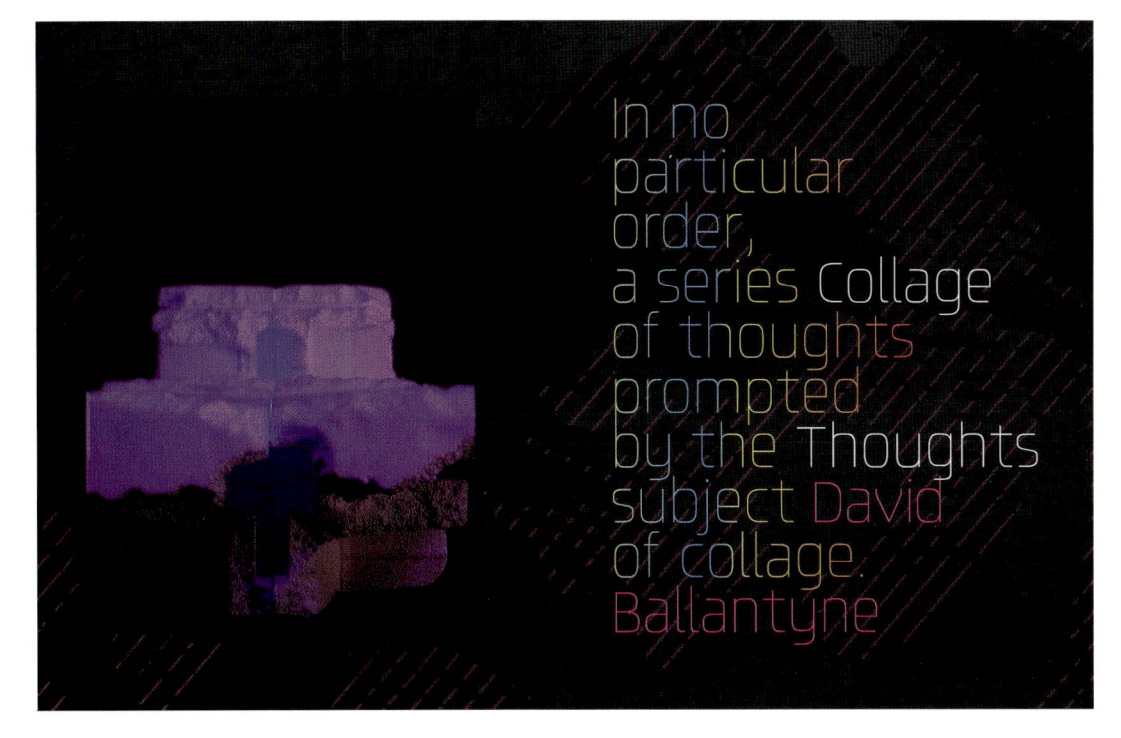

+ CHK Design

Page
40

Client
Keith Talent Gallery London

Origin
London, UK

Title of work
Miser & Now Magazine, Issue 2

Art Director
Christian Küsters

Year produced
2004

Type of work
Magazine

Designer
Christian Küsters

Description
The theme for the second issue was 'Oblique Strategies'. The design followed a strict formula, which was set up beforehand. Every page has a square as the main structure and all material has impact to it one way or another, and it will happen organically or almost mechanically. The result is hopefully subtle enough throughout the whole issue to give the idea of using an oblique strategy.

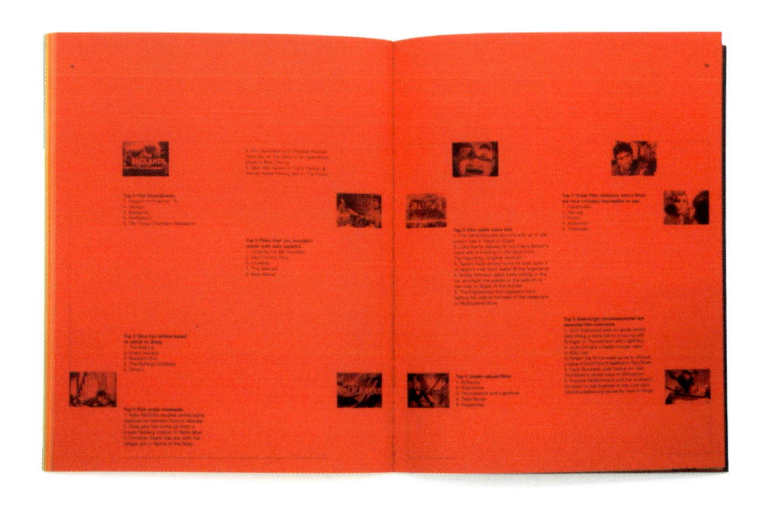

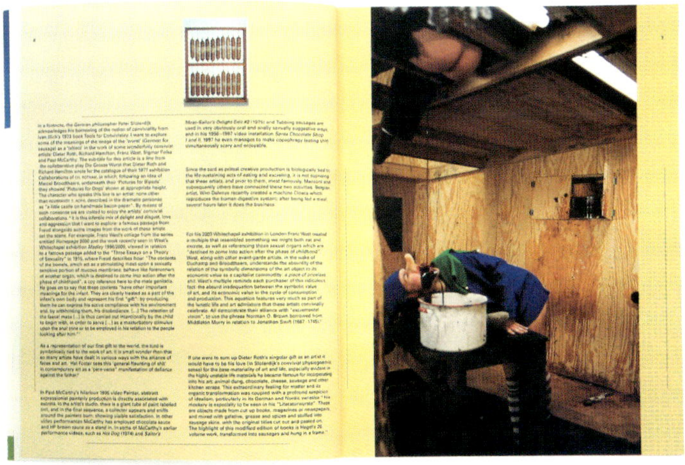

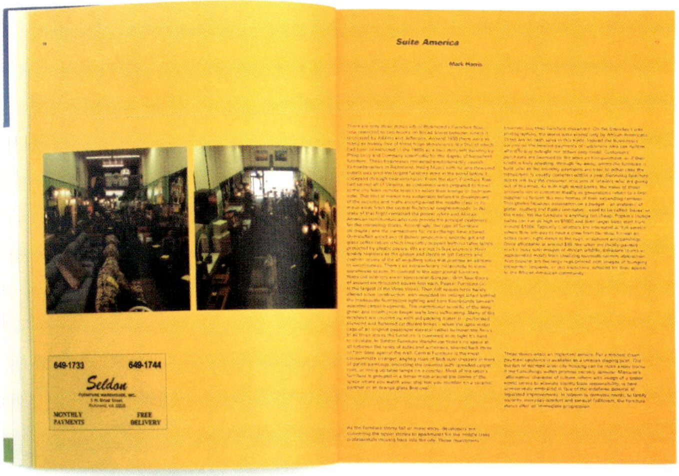
Suite America
Mark Harris
649-1733
649-1744
Seldon
MONTHLY PAYMENTS
FREE DELIVERY

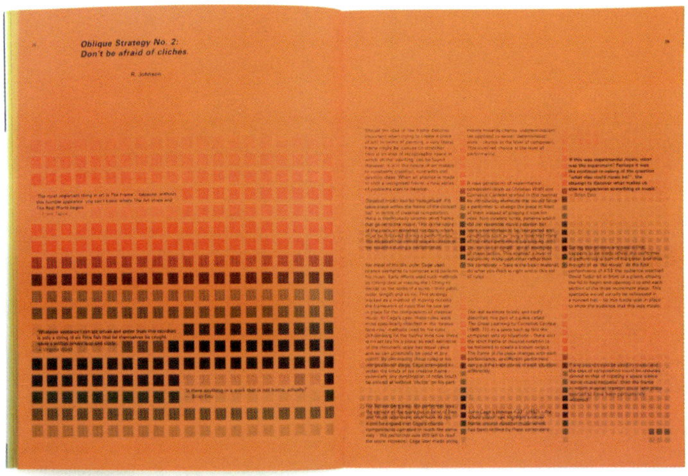
Oblique Strategy No. 2:
Don't be afraid of clichés

Japanese Horror

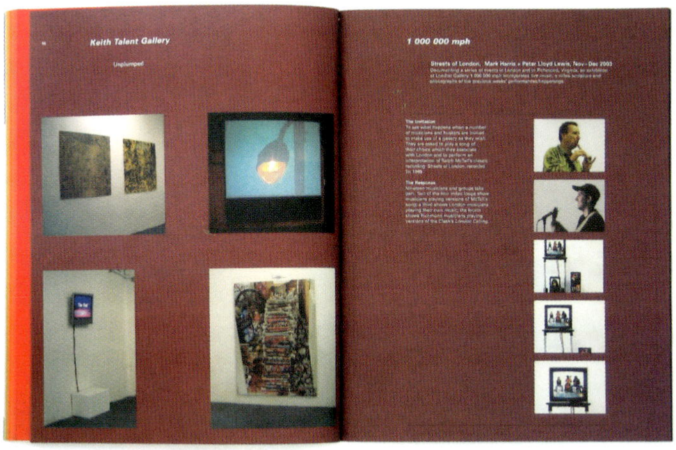
Keith Talent Gallery
Unplumped
1 000 000 mph

MOT

+ Teresa & David

Page
42

Client
Bonzoo

Origin
Stockholm, Sweden

Title of work
Debut

Art Director
Teresa & David

Year produced
2003

Type of work
Magazine

Designer
Teresa & David

Description

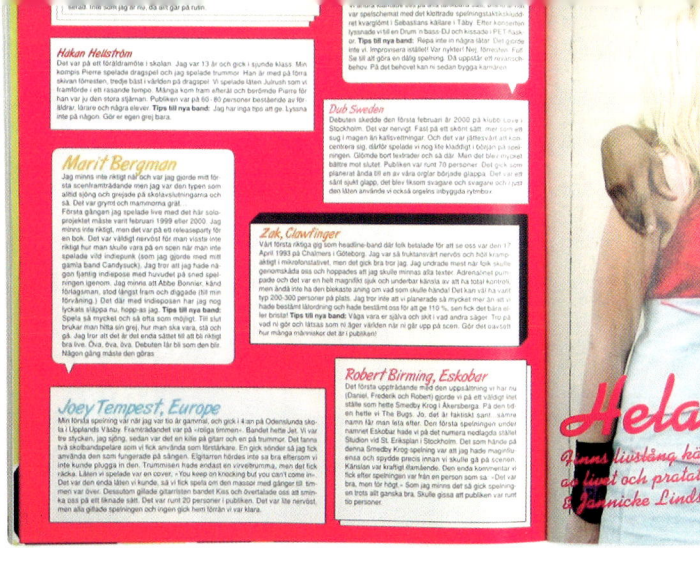

Håkan Hellström
Det var på ett föräldramöte i skolan. Jag var 13 år och gick i sjunde klass. Min kompis Pierre spelade dragspel och jag spelade trummor. Han är med på första skivan föresten. Inrde blått i värld går jag dragspel. Vi spelade låten Julrush som vi framförde i ett rasande tempo. Många kom han efteråt och berömde Pierre för han vi ju den stora stjärnan. Publiken på på 60 - 80 personer bestående av föräldrar, lärare och några elever. **Tips till nya band:** Jag har inga tips att ge. Lyssna inte på någon. Gör er egen grej bara.

Marit Bergman
Jag minns inte riktigt nåt när jag var tio år gammal, och gick i fjärde klass mitt för sta scenframträdande mer jag var den typen som alltid sjöng och grejade på skolavslutningarna och så. Det var grynt och mammorna grät. Första gången jag spelade live med det här projektet måste vart februari 1999 eller 2000. Jag minns inte riktigt, men det var på ett releaseparty för en bok. Det var väldigt nervöst för man visste inte riktigt hur man skulle vara på en scen när man inte spelade vid indiepunk (som jag gjorde med mitt gamla band Candysuck). Jag tror att jag fude någon fjantig indepose med huvudet på sned genomgången. Jag minns att Abbe Bonvier, känd förtalsman, stod långt fram och digade där min förvåning. Det där med indieposen har jag nog lyckats släppa nu, hopps jag. **Tips till nya band:** Spela så mycket och så ofta som möjligt. Till dom brukar man hitta sin grej, hur man ska vara, stå och gå. Alla svenskar har åsikter om att bli riktig bra live. Öva, öva, öva. Debuten lär bli som din. Någon gång måste de göras.

Joey Tempest, Europe
Min första spelning var när jag var 10 år eller 11 år och gick i 4:an på Odensunda skolan i Uppland Våsby. Framträdanaet var på tröliga timmen - Bandet hette Jet. Vi var fyra stycken, jag sjöng, sedan var det en kille på gitarr och en på trummor. Det fanns två skobandsspelare som vi fick använda som förstärkare. En gick stöder så jag fick använda den som fungerade på alperen. Egtalarren fördes inte bra efterson vi inte kunde plugga in den. Trummisen hade endast en vivetummar, men det fick räcka. Låten vi spelade var en coven - King Kong som knocking but you can't come in. Det var den enda låten vi kunde, så vi fick spela om den massor med gånger till timmen vi live. Dessutom gillade gitarristen bandet Kiss och överlakade oss at smikas pås på ett liknade sätt. Det var runt 20 personer i publiken. Det var lite nervöst, men alla gillade spelningen och ingen gick hem förrän vi var klara.

Dub Sweden
Debuten skedde den första februari år 2000 på klub xxxx i Stockholm. Jag var nervös. Fast på ett skönt sätt. Vår grupp hade sug i magen än kalts-stimingar. Och det var gitarriteen i en krockantets sig, därför spelade vi nog lite kladdigt. Det var en sån gång gemensa-skada vi oss hoppades att jag skulle minnas alla texter. Adrenalinet pumpade och det var ett fint magiskt sjuk noch underbara kärnas av att ha total kontroll mer ändå inta ha den behagsba aning om vad som skulle hända! Det kan vält ha varit typ 200-300 personer på plats. Jag tror inte att vi planerade så mycket mer ån att vi hade beslutet tålordning och hade bestämt oss för att ge 110 %, som fick det bra vi bestått! **Tips till nya band:** Våga va er själva och skit i vad andra säger. Tro på vad ni gör och lyckas som ni ligger världen när ni går upp på scen. Gör det ovsätt hur många människor det är i publiken!

Zak, Clawfinger
Vår första riktiga gig som headline-band där folk betalade för att se oss var den 17 April 1993 på Chalmers i Göteborg. Jag var så fruktansvärt nervös och hör kunde åkvejt i mikrofonstativet, men det gick bra tor jag. Jag underde mest när fokulsusu genomskåda oss och hoppades att jag skulle minnas alla texter. Adrenalinet pumpade och det var ett fint magiskt sjuk och underbara kärnas av att ha total kontroll men ändå inte ha den behagsba aning om vad som skulle hända! Det kan vält ha varit typ 200-300 personer på plats. Jag tror inte att vi planerade så mycket mer ån att vi hade beslutet tålordning och hade bestämt oss för att ge 110 %, som fick det bra vi bestått! **Tips till nya band:** Våga va er själva och skit i vad andra säger. Tro på vad ni gör och lyckas som ni ligger världen när ni går upp på scen. Gör det ovsätt hur många människor det är i publiken!

Robert Birming, Eskobar
Det första uppträdandet med den uppsättning vi har nu (Daniel, Frederik och Robert) gjorde vi på ett väldigt litet ställe som hette Smedby Krog i Åkersberga. På den tid ankegt i mikrofonstativet, men det gick bra tor jag. Jag underde mest när fokulsusu genomskåda oss och hoppades att jag skulle minnas alla texter. Adrenalinet pumpade och det var ett fint magiskt sjuk och underbara kärnas av att ha total kontroll men ändå inte ha den behagsba aning om vad som skulle hända! Det kan vält ha varit typ 200-300 personer på plats. Jag tror inte att vi planerade så mycket mer ån att vi hade beslutet tålordning och hade bestämt oss för att ge 110 %, som fick det bra vi bestått! Trots att vad ni gör när ni ligger världen när ni går upp på scen, så om att lätsas som ni ligger världen när ni går upp på scem. Gör det ovsätt hur många människor det är i publiken!

Hela livet

Finns livslång kärlek? Vi har träffat två par i olika åldrar som pratar om långvariga relationer. Möt Pierre & Jeanicke Lindström och Otto & Ruthel Ekzell.

HAN SKA SKITA I VAD JAG SKA HA KONDOMERNA TILL

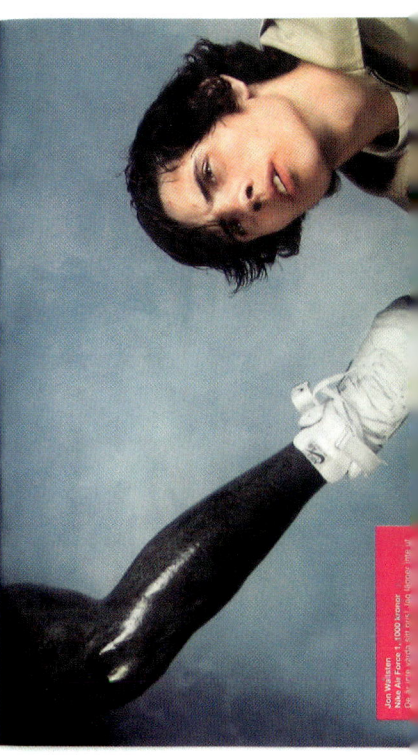

Lolle Widegren
Tiger Wrestling 91, 1,299 kronor:
Jag skulle de nog röligen, men skulle bli visa sa fräta pratskoa. Eftersom de är så höga le för bli värs ett ta så pck på tag. Dessutom holder jag att pruck är för höga. Jag skulle vara nog inte köpta-klossarge plus-fer-tit. Da är vel verde-eft vala rimera och na välds-gt en märkeå-
Utwarding i dn är en genrell kampanj-
sko från Japans!

Betyg: 2

Alla har vi åsikter om hur den optimala dojan ska se ut. Men hur är det egentligen med pris, kvalitet och komfort? Bryr vi oss om det lika mycket? DEBUT gjorde ett urval av tio skor på marknaden, klassiska modeller från kända märken som Nike, Puma och Adidas, men också pjuck från mindre tillverkare som Gola, Le Coq Sportif och Tiger. För en kritisk granskning kallade vi in testpanelen. Sammanlagt genomförde vi tre tester. Efter en svettig och regnig dag på Stockholms gator föll domen.

HÅKAN HELLSTRÖM på turné

TEXT: LOUISE LARSSON
ILLUSTRATION DEBUT

Du uppträder numera som soloartist, men har ett ständigt kompband i ryggen. Blir det samma känsla som med ett "riktigt" band?
- Absolut. Det här är det bästa bandet jag spelat med. Det är handplockade favoritmusiker, ett dröm-band.

Var har du hittat favoritmusikerna?
- Finns spelade jag samba med som tonåring. Stefan satt är den bästa blåsaren i Göteborg, nej förnämsta i hela Sverige, lärde jag känna genom vår förra producent Stefan. Timo är tibottor iti en klass-kompis. Oskar var klasskompis med Timo. Daniel har jag haft massor med band tillsammans med, vi irrade till exempel inop i Broder Daniel. Labbe är en favoritrummis, som jag sett spela tillsammans med Soul. Victor är en fantastisks bläsare och dansare som förut spelade med Monster och Moneybrother.

Hur ser vardagen ut på turné?
- Vi spelar dalaspel, fotboll, sover ibland efter vi repar ni nägan ny grej och bakar om hestar. På bussen lekar vi mycket, lyssnar på musik, lirar för varandra.

Brukar det hända att folk som inte bor till bandet kommer upp på scen och gör saker de inte ska?
- Ja, killar kommer upp ibland och känner att de vill kyssa mig.

Har du någonsin utnytjat, eller anväst, det faktum att du är känd för att få lite kärlek?
- Utnyttjat är fel ord. Då låter det som om det skulle handla om ett vägeltost attar. Nej, det har jag inte använt, inte vad jag kan erinna mig om. Nu har jag ju tjej och det känns från-mande att prata om det här. Jag när inte när jag tänker på sådana saker, det är så långt ifrån det liv jag lever.

Har du några särskilt starka turnéminnen?
- Under första spelningarna på turnén hände det att vi svimmmade. Vi röjde oss gå scenern att plötsligt bler det svårt och så låg man gå gövlot. Det var bara att resa sig upp igen och fortsätta. (En autografjgare kommer in och avbryter: - Min syster tycker du år jättebra och jag tycker du är ganska bra, kan jag få en autograf?-)

Vi är jobbigt när folk reducerar en till ett objekt. Till exempel när folk kommer fram och tar ett kort utan att fråga.

Men det är väl så det blir när man är känd?
- Jo kanske, men jag är ingen kändis. Jag är bara Håkan.

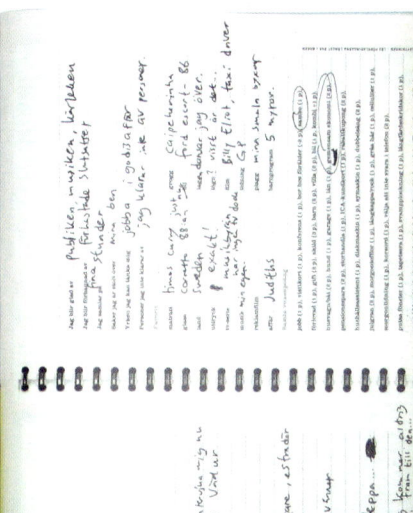

+ Segura Inc.

Page
44

Title of work
Filth

Type of work
Comic

The Filth

GRANT MORRISON CHRIS WESTON GARY ERSKINE

DIRECT SALES VERTIGO

---

02. perfect victim   A SERIES OF 13 BOOKS   USA $0.00 CAN $0.00
SEPTEMBER 2002   SUGGESTED FOR MATURE READERS

VERTIGO

The Filth

Grant Morrison
Chris Weston

23 PAGES

Direct Sales

The Filth

A SERIES OF 13 BOOKS   USA $2.95 CAN $4.95
SEPTEMBER 2002   SUGGESTED FOR MATURE READERS

03. STRUCTURES AND ULTRASTRUCTURES   22 PAGES
GRANT MORRISON
CHRIS WESTON
GARY ERSKINE

Direct Sales

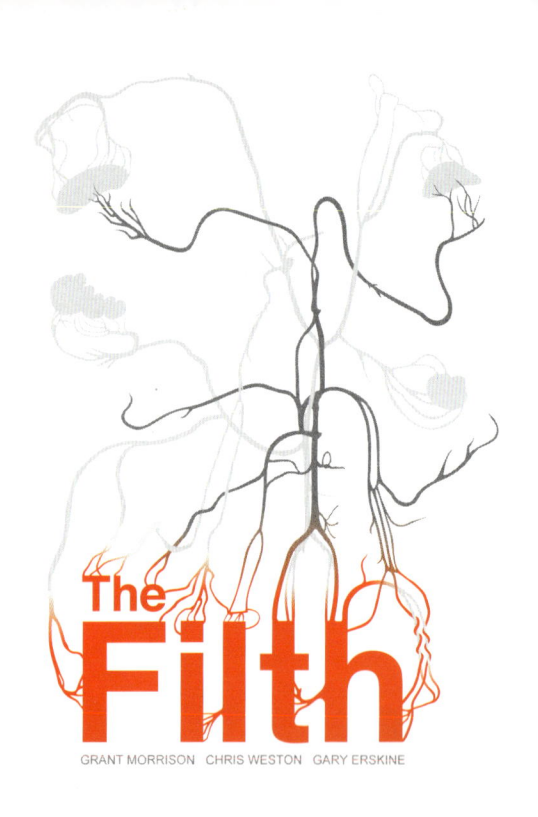

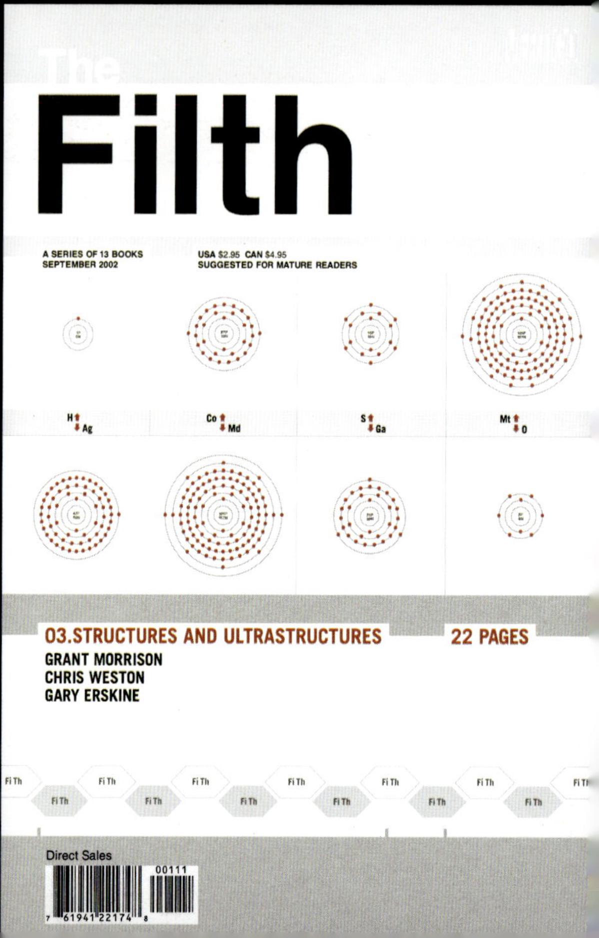

The Filth
VERTIGO
04. s**t happens
DANGER
WARNING
BE CAREFUL
22 Pages
Grant Morrison
Chris Weston
Gary Erskine

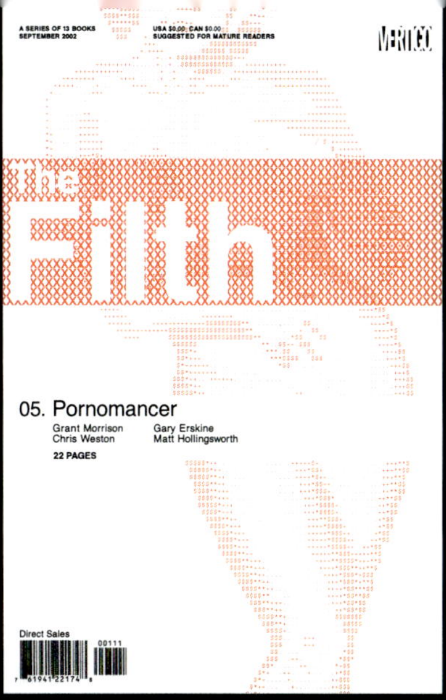
A SERIES OF 13 BOOKS
SEPTEMBER 2002
USA $0.00 CAN $0.00
SUGGESTED FOR MATURE READERS
VERTIGO
The Filth
05. Pornomancer
Grant Morrison
Chris Weston
Gary Erskine
Matt Hollingsworth
22 PAGES
Direct Sales

The Filth
VERTIGO
#06
THE WORLD OF
ANDERS KLIMAKKS
Grant Morrison
Chris Weston
Gary Erskine

The Filth™
VERTIGO
A SERIES OF 13 BOOKS
SEPTEMBER 2002
USA $0.00 CAN $0.00
SUGGESTED FOR MATURE READERS
ISSUE #07
ZERO
DEMOCRACY
GRANT MORRISON
CHRIS WESTON
GARY ERSKINE

A SERIES OF 13 BOOKS
SEPTEMBER 2002
SUGGESTED FOR MATURE READERS
VERTIGO
The Filth
#08
♥*%$ POLICE
Grant Morrison
Chris Weston
Gary Erskine
22 PAGES
DIRECT SALES

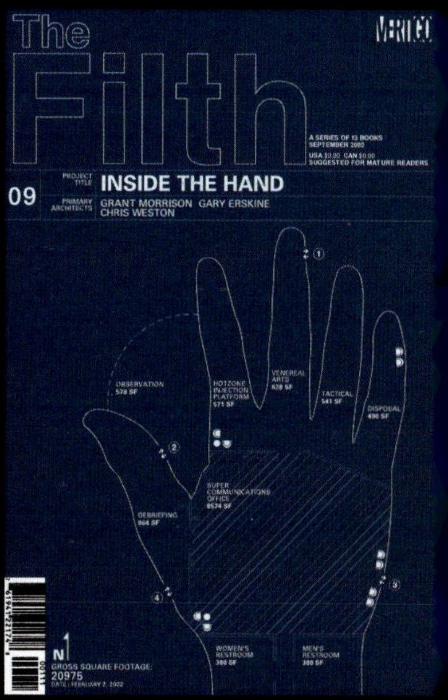
The Filth
VERTIGO
A SERIES OF 13 BOOKS
SEPTEMBER 2002
USA $0.00 CAN $0.00
SUGGESTED FOR MATURE READERS
09
PROJECT TITLE
INSIDE THE HAND
PRIMARY ARCHITECTS
GRANT MORRISON GARY ERSKINE
CHRIS WESTON
OBSERVATION
HOTZONE INJECTION PLATFORM
VENEREAL ARTS
TACTICAL
DISPOSAL
SUPER COMMUNICATIONS OFFICE
DEBRIEFING
WOMEN'S RESTROOM
MEN'S RESTROOM
GROSS SQUARE FOOTAGE:
20975

VERTIGO
The Filth
22 PAGES
Grant Morrison
Chris Weston
Gary Erskine
10. man made god
Direct Sales
A SERIES OF 13 BOOKS
SEPTEMBER 2002
USA $0.00 CAN $0.00
SUGGESTED FOR MATURE READERS

VERTIGO
#12 SCHIZOTYPE
The Filth
22 PAGES
A SERIES OF 13 BOOKS
JULY 2003
USA $0.00 CAN $0.00
SUGGESTED FOR MATURE READERS
SCHIZOTYPE

The Filth
GRANT MORRISON
CHRIS WESTON
GARY ERSKINE
VERTIGO
012
A VERY ENGLISH
NERVOUS BREAKDOWN
A SERIES OF 13 BOOKS
USA $0.00 CAN $0.00
SUGGESTED FOR MATURE READERS

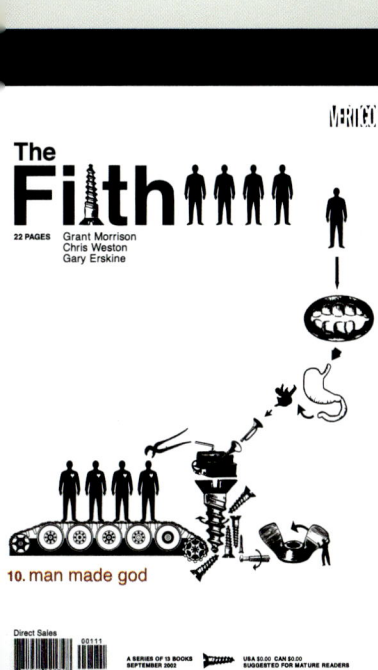

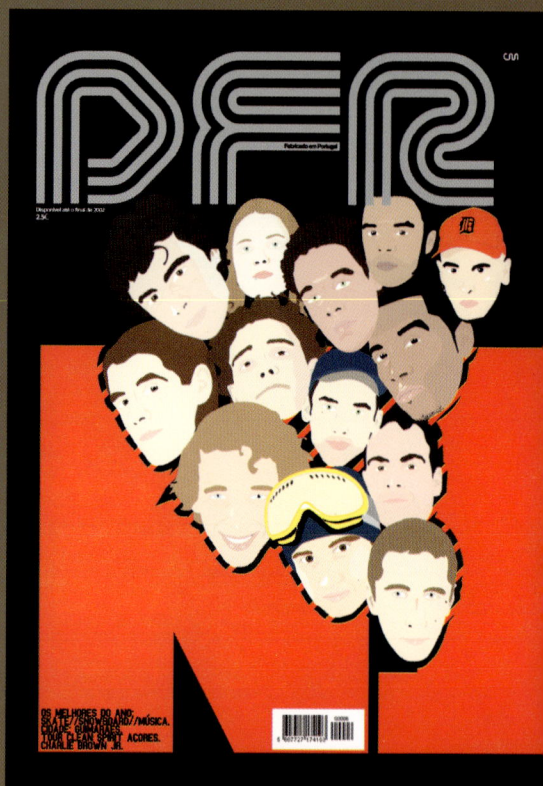

DFR

Fabricado em Portugal

S3t3mbro 2003
2.5€
WWW.DIFERE.COM

ANDRÉ: "KINGSYZE".
PADOCK / KODAP: A RECORTAR, COLAR E CONSUMIR COM OS OLHOS.
BARCELONA: TOUR PORTUGUÊS CIRCA/ LAKAI
ESTÚDIO CIDADE: EXPOSIÇÃO DE ARTE URBANA DA CIDADE ENQUANTO HABITAT CRIATIVO.
OPEN ETNIES 2003: 1ª ETAPA, ALMEIRIM, SKATEPARQUE.
REVELAÇÕES: HUGO MARRAZES & HUGO SILVA.
FESTA ZERO.

N3 2003

DFR

Disponível até o final de 2002
2.5€

OS MELHORES DO ANO:
SKATE/SNOWBOARD/MÚSICA
CIDADE GANADORA
TOUR D-LAX SPORT AÇORES
CHARLIE BROWN JR.

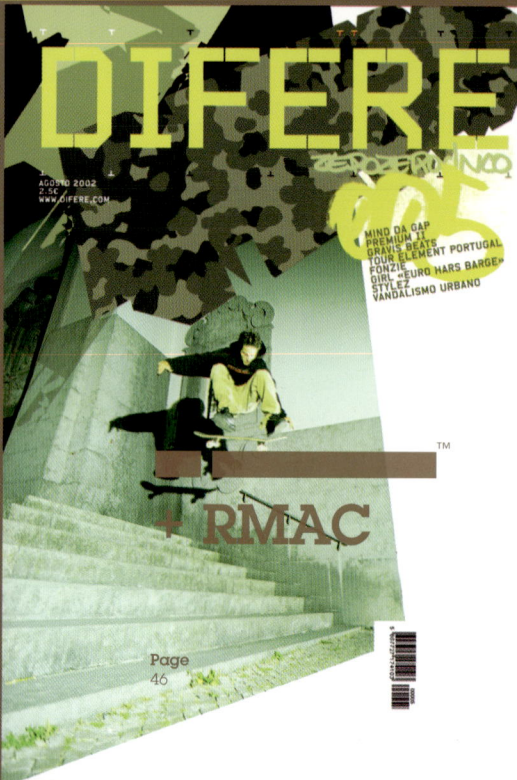

DIFERE

ZERO ZERO UM 001

AGOSTO 2002
2.5€
WWW.DIFERE.COM

MIND DA GAP
PREMIUM II
DRAKE BEATS
TOUR ELEMENT PORTUGAL
FONZIE
GIRL "EURO HARS BARGE"
STYLEZ
VANDALISMO URBANO

+ RMAC

Page 46

OPEN ETNIES

ESTÚDIO CIDADE

+ Build ™

Page
48

Client
Keep Left studios, Sydney, Australia

Title of work
Refill Magazine

Art Director
Michael C. Place

Type of work
Magazine cover

Designer
Michael C. Place

Origin
London, UK

Year produced
2003

Description
Cover design for launch issue of Refill Magazine
The cover is split up into 5 parts:
01: Title/Image area,
02: Tagging/personalisation,
03: Components,
04: Have your Art seen by many +
05: Blank canvas [the reader is encouraged to write/tag on the blank wall].

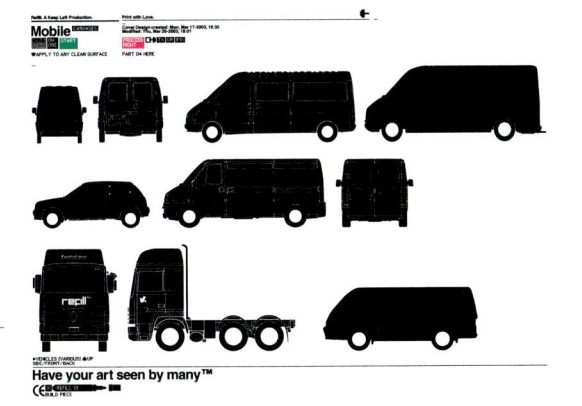

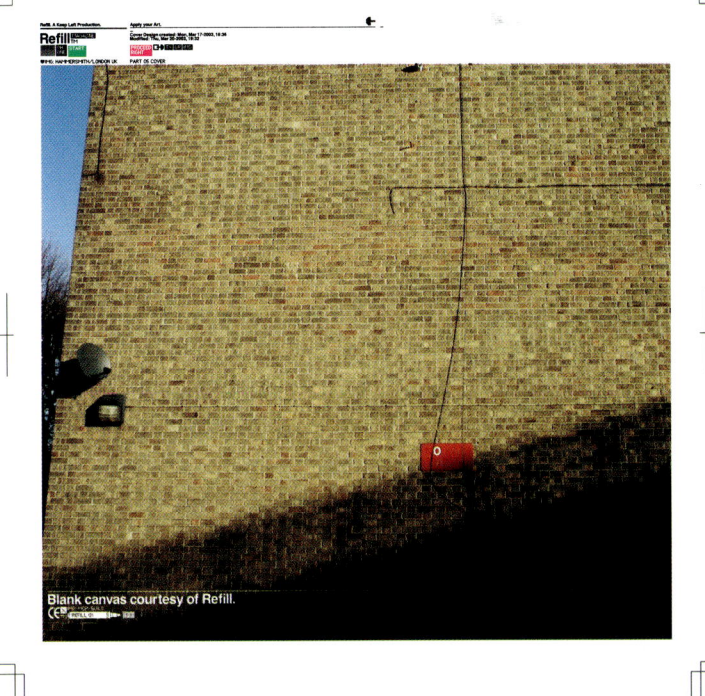

WORDS FOR PICTURES

COPYWRITER MAY BE A REDUNDANT JOB TITLE, BUT WORDS ARE STILL THE BEST MEDIUM FOR THE EXPRESSION OF IDEAS, SAYS GERRY MOIRA

▶ I THINK IT WAS GIBB THE Younger who said "It's only words but words are all I have to take your heart away".

Words were certainly all I had when asked earlier this year to take the stand at Unilever House and address a body of men and women who call themselves "26". So called after the number of letters in the alphabet, 26 is made up of people who write for a living. Otherwise they look and act like perfectly normal human beings. ▶

You may have shared a joke around the water-cooler with one of them, you may have given them money in exchange for words, there is a statistical possibility that you may have been intimate with one or more of them during the last 12 months. It's okay, it's not as though you're suddenly going to become articulate or anything.

My invitation to speak was part of an outreach programme 26 are running toward commercial writers from different disciplines. DDB's Will Awdry and Radio's Owen Paul Burke stood alongside me to try and explain what an advertising writer actually does. Well, there's precious little writing for a start. In almost thirty years as a copywriter I don't suppose I've had more than a couple of thousand words broadcast or published.

"Creative" covers almost every commercial endeavour from the writing of King Lear to the making of drinks coasters from stale digestive biscuits and a coat of yacht varnish.

What we really do is conceptualise. We take the base commercial desires of our clients and fashion them into ideas that "resonate" (a buzzword in every sense) with consumers. Subsequently that idea may need to be expressed in print, radio, on-line or television or whatever the most appropriate medium might be. That might involve some actual writing. For me the real creative work lies in taking those sometimes complex marketing objectives and distilling them down to a simple communicable idea that can change attitudes and, ultimately, behaviour. ▶

The concept behind the Nike brand for example is "irreverence justified". Two words worth about a billion dollars each. Together they make Nike a brand and not just a shoe. Those two little words inform all of Nike's communications from the ads they run to the people they hire to the stars they choose to sponsor. Any self-respecting street kid can tell you the difference between Nike and Adidas. The shoes may be interchangeable but the brands are distinct. That's what we do, we create those differences and make them worth something. Everything else is subservient to that objective.

Someone once suggested the title "concepteur" to describe our primary function. Obviously this sounds hopelessly French and pretentious. It reminds me that the most famous of all French copywriters Jacques Seguela, called his autobiography "Don't tell my mother I work in advertising, she thinks I play piano in a brothel".

This tells us a lot about French intellectual snobbery and the sexual mores of the bourgeoisie but is no help in providing us with a modern and relevant job descriptor. Only think it's important because I sense there's a ceding of the high ground by today's creative thinkers from having big ideas to just making ads. I'm certainly not denigrating the latter skill-set but if that's really our sole "raison d'etre" then perhaps we should be working for production companies not advertising agencies. But I digress, a funny thing happened to me on my way to this 26 gig.

Whenever you're put in a position of having to explain what you do to people who are not "in the life", you inevitably start to regain some objectivity toward your job function. This reappraisal was made all the more poignant for me by watching my son Dominic take his first faltering steps as a copywriter. He's decided to take up the Moira baton and let's hope he'll be showing it up an account man's arse near you in the near future. But what kind of future will it be? I don't think the business of writing in advertising has ever been under such intense pressure. Firstly you have the established tectonic plates of Compression and Abstraction. These two, often conflicting, forces are rubbing against each other with more friction than ever before. Compressing the global ambitions of giant conglomerates into 30 seconds has never been as easy as it looked. Now, any self-respecting CEO wants to see his corporate face reflected in an online banner! The ad-byte is with us and the USP is no longer. Compression was a relatively simple exercise when you could reduce it to simple product superiority. Creating a differentiated brand personality takes longer. Barclays (or any other high street bank) has long since abandoned any pretence to a "better mouse trap" but they've got Samuel L Jackson and your bank hasn't… huh? It's no wonder that cliché, parody and celebrity endorsement are the copywriter's best friends. There's no time and less and less media money for character development, a back story or second act in contemporary TV campaigns. Imagine the cost of establishing a Heineken or Hamlet at today's rate of media inflation and audience fragmentation.

If Compression is about reducing our client's offering to its most condensed and compelling expression, then Abstraction is about acknowledging that nobody else gives a fuck.

Nobody pays their Sky subscription or TV license to watch the ads. We have to make things interesting. And in setting out one's stall, it's no longer enough to give the apples a good polish. These days you have to pose naked with a banana and a couple of kiwi fruit to raise an eyebrow let alone anything more substantial. We have to create new news and the quest for novelty almost inevitably that takes us further and further away from our overt purpose. The average UK citizen receives around 3000 advertising hits each day. By the time the average Brit reaches his or her thirty-fifth birthday, she or he will have already seen 150,000 commercials. What space do your efforts occupy in their overloaded, over-stimulated memory banks? In the struggle for cut-through, the word is the words are no longer up to the job.

There are only three kinds of word-dependent TV advertising left. There's the old Persuasion Model from advertising's Jurassic period. This is still used by the P&Gs, L'Oreals and "better mouse trap" people who believe that 30 seconds of rational argument can affect behavioural change. Marks are from the Jurassic period too and they've survived because they're efficient. This model must work for those with sufficient NPD programmes to support it.

Next you have that rare visitor to our shores, The Corporate Philosopher. Really an American native, the "let's talk about us" approach has failed to find popularity or talented practitioners here, early Orange work and the Honda UK spot being the exceptions. Lastly there's the overwhelming British favourite, The Sponsored Sketch. Invented by CDP in the 70s, refined by BMP in the 80s and then roughed up a bit by HHCL in the 90s. The Sponsored Sketch has become the preferred form of expression for most UK copywriters. This is their last redoubt against the serried ranks of art college clones, of post-production trickery, MTV cliché and minimalist cool. Not to mention some of the most reductive and conformist research techniques ever devised by man to squeeze life and individuals out of an idea.

We've come a long way since the Abbott Hegarty Arts and Crafts Movement of the early 80s. There's a New Brutalism about the agencies that making good TV ads is a purely instinctive process, like producing good rock n'roll. It's all about feel and texture and image man. The New Brutalists are suspicious of words, they believe brainy, articulate people should be confined to the Planning Department. But the truth is that words have never been cooler. Britons buy more newspapers than any other nation. We read more books than any other nation. Indeed, book sales rose by over 40 per cent from 1997 to 2001. Radio 4 is one of the great media success stories of the last five years. Words are still the best medium for the expression of ideas and Maurice Gibb was right about the innate emotional power. The question is, are our writers up to the challenge?

Gerry Moira, the former executive creative director and chairman of Publicis, now writes commercials for a list. For more information about 26, the not-for-profit association of professional writers and language specialists, go to www.26.org.uk

+ Build

Page
51

Title of work
+ Creative Review Magazine
++ Graphic 03

Type of work
Magazine
+ Inside pages/spreads
++ Double page spreads

Compression /File Formats. Graphic, Design by Build.

dotsuffix here.
iso/iec number.
Example:
hyper-text links placed here.
non-clickable examples.

Compression /File Formats. Graphic, Design by Build.

dot.jpg
itu-t t.81/ iso/iec 10918-1.
Example:
http://newswire.spaceimaging.com/images/launch/sanfran/deg4_1_300.jpg

Compression /File Formats. Graphic, Design by Build.

dotmpg[2]
iso/iec 11172-1.
Example:
http://www.argo.ce.unipr.it/ARGO/movies/vd2.mpg

Compression /File Formats. Graphic, Design by Build.

dotwmv[3]
iso/iec jtc1/sc29/wg11
Example:
http://www.centralsingapore.org.sg/site/pif/pif_video_56k.wmv

---

Client
+ Creative Review Magazine, UK
++ Magma/Graphic

Origin
London, UK

Art Director
Michael C. Place

Year produced
+ 2004
++ 2003

Designer
Michael C. Place

Description
+ Editorial design [x3 pages].
Keyboard layout as image-maker.
Extended keyboard layout determines image process and execution.
++ Design as Pornography.
dot suffix here.
iso/iec number.
Example: Hyper-text links placed here.
Non-clickable example [input by hand only].

Compression: dotmpg/dotmpg/dotwmv.
The everyday suffix you click on/use everyday.
00:03:47 download time remaining...
Download link to disc?

+ Build

Page
52 - 54

Client
Magma/Graphic

Title of work
Graphic 01, Asthma, Eczema

Art Director
Michael C. Place

Type of work
Double page spreads

Designer
Michael C. Place

Origin
London, UK

Year produced
2003

Description
My Asthma/Eczema presented in graphic form. My frustrations. My medication.
Link. CMYK + Scratch resistant Spot U/V Varnish.
I love my Ventolin Inhaler™

Here:
Photography, Design
by Michael C. Place

BUILD

Upside down

Asthma, Eczema.

Hello, my name is Michael. I am asthmatic. I also suffer from Eczema.

A piece titled:

A print piece for G/'01.

Shake before use.

Do not scratch.

Continue ▶

Font: B-DKL/01™
Labeled:

▶ Cannister label:

100 micrograms per spray

200 doses FOR INHALATION USE

Beclomethasone Dipropionate
100 micrograms Inhaler

Each actuation delivers: 100 micrograms beclomethasone dipropionate per actuation. The patient should read the enclosed patient leaflet before use. Shake before use. Caution: Pressurised vial. Do not puncture or burn, even when empty. Store below 30°C. Protect from direct sunlight or heat. KEEP OUT OF THE REACH OF CHILDREN.
PL holder: 3M Health Care Limited, Loughborough, LE11 1EP, England
Distributed by: Generics (UK) Limited,
Patents: Herts CD640 Bc-L37
PL 68/0144

[POM]

[◆ actual size label]

▶ Becotide Inhaler

▶ Outer Casing/Body.

Body.

Cap.

▶ Preventer

Made 2002-02
Exp 2005-02
Lot GDB023A

Serevent 25mcg
Preventer

Body.

Cap.

▶ Reliever

100 mcg
200 ACTUATIONS
Salbutamol Inhaler CFC-Free
Shake before use

For inhalation use. The patient should read the enclosed patient leaflet before use. Each actuation delivers: Salbutamol Sulphate B.P. equivalent to 100 mcg Salbutamol. Dosage: As directed by the physician.
KEEP OUT OF THE REACH OF CHILDREN. Caution: Pressurised vial. Do not puncture or burn, even when empty. Store below 30°C. Protect from direct sunlight or heat.
PL holder: 3M Health Care Ltd, Loughborough, LE11 1EP, UK.
Distributed by: Generics (UK)
PL 66/0179
[POM]

SG-L63
B00137

Made 2001-11
Exp 2003-11
Lot FCK005A

▶ Label application:

Packaging Top

▶ Fold page here

Eczema Inform:
http://www.eczema.org/

See over.

Salbutamol Inhaler
CFC-Free
200 actuations
Made 2002-02
Exp 2004-02
Lot FDB005A

READ NEW LEAFLET INSIDE

Affix Dispensing Label Here

READ NEW LEAFLET INSIDE

Continues over.

TITLE: ASTHMA, ECZEMA.
END USER NOTE: DO NOT RE-PRODUCE [] THIS PIECE HAS BEEN PRINTED WITH SPECIALLY DESIGNED COPY-PROOF INK.]

I ♥ MY HEART

0BV/ Breathing

50/

0170V3-8U170
8 2610 10802 4

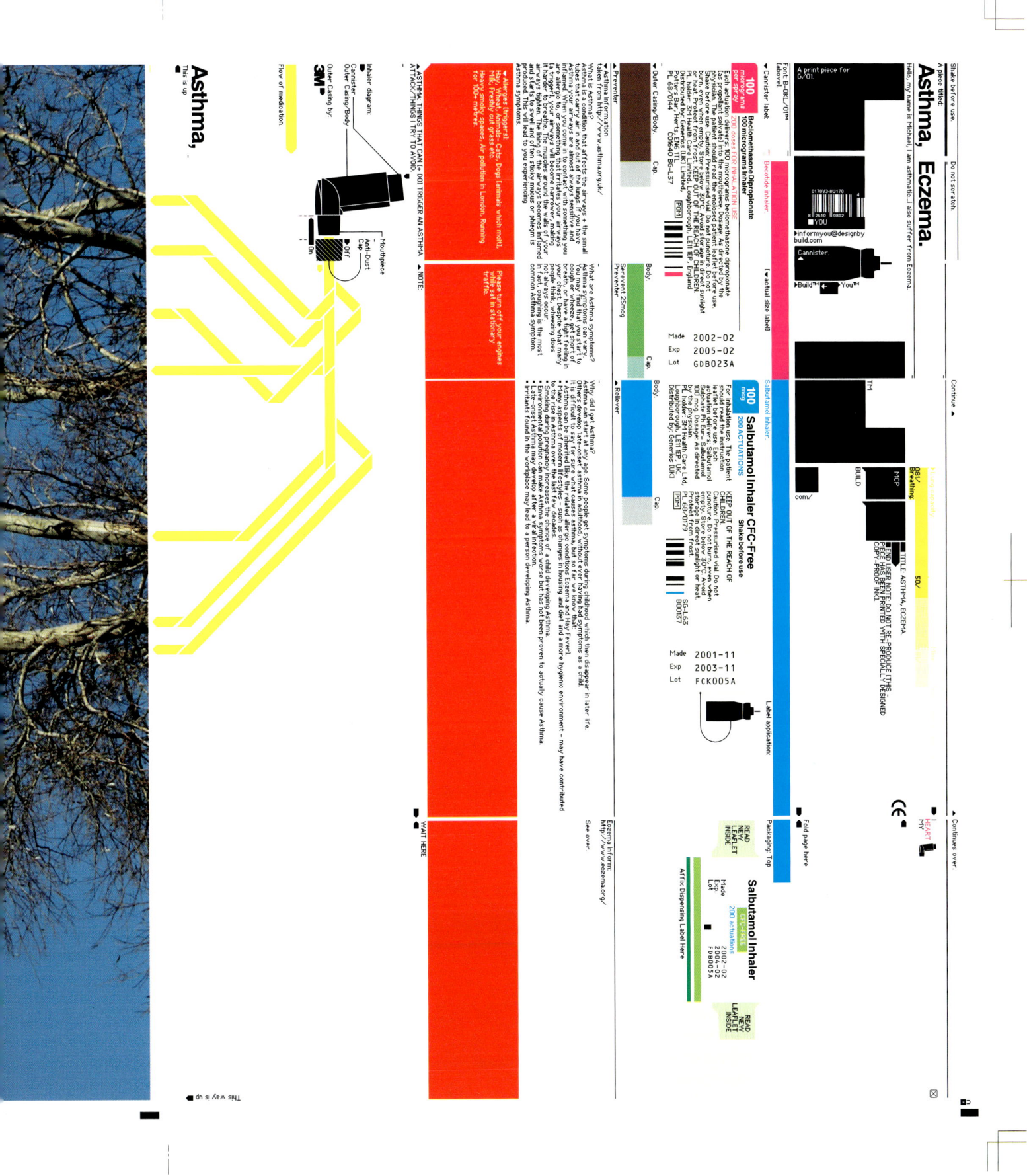

▶ YOU

▶informyou@designbybuild.com

▶Build™ ▶You™

Cannister.

TM

BUILD

MCP

com/

CE

Asthma,
■ This is up

▶ Flow of medication.

Outer Casing by:
3M

Cannister:
Outer Casing/Body:

Inhaler diagram:

Mouthpiece
Anti-Dust Cap
Off
On

▶ ASTHMA, THINGS THAT CAN I-DO! TRIGGER AN ASTHMA ATTACK./THINGS I TRY TO AVOID.

• Allergies triggers?: Cats, Dogs (animals which moth), Milk. Freshly cut grass etc.
Heavy smoky spaces, Air pollution in London. Running for 100+ metres.

▶ Asthma Information:
taken from http://www.asthma.org.uk/
What is asthma?
Asthma is a condition that affects the airways – the small tubes that carry air in and out of the lungs. If you have asthma, your airways are almost always sensitive and inflamed. When you come in to contact with something that irritates your airways (a trigger), your airways will become narrower, making it harder to breathe. The muscles around the walls of your airways tighten. The lining of the airways becomes inflamed and starts to swell and often sticky mucous or phlegm is produced. This will lead to you experiencing common Asthma symptoms.

What are Asthma symptoms?
Asthma symptoms can vary. Others develop 'late-onset' asthma in adulthood, without ever having had symptoms as a child. You may find that you start to cough, or wheeze, get short of breath, or have a tight feeling in your chest. Despite what many people think, wheezing does not always occur. In fact, coughing is the most common Asthma symptom.

Please turn off your engines while sat in stationary traffic.

▶ NOTE

Why did I get Asthma?
Asthma can start at any age. Some people get symptoms during childhood which then disappear in later life. It is difficult to say for sure what causes asthma, but so far we know that:
• Asthma is an inherited condition.
• Many aspects of modern lifestyles – such as changes in housing and diet and a more hygienic environment – may have contributed to the rise in Asthma over the last few decades.
• Smoking during pregnancy increases the chance of a child developing Asthma.
• Environmental pollution can make Asthma symptoms worse but has not been proven to actually cause Asthma.
• Late-onset Asthma may develop after a viral infection.
• Irritants found in the workplace may lead to a person developing Asthma.

▶ WAIT HERE

▶ This way is up

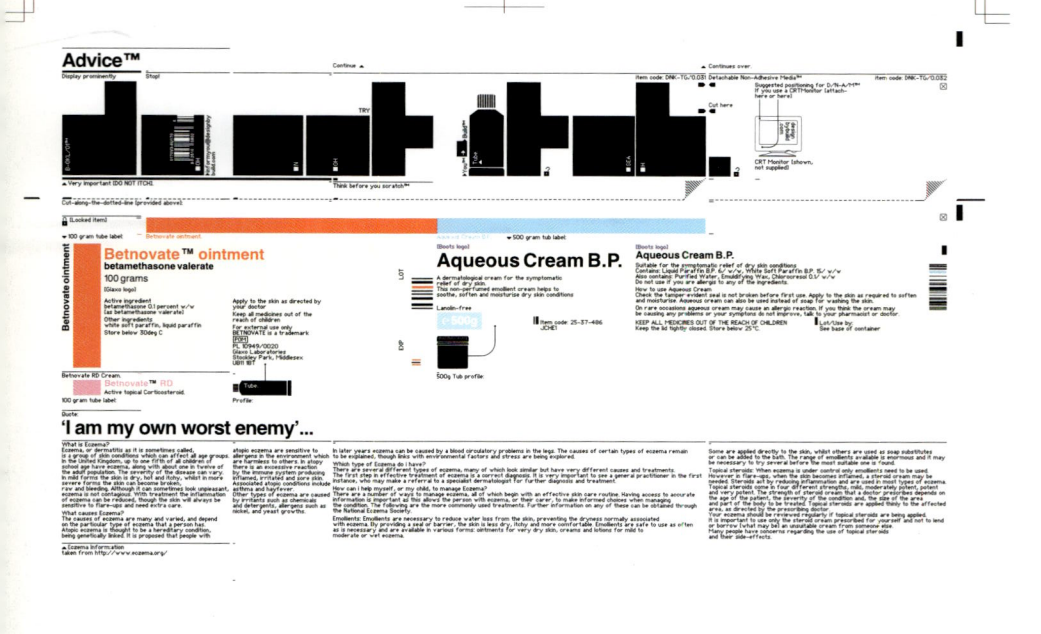

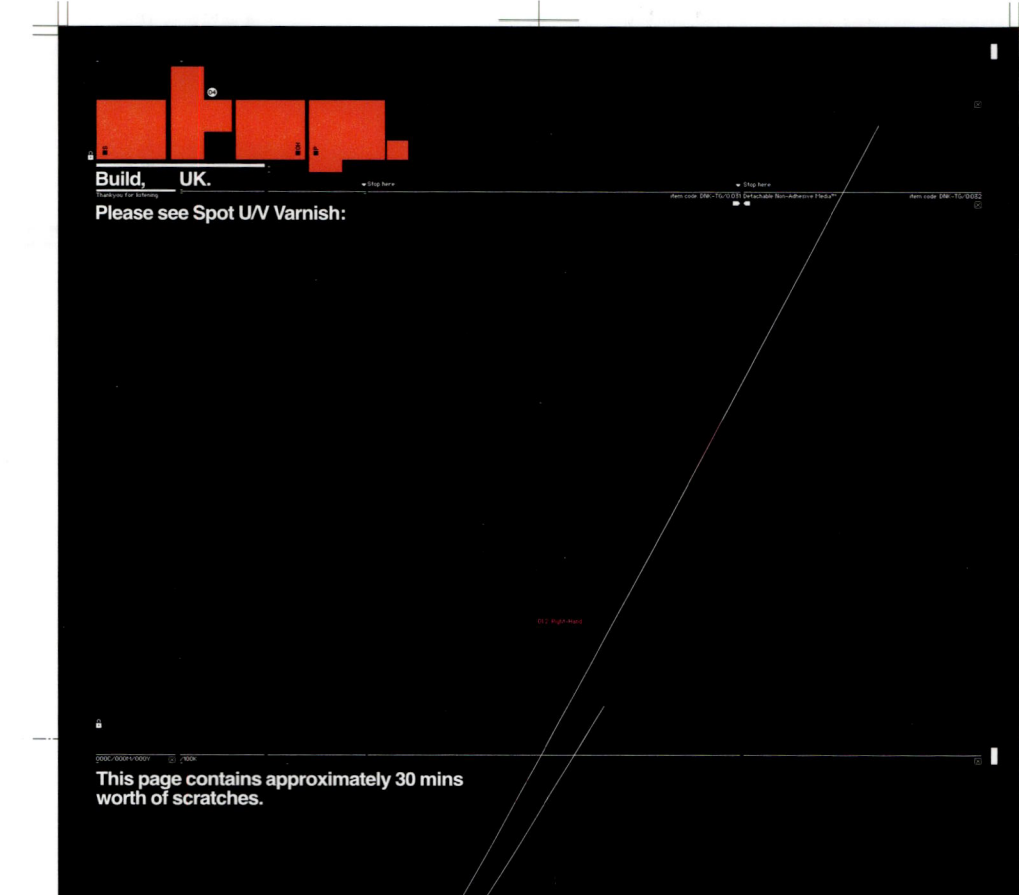

Eczema

'I am my own worst enemy'...

Quote

Betnovate ointment
betamethasone valerate
100 grams

Aqueous Cream B.P.

Advice™

Build, UK.
Please see Spot U/V Varnish:

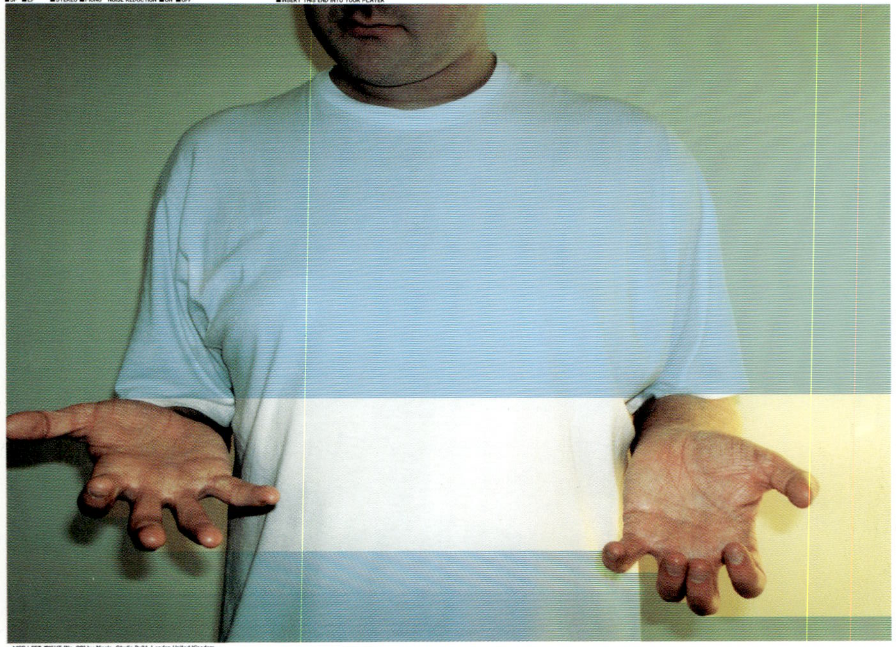

scratch, repeat.

This page contains approximately 30 mins worth of scratches.

+ Build™

Page
55

Client
IdN Magazine

Origin
London, UK

Title of work

Art Director

Year produced

+ Meiré und Meiré

Page
56

Client
Dornbracht Armaturenfabrik

Origin
Zurich, Switzerland

Title of work
ISERLOHN the Dornbracht Culture Projects Vol.1

Art Director
Mike Meiré (creative director)
Florian Lambl (art director)

Year produced
2003

Type of work
Magazine

Designer
—

Description
Development of a high-quality art and culture magazine that in terms of content and design reflects and credibly presents the standards and cultural image of Dornbracht. Iserlohn unites the documentation of the company's pioneering art and cultural involvement with writings on art theory, interviews, and extensive image sections, providing an independent platform for lifestyle and cutting-edge culture in terms of form and content.

MÄRCHENSTÜBERL
Juergen Teller

TOTES HAUS UR

„Ich bin in einer Falle. Ich werde gezwungen, das Ding weiter durch die Welt zu bekommen."
Gregor Schneider

E-R-S
Energetic Recovery System
MIKE MEIRÉ

NEW YORK
Statements (six)

Rita Ackermann, Mark Borthwick, Nicola Tyson

BERNHARD WILLHELM
Mode, die lacht

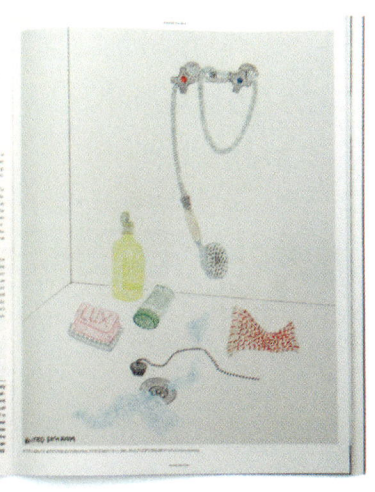

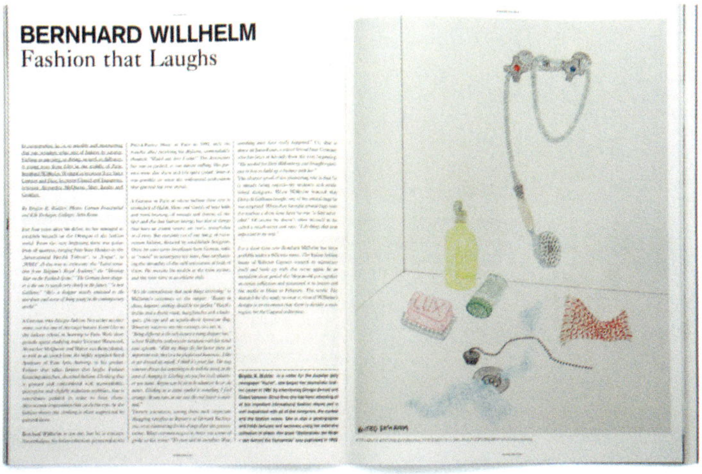

BERNHARD WILLHELM
Fashion that Laughs

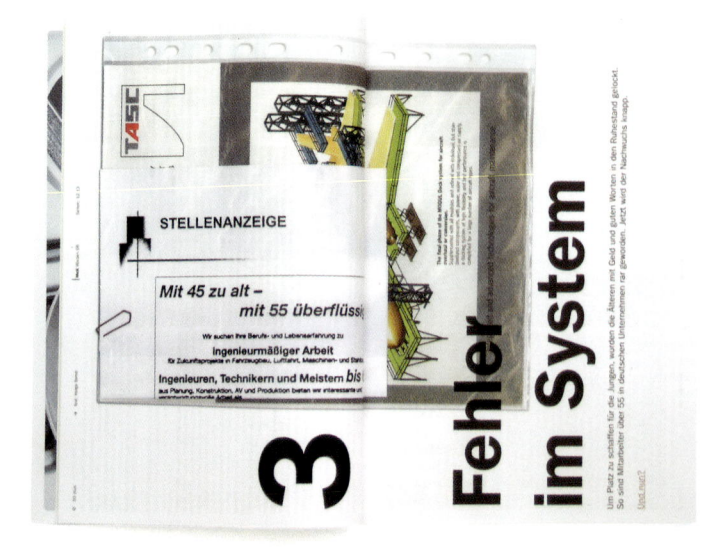

+ Meiré und Meiré

Page
58

Client
McKinsey

Origin
Zurich, Switzerland

Title of work
McK Wissen 06 Mobilität
McK Wissen 07 Strategie
McK Wissen 08 Menschen

Art Director
Mike Meiré (Creative director)
Katja Fössel
Katja Fössel, Alice Chi (07 Strategie)

Year produced
2003 - 2004

Type of work
Magazine

Designer
—

Description
An unusual magazine both in terms of content and form that for the first time unites the expertise of a company, the consulting firm McKinsey & company, with independent business journalism. The result is a medium that appropriately represents the consulting firm as a highly credible and competent company.

14
Die Evoluzzer

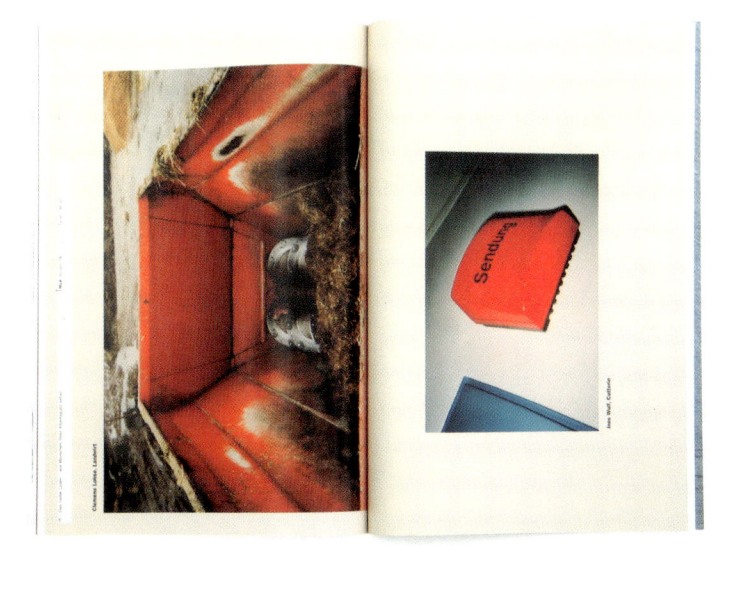

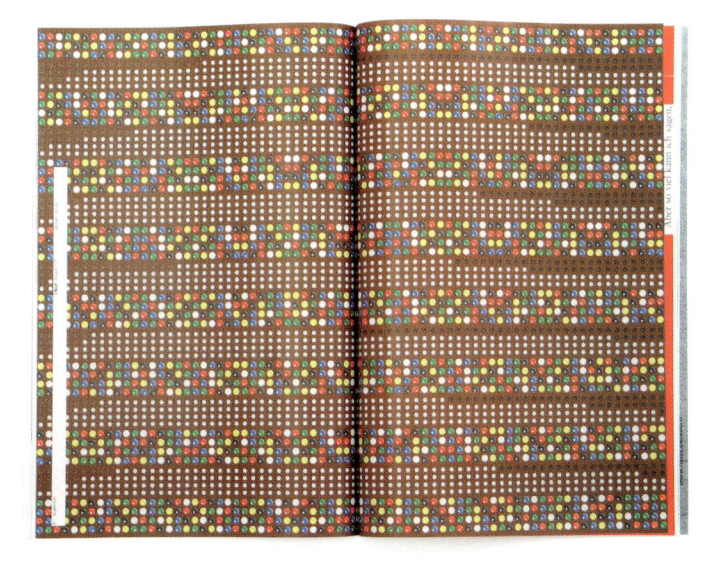

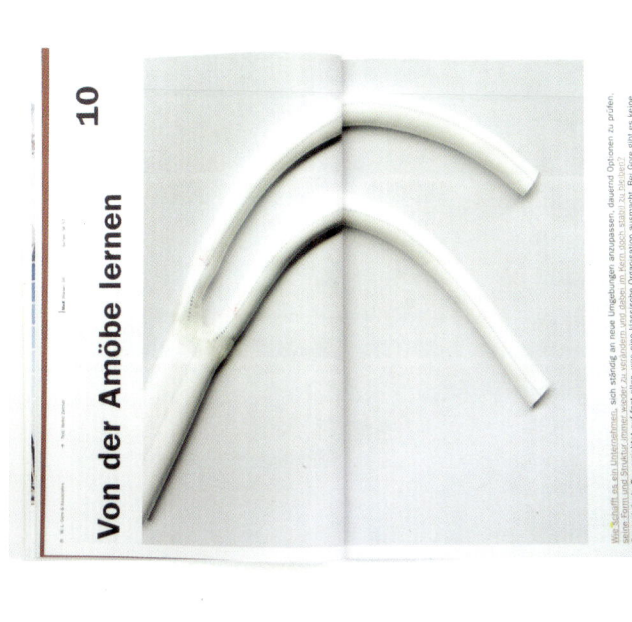

Krabbeln, brabbeln, entdecken
8

10
Von der Amöbe lernen

+ Meiré und Meiré

Page
60

Client
+ BMW Mini
++ BMW AG

Title of work
+ MINIInternational Shanghai
++ MINIInternational Montreal

Art Director
Mike Meiré (creative director)
Mirko Borsche

Type of work
Magazine

Designer
Henrike Schrader (Meiré und Meiré),
Florin Preußler, Kurt Wilhelm

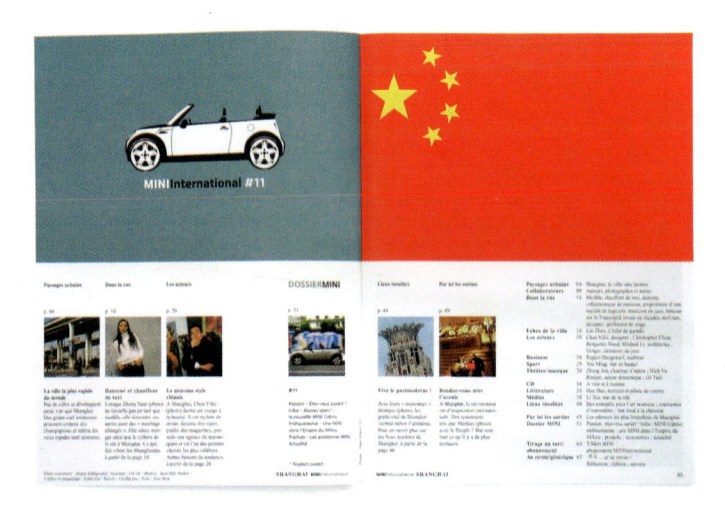

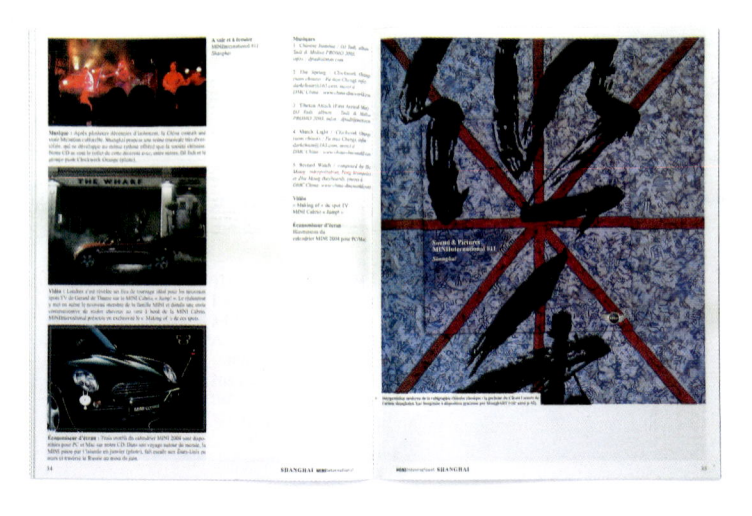

+ CD
SOUND & PICTURES

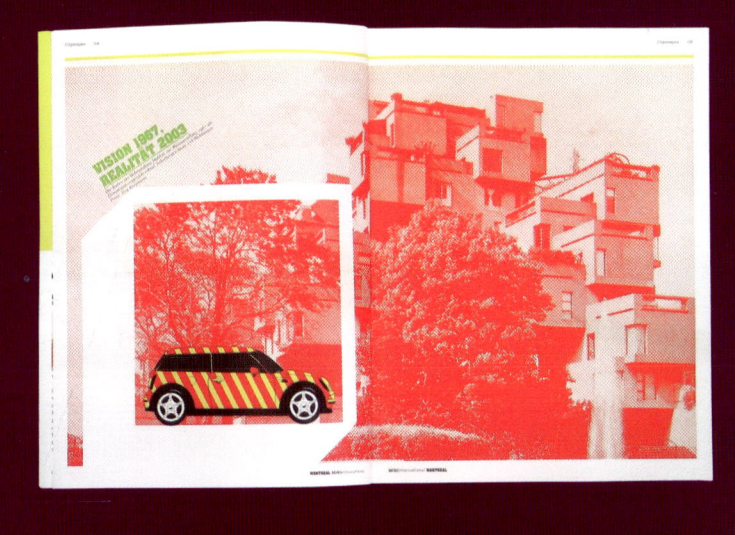

Origin
Zürich, Switzerland

Year produced
+ 2004
++ 2003

Description
Each individual edition of MINIInternational is dedicated to a different city. In a unique combination of the creative impulses from design, music, fashion, art and architecture, each magazine conveys the typical lifestyle and spirit of the respective city it covers.

MINIInternational
MONTREAL

Kanada's Sexiest City

Page
62

Type of work
Magazine

Client
BMW AG

Art Director
Mike Meiré (creative director)
Mirko Borsche

Designer
Henrike Schrader (Meiré und Meiré),
Florin Preußler, Kurt Wilhelm

Title of work
MiniInternational Mailand

Origin
Zurich, Switzerland

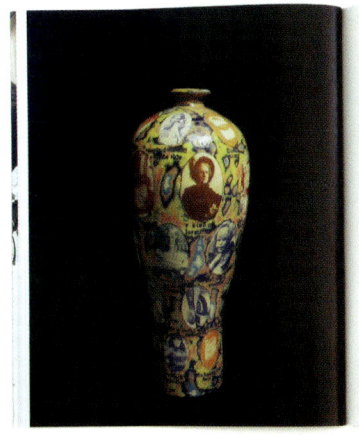

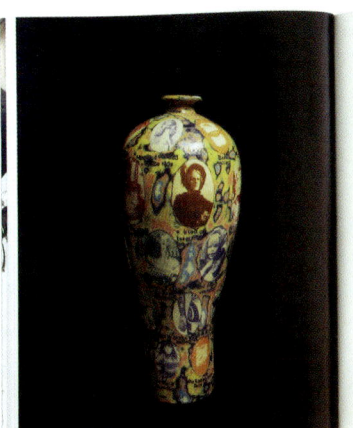

+ A2-Graphics/SW/HK

Page
63

Title of work
Quarterly Magazine, Issue no.1

Type of work
Magazine

Client
Kunstuff

Art Director
Scott Williams, Henrik Kubel

Designer
Scott Williams, Henrik Kubel

Origin
London, UK

Year produced
2004

Description
A 48-page quarterly magazine on Danish Art and Craft, *Quarterly Magazine* is bilingual in Danish and in English and is printed in 5-colours. In issue no.1 the KUNSTUFF cover has a removable sticker acting as masthead (rotating clockwise from issue to issue). The design employs a simple grid with two custom-made typefaces.

+ A2-Graphics/SW/HK

Page
64

Title of work
Afterall

Type of work
Journal

Client
Afterall

Art Director
Scott Williams, Henrik Kubel

Designer
Scott Williams, Henrik Kubel

Origin
London, UK

Year produced
2003

Description
Afterall is published twice yearly by Central Saint Martins College of Art & Design and the California Institute of the Arts.
The narrow format is part of the journal's overall visual identity and clearly distinguishes it from similar publications. The design employs three different paper stocks and four specially developed typefaces with extensive use of ligatures. *Afterall* employs a simple two-column grid with images intersected into the text when referenced. Footnotes and image captions are displayed in the inner column.

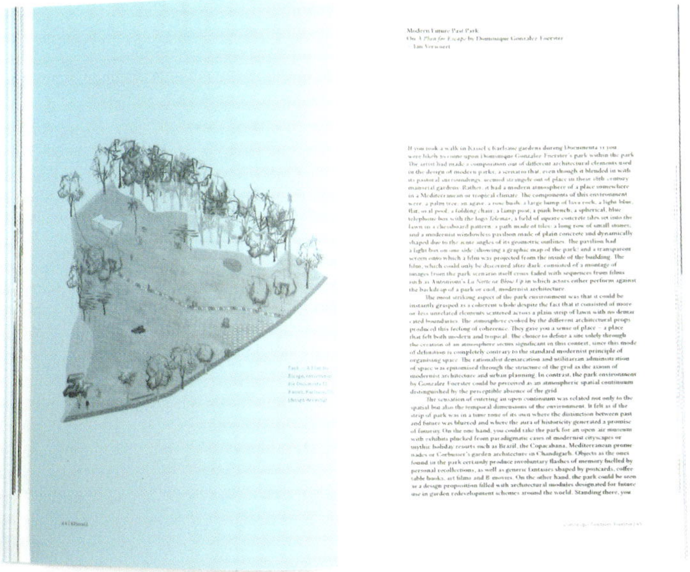
Modern Future Past Park
On A Plan for Escape by Dominique Gonzalez-Foerster
– Jan Verwoert

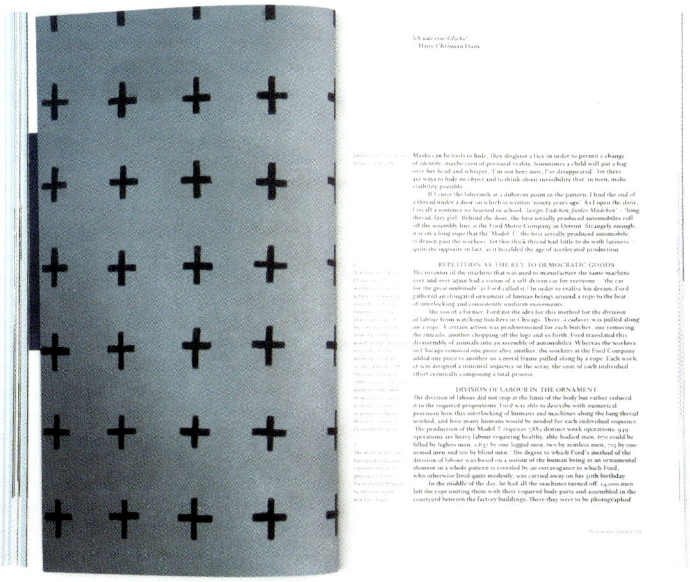
Ich war eine Glocke!
– Hans Christian Dany
REPETITION AS THE KEY TO DEMOCRATIC GOODS
DIVISION OF LABOUR IN THE ORNAMENT

III. MAELSTROM OF DESCRIPTION

Notes on the Subject Without Qualities
From the Cowboy Flaneur to Mr Smith
– Walead Beshty

+ Envision+

Page
66 - 69

Client
20/20 Media Ltd.,
London, GB

Origin
Bühlertal, Germany

Title of work
themepark

Art Director
Brian Switzer
Esther Mildenberger

Year produced
2000 - 2002

Type of work
Magazine

Designer
Brian Switzer
Esther Mildenberger

Description
Authors, artists, designers, photographers and people with something to say or show are all invited to contribute to *themepark*. A new website is produced in tandem with every magazine and presents articles or pieces in ways not possible in print. Previous websites are expanded rather than replaced to build into the thematic collection.

violence

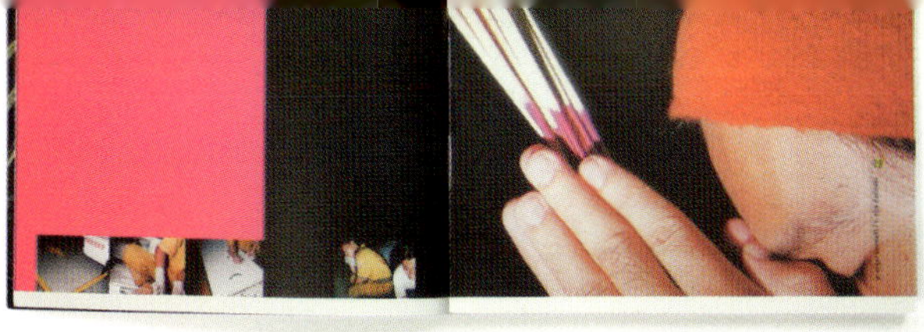

north south view
Pizza
Hut

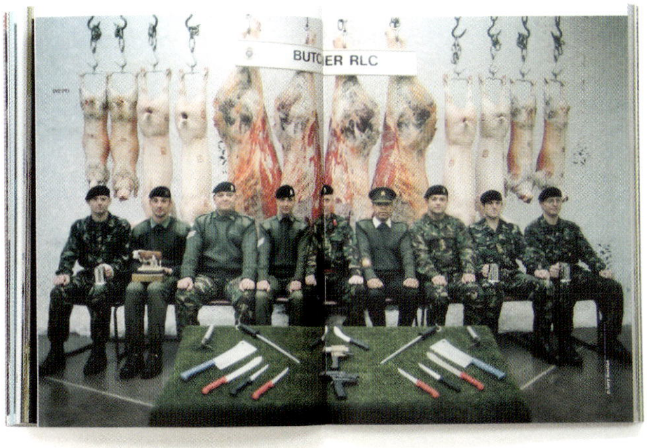

Wohlstand durch
Anlage oder Steuertricks
1975 1980 1985 1990 1995 2000
im Wertewechsel

themepark

emepark
home

«BOLOU; "DOUHIBO" : LA MER CITADINE · BOLOU EST UN NOM PROPRE DONT ON BAPTISE LES PERSONNES 77

themepark
£4.95
motion

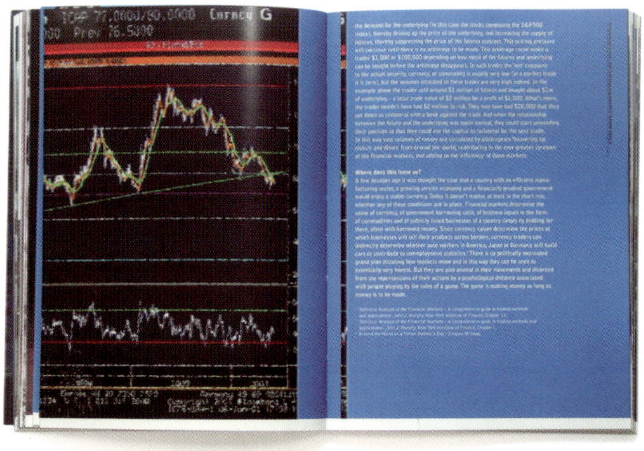

rop the pearls

limited edition t-shirt
by frank leder
make a
run for it
FRANK LEDER
themepark
mobile phonics
temporama
themepark
economy

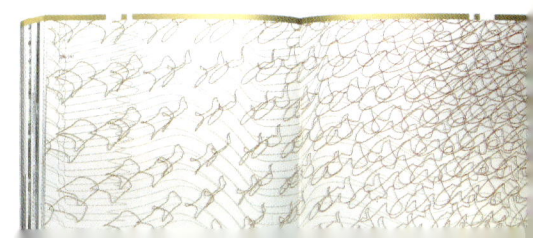

+ Segura Inc.

Page
70

Title of work
CROP Series

Type of work
Catalogue

Client
Corbis

Art director
Carlos Segura

Designer
Carlos Segura, Tnop, Chris May, Dave Weik, Ryan Halverson

Description
CROP Series aims to reposition Corbis as a brand through large format catalogues intended to reinforce the craft.

Origin
Chicago, USA

Year produced
2004

CROP/4 corbis
RM
CONSUME_PG.28

CROP/4 corbis
RM
CONSUME_PG.29

CROP/4 corbis
RM
EVOLVE_PG.38

CROP/4 corbis
RM
EVOLVE_PG.39

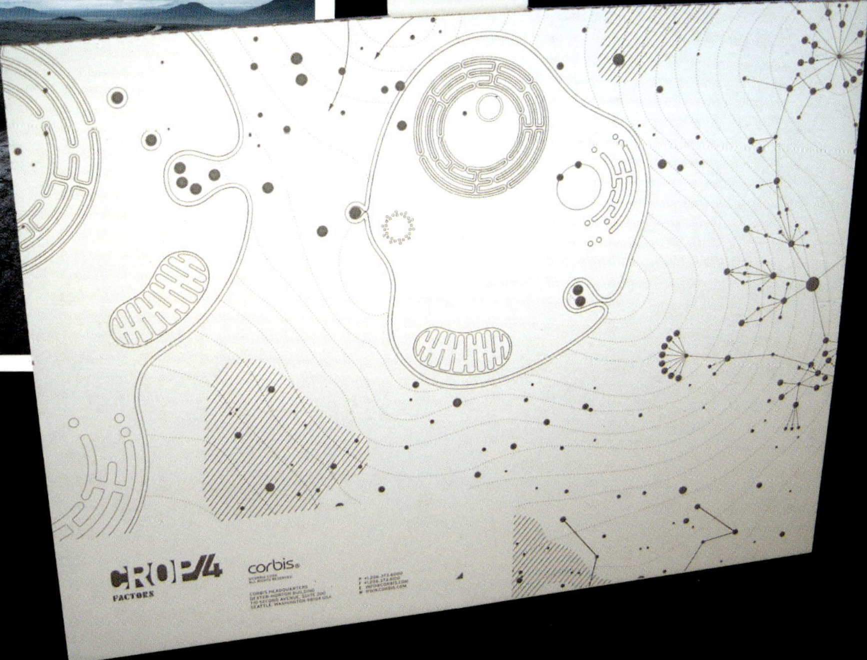
CROP/4
FACTORS
corbis

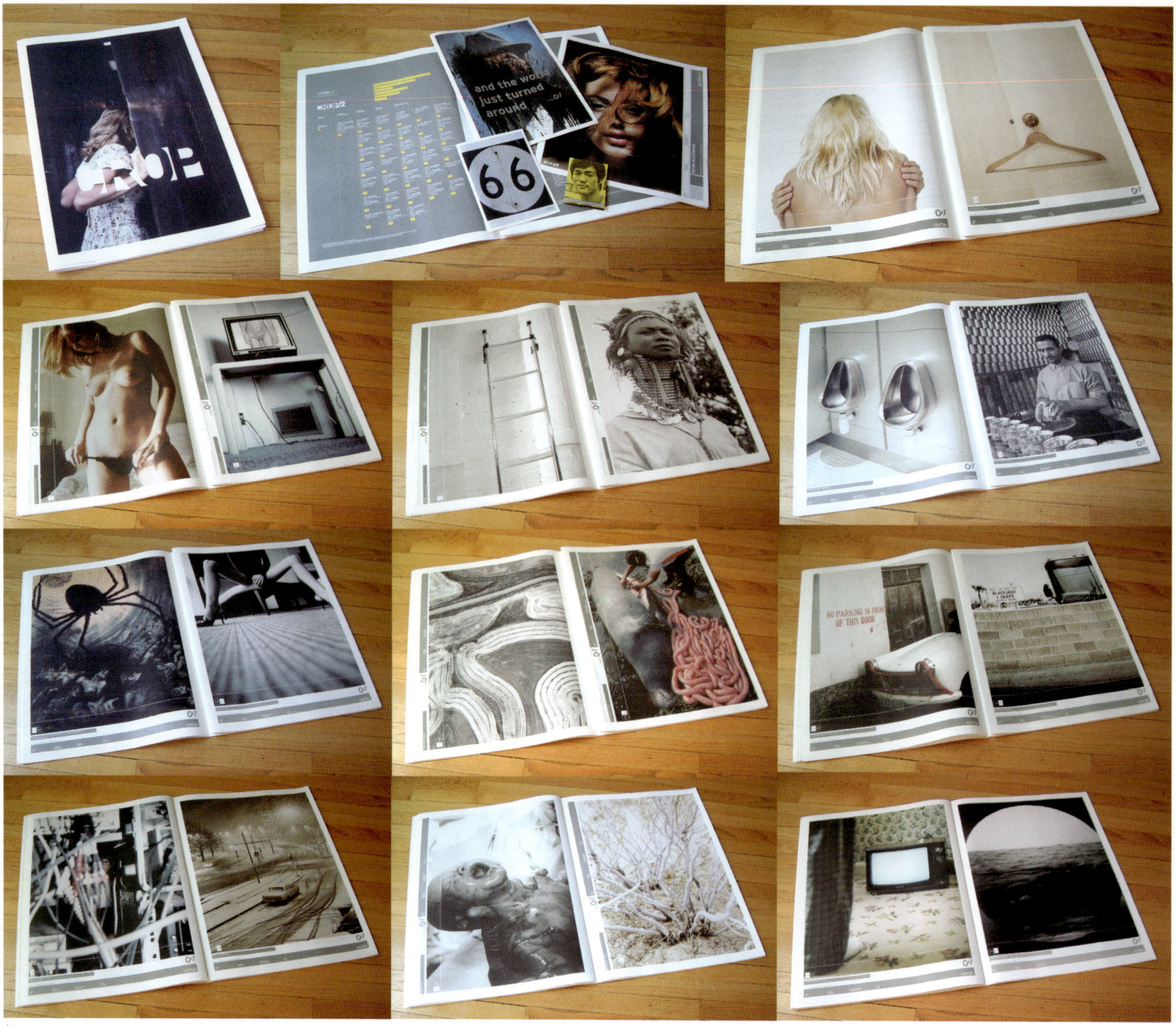
CROP
just turned
around
66
OF THIS DOOR

+ Segura Inc.

Page
73

Client
Corbis

Origin
Chicago, USA

Title of work
+ CROP Series
++ Sample

Art Director
Carlos Segura

Year produced
2004

Type of work
Catalogue

Designer
+ Carlos Segura, Tnop, Chris May, Dave Weik, Ryan Halverson
++ Tnop

Description
+ CROP Series aims to reposition Corbis as a brand through large format catalogues intended to reinforce the art of the craft.
++ Sample is a catalog of specific images licensed for product applications.

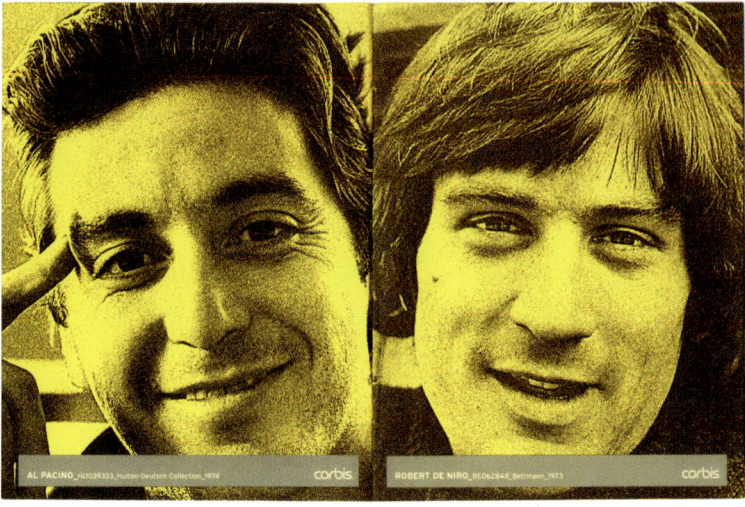

+ Segura Inc.

Page
74

Client
Corbis

Origin
Chicago, USA

Title of work
CROP Series

Art Director
Carlos Segura

Year produced
2004

Type of work
Catalogue

Designer
Carlos Segura, Tnop, Chris May,
Dave Weik, Ryan Halverson

Description
CROP Series aims to reposition Corbis as a brand through large format catalogues intended to reinforce the art of the craft.

DUSTIN HOFFMAN_BE020812_Bettmann_1968
corbis

JOHN WAYNE_JS1562238_John Springer Collection_ca. 1960s
corbis

JACK NICHOLSON_HU046897_Hulton-Deutsch Collection_1978
corbis

MARTIN SHEEN_HU049490_Hulton-Deutsch Collection_1980
corbis

KIRK DOUGLAS_HU055615_Hulton-Deutsch Collection_1958
corbis

MICHAEL CAINE_HU019560_Hulton-Deutsch Collection_1966
corbis

GENE HACKMAN_JS1562545_John Springer Collection_1971
corbis

MARLON BRANDO_HU039961_Hulton-Deutsch Collection_1968
corbis

PAUL NEWMAN_U1795783_Bettmann_1974
corbis

ROBERT REDFORD_BE070385_Bettmann_1976
corbis

STEVE McQUEEN_JS1566516_John Springer Collection_1968
corbis

+ Public

Page
76

Client
San Francisco Museum
of Modern Art

Origin
California, USA

Title of work
SFMOMA 1998 - 1999
Annual Report

Art Director
Todd Foreman

Year produced
1999

Type of work
Annual report

Designer
Todd Foreman
Tessa Lee

Description
This annual report is an exhibition and program guide, serving as membership collateral for a modern art museum.

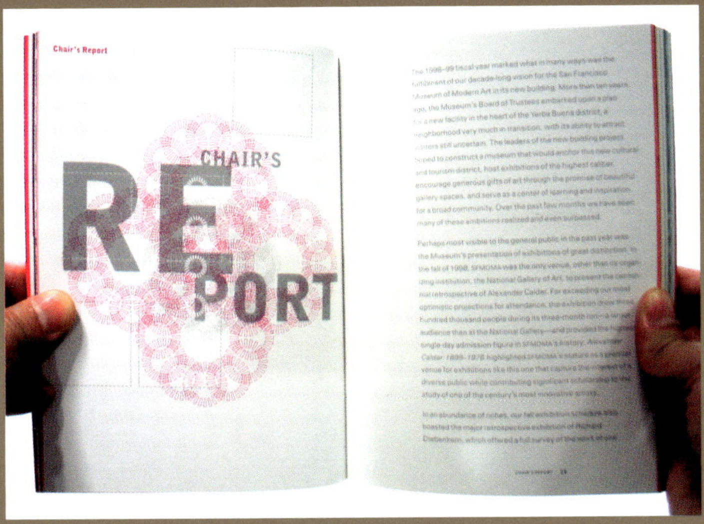
Chair's Report
CHAIR'S
REPORT

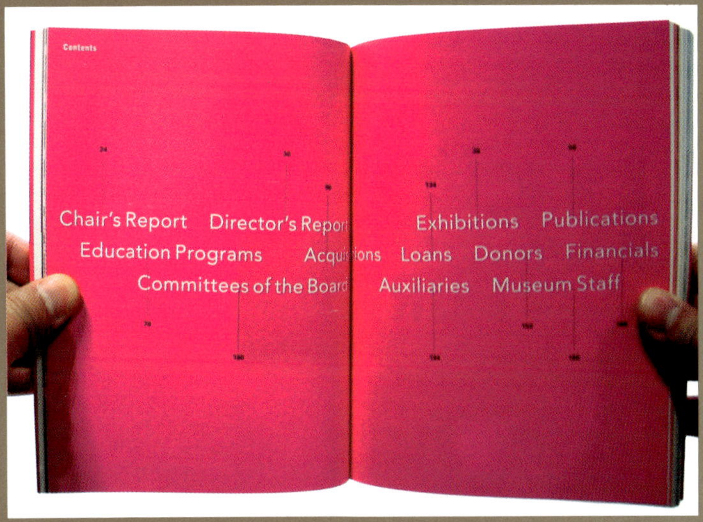
Contents
Chair's Report
Director's Report
Exhibitions
Publications
Education Programs
Loans
Donors
Financials
Committees of the Board
Auxiliaries
Museum Staff

Langston Hughes
Dorothy Dandridge
Warrick Fuller

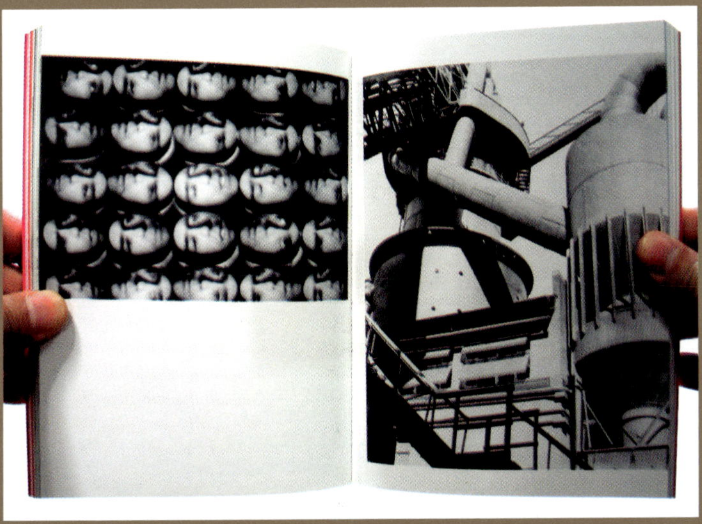

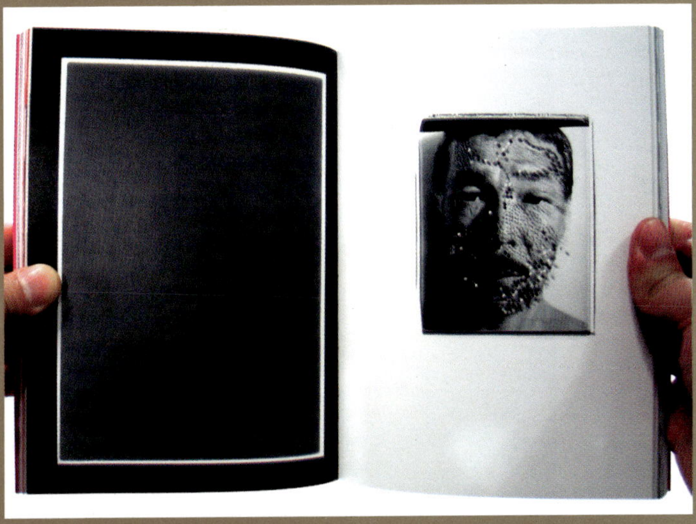

+ Public

Page
78

Client
San Francisco Museum
of Modern Art

Origin
California, USA

Title of work
SFMOMA 2001- 2002
Annual Report

Art Director
Todd Foreman

Year produced
2003

Type of work
Annual report

Designer
Todd Foreman
Lindsay Wheeler

Description
This annual report is an exhibition and program guide, serving as membership collateral for a modern art museum.

Lee Bul, *Supernova*, 2000; Courtesy of the artist and Kukje Gallery, Seoul

Ellen Lupton and J. Abbott Miller, on/off, 1999; Collection SFMOMA, gift of Ellen Lupton and J. Abbott Miller

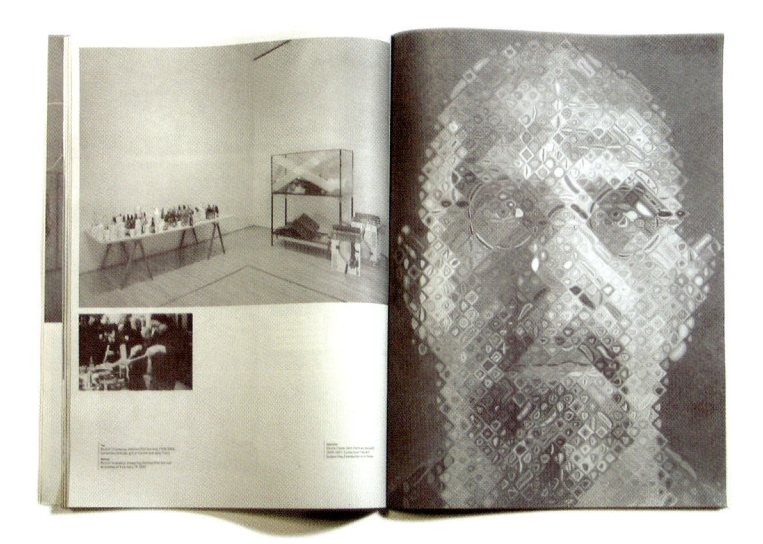

+ PRESENTATIONS
# EXHIBITIONS

During fiscal years 2001 and 2002, the Museum presented thirty-eight exhibitions and seven traveling presentations, showcasing an extraordinary range of modern and contemporary art. These shows drew 1.5 million visitors to the Museum on the two-year period, with countless more employing virtual refractors on sfmoma's Web site. Offering something for everyone, the Museum's presentations won accolades from scholars, members, press, and visitors alike.

Fiscal year 2001 saw the biggest exhibition in sfmoma's early seventeen history, *Celebrating Modern Art: The Anderson Collection*. With 230 works of art on display over three floors of the Museum, *Celebrating Modern Art* was truly a massive undertaking. *010101: Art in Technological Times* explored technology-based artistic expression, acknowledging the Bay Area's central role in the digital realm and expanding traditional notions of a museum exhibition to include a simultaneous Web component. *Revelatory Landscapes* also challenged the gallery format by presenting site-specific works of landscape architecture around the Bay Area. *Points of Departure: Connecting with Contemporary Art* broke new curatorial ground, reconditioning how the permanent collection can be displayed and highlighting the Museum's key holdings. Honoring outstanding local talent, 2000 SECA Art Award featured the work of Rachael Neubauer and Kathryn Van Dyke.

Fiscal year 2002 opened with *Ansel Adams at 100*, which brought 180,000 visitors to the galleries during its run, and, in the fall of 2001, proved an invaluable resource for a community mourning the tragedies of September 11. Debuting in fiscal year 2002 was *The Seventh Art: New Dimensions in Cinema*, a monthly film series jointly organized by sfmoma and the San Francisco Film Society. February 2002 brought the much-anticipated *Eva Hesse*, a retrospective of the important Post-Minimalist that with the International Association of Art Critics/USA award for "Best Monographic Exhibition outside New York" in 2002. *Sampling/Christian Marclay* presented the media-based work of rising artist Marclay, including his celebrated *Video Quartet* (2002), commissioned by sfmoma. *Points of Departure II* continued the imaginative, thematic exploration of the permanent collection begun in fiscal 2001. Presenting indelible photographs of people across the nation, *Stranger Passing: Collected Portraits by Joel Sternfeld* was both a critical and a popular success. Traveling exhibitions in 2002 included *Ultrabaroque: Aspects of Post-Latin American Art*, which attracted new audiences to sfmoma, and *Yoko Ono: One*, a retrospective that included a special *War is Over* billboard installation behind the Museum on New Montgomery Street.

+ Époxy

Page
80

Title of work
Millilite

Type of work
Corporate magazine

Client
Labatt

Art Director
Daniel Fortin, George Fok
(creative director)
Éric Dubois, Stephane Legault
(art director)

Designer
Éric Dubois, Stephane Legault
(designer, illustrators, photographers)
Andr/renaud, Eric Pelletier,
Gilles Blain (computer graphics)

Origin
Québec, Canada

Year produced
2003

Description
This guide to the Quebec brewing industry, designed for La Brasserie Labatt's sales team, serves as an informational tool to present statistics in an interesting and attractive fashion. Époxy designed the guide in a game-like format to resemble a six-pack of beer. Eschewing a rigid graphic standard, every page is unique, displaying the charts and graphs in a lighthearted and original light. The photos and illustrations were produced by the agency and the project was created digitally

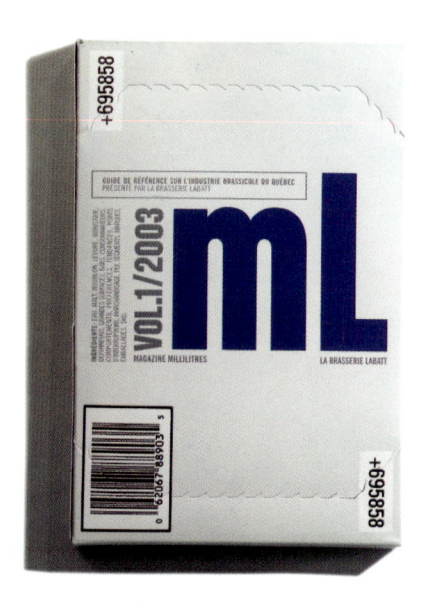

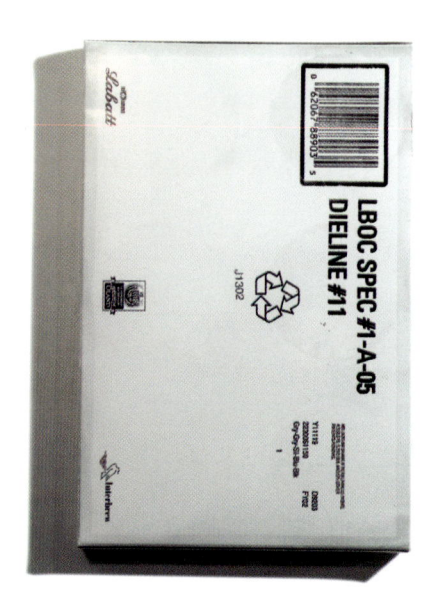

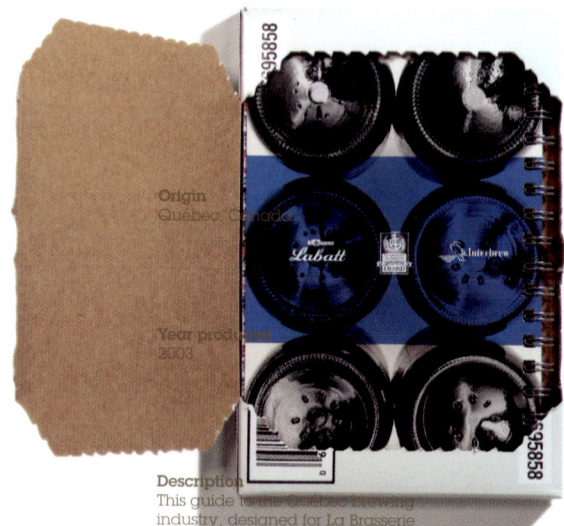

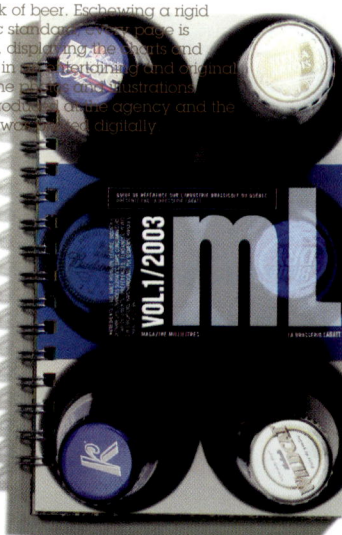

LA BIÈRE : UNE INDUSTRIE DE 1,85 MILLIARD DE DOLLARS ET TOUJOURS EN CROISSANCE

IMPORTANCE DES SEGMENTS DE PRIX DANS LES GRANDES SURFACES

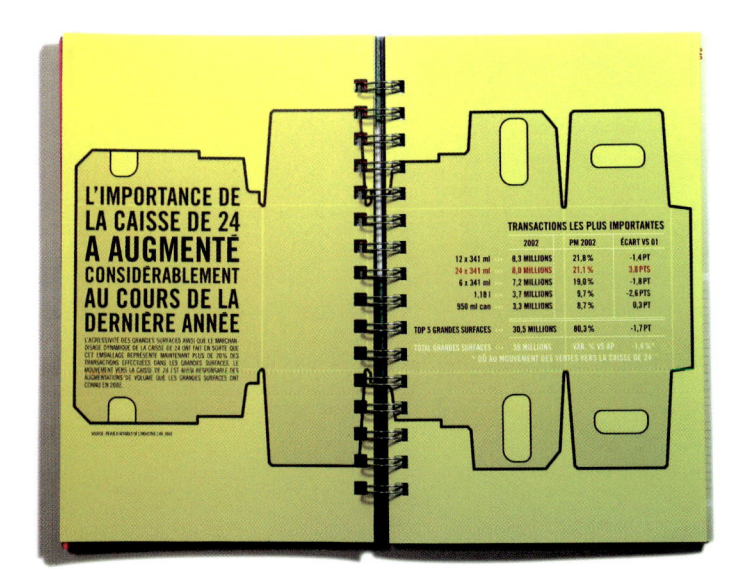

L'IMPORTANCE DE LA CAISSE DE 24 A AUGMENTÉ CONSIDÉRABLEMENT AU COURS DE LA DERNIÈRE ANNÉE

LES PETITS FORMATS REPRÉSENTENT PRÈS DE 70 % DES TRANSACTIONS EN DÉPANNEUR

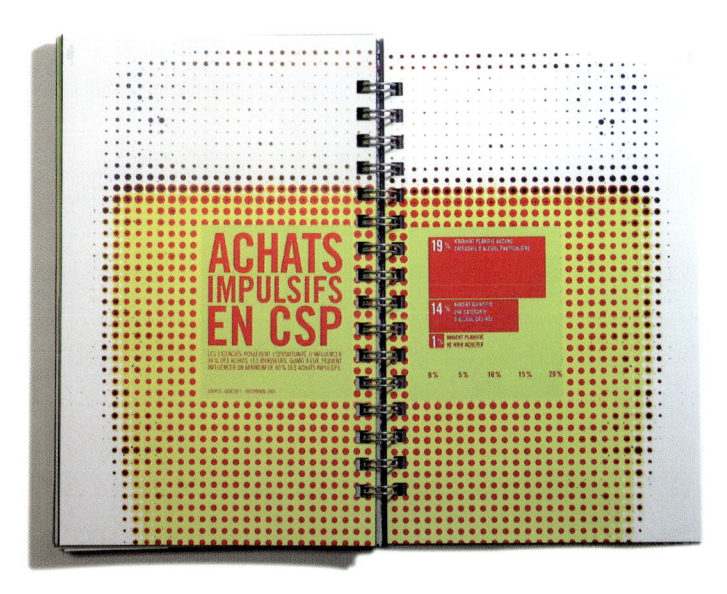

ACHATS IMPULSIFS EN CSP

+ Envision+

Page
82

Client
Interaction Design Institute
Ivrea (IDII), Ivrea, Italy

Origin
Bühlertal, Germany

Title of work
Interaction Design
Almanacco 2003

Art Director
Britta Boland, associate
professor at IDII

Year produced
2003

Type of work
Yearbook

Designer
Esther Mildenberger

Description
The Interaction Design Institute Ivrea is an industry-funded research institute and school. Located on the grounds of Italian industrial giant Olivetti, the heritage of the school is ever present, especially in the buildings designed by Ettore Sottsass.
This book is the first collection of projects from the Institute in a planned series of publications.

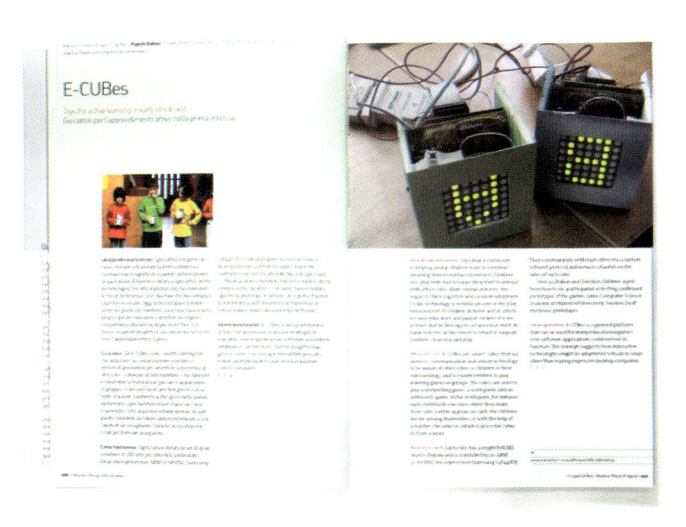

- Digital Peacock Tails
- E-CUBes
- Harmony in Architecture
- Progetti di Innovazione | Innovation Projects
- Design for Future Needs

+ AdamsMorioka

Page
84

Client
Sundance Film Festival

Title of work
2004 Sundance Film Festival

Art Director
Sean Adams
Noreen Morioka
Jan Fleming

Type of work
+ Catalogue
++ Brochure

Designer
Sean Adams
Noreen Morioka
Jennifer Hopkins
Cynthia Jacquette
Brian Goodman

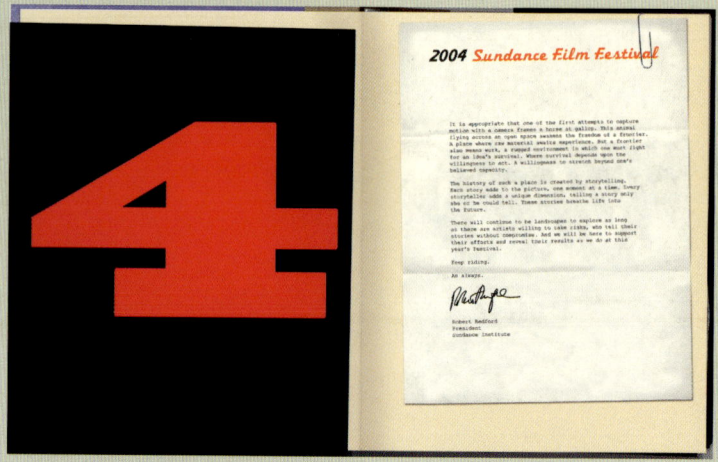

THE BIG BOOK OF
SUNDANCE FILM FESTIVAL

Origin
California, USA

Year produced
2003 - 2004

Description
The graphics for this year's festival were inspired by the idea of an eclectic set of limited edition books. The goal of the design concept is to express the contradiction of diversity and a sense of place, Park City, which is a western town, as well as a sense of playfulness and humour.
+ The catalogue evokes keepsake fine art books.
++ The registration brochure resembles a children's book on cowboys.

CONTENTS

4   Sundance Institute Presents
6   How to Sundance
8   Festival Passes and Ticket Packages
10 Support Sundance Institute
12 Festival Lodging
14 How to Get There
15 Lodging Outside Park City

2004 Sundance Film Festival January 15–25, 2004 • Park City, Utah

THE DIRECTOR

THE ACTOR

THE PRODUCER

AUDIENCE MEMBER

HOW TO SUNDANCE • The best and most convenient way to enjoy the 2004 Sundance Film Festival is to purchase a Festival Pass or Ticket Package. Festival Passes allow you to walk into screening venues by showing your credentials—there's no need to purchase tickets or plan ahead. Ticket Packages allow you to select your screening tickets in early January, based on availability, so you don't have to wait in line at the Festival.

This year, we're introducing a completely new Pass and Package ordering system that's easier and faster. We've enhanced our online service and expanded the number of Customer Service operators. Plus, you'll receive instant confirmation of a Pass or Package when you order. But Passes and Packages sell out quickly so don't be left in the dust.

View innovative filmmaking for the web, the Sundance Online Film Festival, throughout its broadcast by purchasing a digital ticket for just $10 when you order your Festival Pass or Ticket Package. Visit www.sundance.org for broadcast dates.

NEW PAPERLESS ORDER SYSTEM • On October 20, 2003, at 8:00 a.m. MST, we begin taking orders for Festival Passes and Ticket Packages 24 hours a day at www.sundance.org. You can also place orders by telephone toll-free Monday through Saturday at (877) SFF-TDXS or (877) 733-8497 from 8:00 a.m. to 6:00 p.m. MST on October 20 and from 10:00 a.m. to 6:00 p.m. MST thereafter. This year, we're accepting online and telephone orders only.

Individual tickets can be purchased beginning January 6, 2004 at 10:00 a.m. MST at www.sundance.org or by telephone toll-free Monday through Saturday at (877) SFF-TDXS or (877) 733-8497 from 10:00 a.m. to 6:00 p.m. MST. Individual tickets are also available for purchase during the Film Festival at the Festival box offices.

NEW OPTIONAL EXPRESS DELIVERY SERVICE • You can choose to have your Festival Passes and Ticket Packages expressed to you for in-person delivery before the Festival. Skip the at-Festival registration process, and arrive ready to go with Pass or tickets in hand. A $25.00 shipping fee applies. VISIT www.sundance.org REGULARLY FOR UPDATED FILM FESTIVAL INFORMATION.

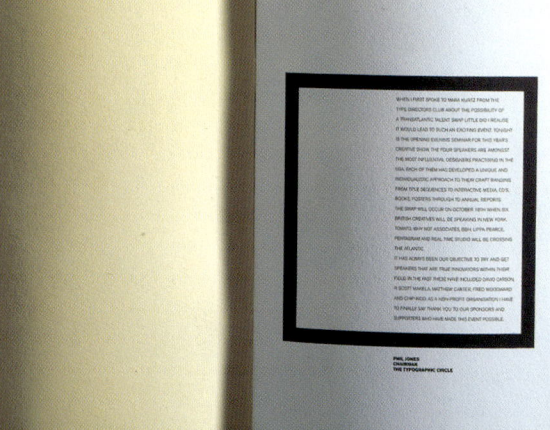

STEFAN SAGMEISTER
CARIN GOLDBERG
DANA ARNETT
ROBERT GREENBERG

LONYC

+ Lippa Pearce

Page
86

Client
The Typogra[phic]

Title of work
+ LONYC Magazine
++ Circular 11

Art Director
Domenic Lipp[a]

Type of work
Magazine

Designer
Domenic Lip[pa]

CIRCULAR 11 contains work from the five speakers we have had during the last year. Chronologically we began with the maverick and experimental *Graphic Thought Facility*. This was followed by the precision and detail of *North*. In contrast *Alan Fletcher* proved that you didn't have to be young to provide the inspiration. *SEA* were next up, continuing the modernist theme. We then finished with *Vince Frost* who is one of the few designers able to straddle the 'old school' ideas-based approach with a sensitivity to the final look of the design.

'Probably the best way to describe this issue of Circular is a visual scrapbook, a compendium of work some of you may have seen but many might not. So what has been the the common thread?' All of them use typography in different ways, to different degrees. But all of them use it with care. They all put their heart and soul into their work - they all have integrity - enjoy.'

VINCE FROST is a very, very good designer. Let's get that out of the way from the outset. His work peppers many of the most prestigious design awards and annuals worldwide. The 36 year-old Canadian began his career working for *Pentagram Design*. Anyone who knows how that company works will say its a tough training school. Its not for the weak-minded. First there's the long hours, and then there's the tough and very competitive environment - all for little financial reward.

The talk continued for a good couple of hours with plenty of anecdotal stories about each of his projects. A bit too candidly he showed some of the work for the *Spice Girls*. Talking to people afterwards, many seemed surprised by its inclusion, especially as *Frost* hardly defended the work and offered a slight apology for its presence. But this is the point - it's the confidence of *Frost* that he can stand in front of 250 people and describe how the project developed with a smile on his face. That is what makes the difference. That taken with the story about the disastrous trip to try and set up Japanese *Vogue* gave the talk an openess rarely seen or heard from designers today.

Origin
London, UK

Year produced
+ 1996

8

TO DESIGN TOTAL

9

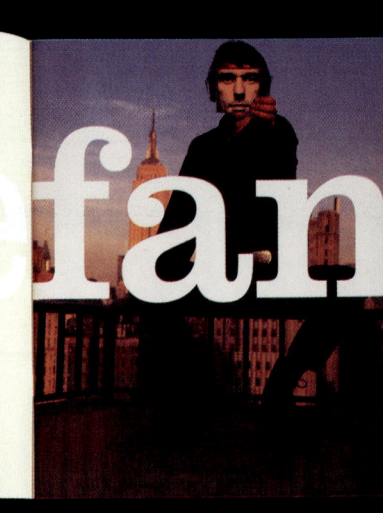

stefan sagmeister

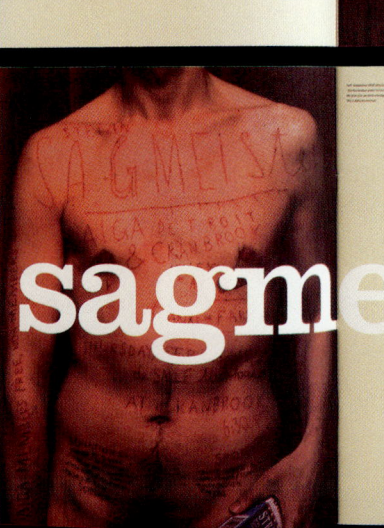

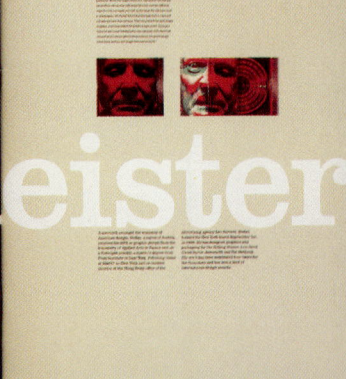

+ Lippa Pearce

Page
39

Title of work
+ Circular 8
++ Circular 9
+++ Circular 10

Type of work
Magazine

Client
The Typographic Circle

Art Director
Domenic Lippa

Designer
+/++/+++ Domenic Lippa
+ Richard McGillan
+++ Mukesh Parmer

Origin
London, UK

Year produced
+ 1999
++ 2000
+++ 2001

Description
Circular is a magazine designed for the typographic organisation in London, UK.

+ Chen Design Associates

Page
90

Client
California Pacific Medical Center

Origin
California, USA

Title of work
California Pacific Medical Center
Annual Report

Art Director
Joshua Chen, Max Spector,
Jennifer Tolo

Year produced
2003

Type of work
Annual report

Designer
Max Spector
Jennifer Tolo
Susan Sharpe (writer)
Todd Hido (photographer)

Description
Looking to the people and places that comprise and surround CPMC, the *2002 Annual Report* demonstrates how California Pacific Medical Center is an integral part of the Bay Area community; how there is often more than meets the eye; and how giving to the medical center is not just a donation, it is also an investment and commitment to the growth and health of a community.

Frances Rose

INFORMATION DESK VOLUNTEER
GREAT GRANDMOTHER

MOVED FROM TEXAS TO SAN FRANCISCO
IN 1920. GOT HER FIRST VOLUNTEER
JOB DURING WORLD WAR II AND IS
STILL GOING STRONG. GRANDMOTHER OF
SIX AND GREAT GRANDMOTHER OF TWO —
WITH TWO MORE ON THE WAY.

Stephen Lockhurst, M.D., Ph.D.

ANESTHESIOLOGIST
VOLUNTEER, MARIN HEADLANDS INSTITUTE

INTRODUCES TEENAGERS TO THE
WONDERS OF THE NATURAL WORLD
AND TEACHES THEM TO RESPECT THE
ENVIRONMENT. DECIDED TO BE A DOCTOR
AT AGE TEN WHEN A NEUROSURGEON
SAVED HIS MOTHER'S LIFE.

ATTENDS DIABETES SUPPORT GROUP

DONATES ANNUALLY TO THE FOUNDATION

WORKS NIGHTS IN THE INTENSIVE CARE UNIT

Caffe Trieste

VALLEJO AND GRANT
SAN FRANCISCO

CALIFORNIA PACIFIC MEDICAL CENTER IS THE PRESENCE OF LIFE IN YOUR COMMUNITY. In schools and playgrounds, at street markets and cafés, on park benches and cable cars, a common thread connects people to one another in the neighborhoods where we live and work. At one time or another, their lives have been, or will be, touched by the caregivers of California Pacific Medical Center.

California Pacific gave the future to a happy baby you see in passing who once fought for life in our Neonatal Intensive Care Unit. We offered a safe place at our Child Development Center for a teenager to overcome a learning disability. Our Medical Center offered solace to a woman who attended our weekly Breast Cancer Support Group after getting off work at a local supermarket. We provided educational resources for a worried son whose elderly mother is exhibiting signs of Alzheimer's Disease. We navigated the rehabilitation process for a middle-aged man who had his second open-heart surgery and needed to get back to his job so he could support his family.

As you go about your daily life in and around San Francisco, people with stories like these are all around you. You may not realize who they are, but they create unseen and very real connections between individuals who have never met, and those whose lives are intertwined through work, family, and friendship.

During 2002, from our trio of San Francisco-based campuses, California Pacific Medical Center served patients from 47 California counties, 44 states, and 3 nations. More than 42% of California Pacific's patients speak Chinese, Russian, Spanish, or Tagalog as their first language, so we provide interpreters to assist them in person, by telephone, and with document translation. As the diversity of our patient population changes — as it surely will — so will our services to provide for them.

California Pacific's community education and outreach programs touched the lives of more than 200,000 people last year. Over 6,000 new and expectant parents borrowed books and videos from our lending library, *Newborn Connections*. More than 1,200 parents, teachers, and children participated in *Health Champions*, a school-based program to prevent health problems in young people. We provided health screenings for low-income

+ Büro International London

Client
Calouste Gulbenkian Foundation, London

Origin
London, UK

Art Director
Oliver Klimpel

Year produced
2003

Designer
Oliver Klimpel

Description
The title of this magazine, which is printed on newsprint paper, reflects the bilingual character of the publication as 'do' also reads in Portuguese as "about" or "on". Both the cover and back use the word to address the readers with changing title sentences.

Printed materials made to last

The second section of this book explores books and corporate brochures. Books and brochures may not have as wide a readership as most magazines, catalogues and periodicals; however, they are usually more substantial and have a much longer shelf life. They are also more expensive and tailor-made, allowing the art director greater freedom to challenge the editorial confines that market forces place on other printed formats.

Interview #03 / Sagmeister Inc.

Interview with Stefan Sagmeister

Born in 1962 in Bregenz, Austria, Stefan Sagmeister has an MFA in graphic design from the University of Applied Arts in Vienna and a master degree from Pratt Institute in New York. Following stints at M&Co. in New York and Leo Burnett in Hong Kong, where he was Creative Director, Stefan set up the New York based graphic design studio Sagmeister Inc. in 1993. Projects undertaken include design jobs for all things printed – from posters, brochures, books and annual reports to identity systems, perfume packaging and CD covers.

He has designed graphics and packaging for the Rolling Stones, David Byrne, Lou Reed, Aerosmith and Pat Metheny. His work has been nominated four times for the Grammies and has won numerous international design awards. He currently lives in New York.

When did you set up Sagmeister Inc?
Properly in 1993 in New York, but there was an earlier incarnation in Vienna in 1990.

Could you describe a bit about the company?
We are a small design company trying to do work that we, our clients, our audience are all happy with.

You have worked in the design industries in Europe, HK and now in New York. Do you see any difference being a designer in these places?
Less than I would have thought. There are some different ground rules that colour and border play. But in general, I do think people are surprisingly similar everywhere I go.

Made You Look is a great book, I'm particularly impressed by the red filter slip case and the flip book animation. How did you come up with the design concept and filter the ideas?
I saw a little girl in the subway with a math book: the answers were overprinted with red X's, and she had a little red filter making these answers visible again. I just made a little note to myself: try, see if this would also work with photography. It did.

What is the biggest challenge in designing a book?
Different books have completely different challenges. In our case, the aim was to design *Made You Look* so that it would be readable for different audiences who have differing amounts of time to devote to it. So that it works for somebody leafing through it in the bookstore spending 30 seconds on it; and also for somebody who spends 30 minutes looking at it at a friend's house. And it should still yield information for those who want to read the entire thing and spend 30 hours on it.

We got much more feedback on the book than we got on all our other projects combined. Some of that came from young designers. My favorite line was: 'After I read your book, I had to go and do a lot of work.' That's exactly how I felt as a student after reading a design book I enjoyed.

We also included a rating system at the end of the book (1-5, 1 being the best grade), where readers can look up our opinion of the projects.

TITLE // Sagmeister, Made You Look
TYPE OF WORK // Self-promotional book
CLIENT // Booth Clibborn Editions
YEAR PRODUCED // 2001
ART DIRECTION // Stefan Sagmeister
DESIGNER // Stefan Sagmeister and Hjalti Karlsson

DESCRIPTION OF WORK //
Made You Look contains practically all the work Sagmeister Inc. ever designed, including the bad stuff. The work is published as a paperback in a red transparent slip-case. Removing the book from the red tinted transparent slip-case causes the mood of the dog to worsen considerably. Bending it one way results in the title *Made You Look*; in the other direction dog food shows up on the fore edge.
Peter Hall wrote a very detailed text (for a design book), and Stefan Sagmeister included handwritten excerpts from his diary and many comments from his dear clients.

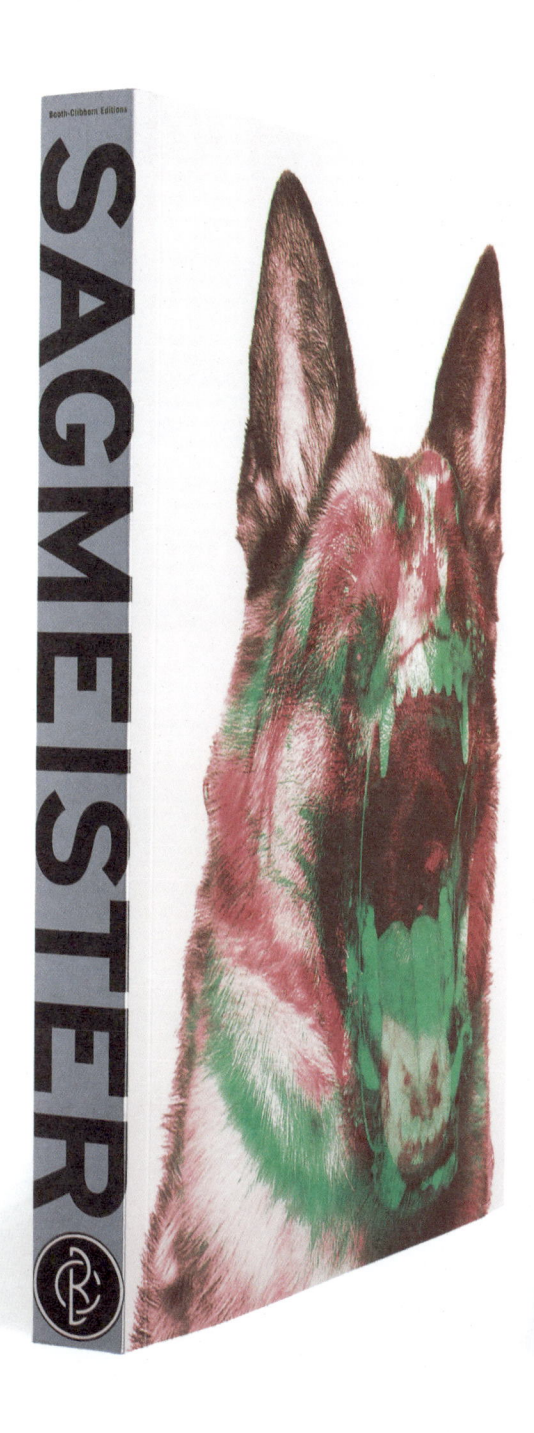

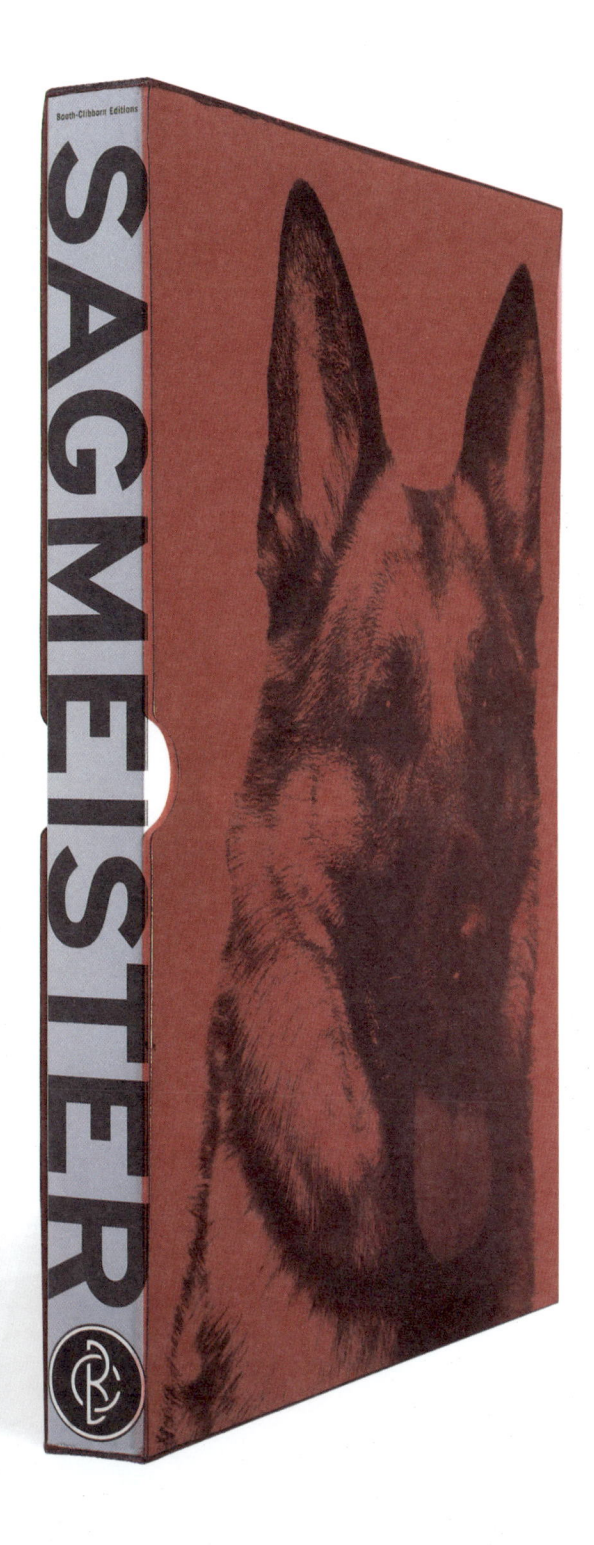

Could you tell us more about your favourite book projects you've handled so far? Any positive/negative experiences during the process?

Altogether, I don't think we have designed more than 10 books overall. In general, the reason we like to do them is because they enter people's homes, live in their living-groom or bedroom, won't get thrown out easily like so many other forms of graphic design.

Do you have any special design concept that you want to be implemented in the near future?

I never feel comfortable talking about things I have not done yet, because by discussing them I feel I am already in the process of doing them and then have less of a desire to actually do them.

Name some of your favourite artists/designers. What is it that you like about them? Do you think you've been influenced by them?

The most influential person in my design life and my one and only design hero: Tibor Kalman.

15 years ago, as a student in NYC, I called him every week for half a year and I got to know the M&Co receptionist really well. When he finally agreed to see me, it turned out I had a sketch in my portfolio rather similar in concept and execution to an idea M&Co was just working on. He rushed to show me the prototype out of fear I'd later say he stole it out of my portfolio. I was so flattered.

When I finally joined M&Co five years later, I discovered it was, more than anything else, his incredible salesmanship that set his studio apart from all the others. There were probably a number of people around who were as smart as Tibor (as there were certainly a lot who were better at design), but no one else could sell these concepts without any changes, get these ideas with almost no alteration out into the hands of the public. No one else was as passionate.

As a boss, he had no qualms about upsetting his clients or employees. (I remembered his reaction to a logo I had worked on for weeks and was very proud of: 'Stefan, this is TERRIBLE, just terrible. I am so disappointed.') His big heart was shining through, nevertheless.

He had the guts to risk everything. I witnessed a very large architecture project where he had collaborated with a famous architect and spent a year's worth of work. He was willing to walk away when the question arose of who would present to the client.

Tibor had an uncanny knack for giving advice, for dispersing morsels of wisdom, packaged in rough language later known as Tiborisms: 'The most difficult thing when running a design company is not to grow,' he told me when I opened my own little studio. 'Just don't go and spend the money they pay you or you're going to be the whore of the ad agencies for the rest of your life,' was his parting sentence when I moved to HK to open up a design studio for Leo Burnett.

These insights were also the reason why M&Co got so much press. Journalists could just call him and he would supply the entire structure for a story and some fantastic quotes to boot.

He was always happy and ready to jump from one field to another: corporate design, products, city planning, music videos, documentary movies, children books and magazine editing. All were treated under the mantra: 'You should do everything twice; the first time you don't know what you're doing; the second time you do; the third time it's boring.'

He did good work containing good ideas for good people.

Are you happy with what you're doing now? What is the greatest satisfaction in your career so far?

Yes, I am doing fine and I still really like being a designer. At the moment I'm in Berlin teaching at the UDK for one semester, which is a nice change after ten years in New York. Literally, my biggest satisfactions in design are these little moments of pure happiness I experience every now and then. I am talking about shivers down my spine, rush to the head kinds of situations. Of course they happen too rarely and far in-between. The ones I remember in a second (also because I wrote them down for a talk recently) include:

Interview #03 // Sagmeister inc.
Page 96/97

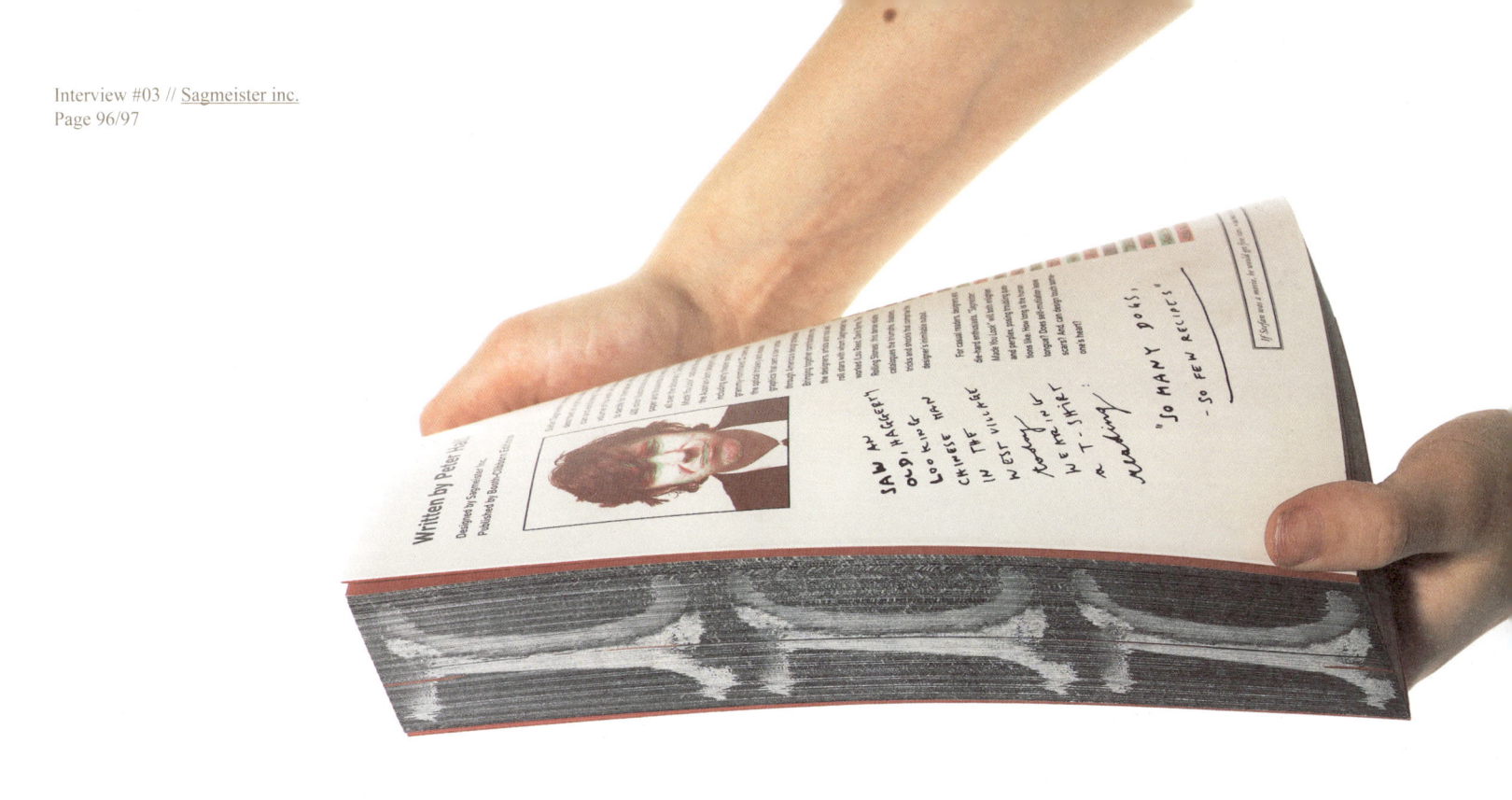

- walking home in Vienna when I suddenly had the idea for a campaign for the Ronacher Theatre, 20 years ago;

- being driven in Keith Richards' limo through the wastelands in New Jersey, the sun setting, on my way to meet the Stones in LA and having to pinch myself in order to believe this is really happening;

- sitting in a very nice hotel in Bombay working on free ideas without any clients attached while Six by Seven was running on the stereo.

What sort of publications do you usually read?

We get a whole slew of design publications in the studio, I leaf through them after work here and there. The one publication I really read is the *New York Times*.

Finally, could you recommend some good publications to our readers?

My favourite and for free: www.underconsideration.com and www.thisisamagazine.com

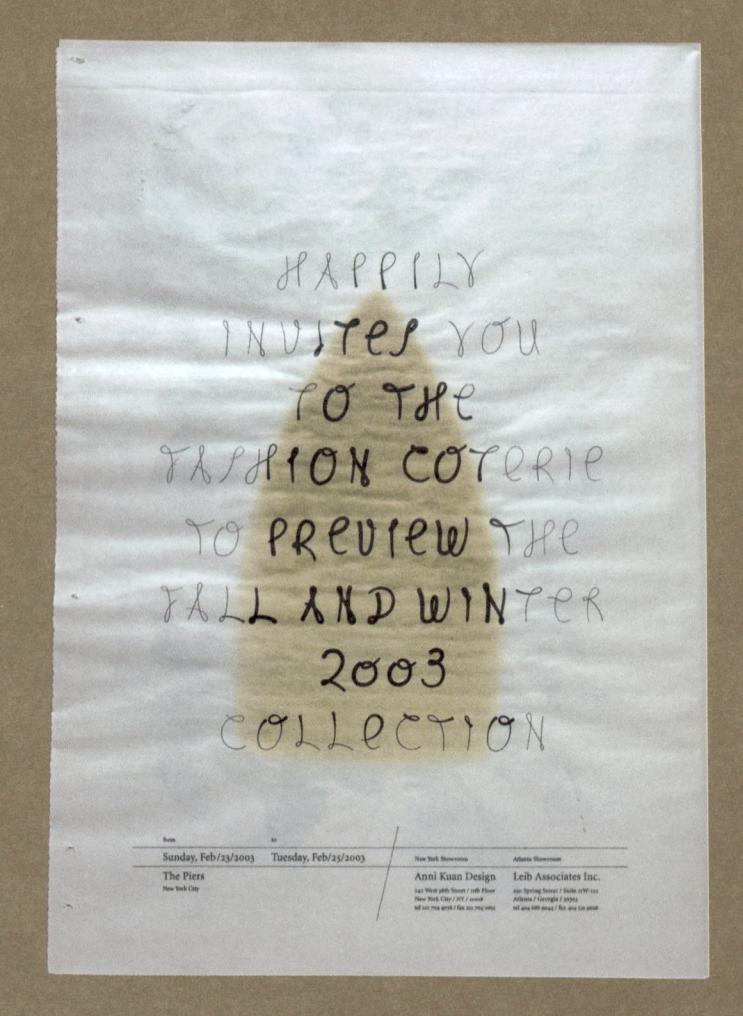

Interview #03 // Sagmeister inc.
Page 98/99

TITLE // Anni Kuan Brochure, Iron
TYPE OF WORK // Brochure
CLIENT // Anni Kuan
YEAR PRODUCED // 2003
ART DIRECTION // Stefan Sagmeister
DESIGNER/ILLUSTRATOR/PHOTOGRAPHER // Julia Fuchs
TYPOGRAPHY // Matthias Ernstberger

DESCRIPTION OF WORK //
Burn-marked Fall/Winter 2003 brochure for Anni Kuan, an Asian fashion designer working in New York.

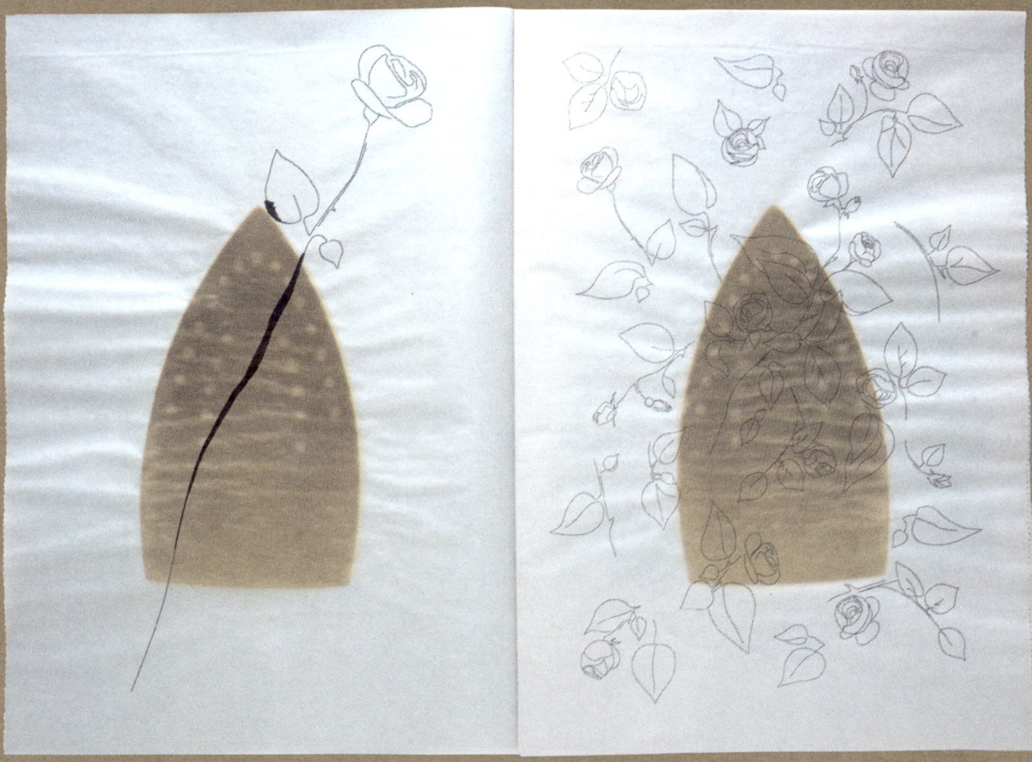

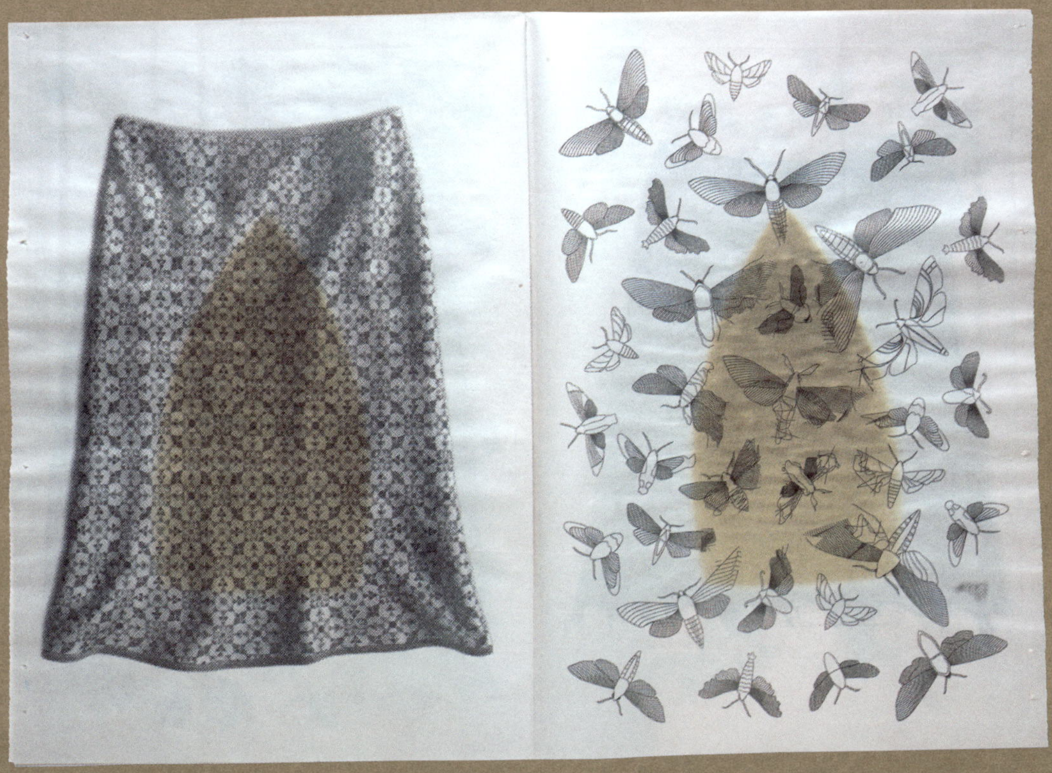

Interview #03 // Sagmeister inc.
Page 100/101

TITLE // Zumtobel Annual Report
TYPE OF WORK // Annual report
CLIENT // Zumtobel AG
YEAR PRODUCED // 2002
ART DIRECTION // Stefan Sagmeister
DESIGNER // Stefan Sagmeister, Matthias Ernstberger
PHOTOGRAPHER // Bela Borsodi
PROTOTYPE // Joe Stone

DESCRIPTION OF WORK //
Zumtobel is a leading European manufacturer of lighting systems. The cover of this annual report features a heat-molded relief sculpture of five flowers in a vase, symbolizing the five sub-brands under the Zumtobel name.

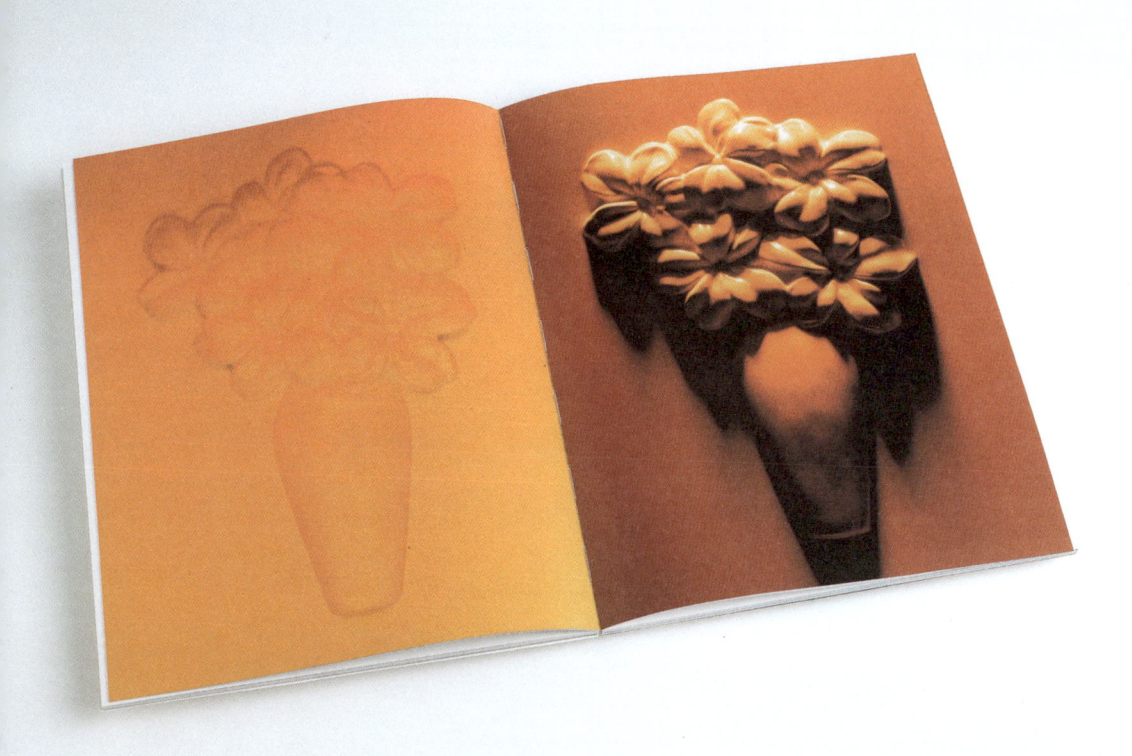

ZUMTOBEL AG

HETEROGENER GESCHÄFTS- VERLAUF BELASTET

Das Geschäftsjahr 2001/02 prägte ein äußerst heterogener Verlauf. Innerhalb des Zumtobel Konzerns mussten einerseits alle Anstrengungen auf den Fortgang der erfolgreichen Integration des im vorherigen Berichtszeitraum übernommenen britischen Leuchtenherstellers Thorn gelegt werden. Andererseits führten die sich rapide verschlechternden internationalen konjunkturellen Rahmenbedingungen in der zweiten Hälfte des Geschäftsjahres im Unternehmensbereich Leuchten und Lichtlösungen zu teilweise erheblichen Rückgängen. Der Gesamtumsatz sank daher um 7,1 Prozent auf EUR 1.240,3 Mio. Das im vorherigen Bilanzergebnis stabilisierte sich. Die Zahl der im Jahresdurchschnitt beschäftigten Mitarbeiter verringerte sich auf 9.014 Beschäftigte.

Pg.102 / Interview #04 / Flink

Interview with Fanny Khoo

Art direction, good design and interesting content are what Flink does best.

Flink is a multi-disciplinary creative studio based in Antwerp, Belgium. Their work crosses over a wide variety of disciplines, including brand development, corporate identity, interactive media, packaging and print.

Flink has an open and flexible structure, which allows the company to grow organically. Thinking with their hearts and minds has always been their greatest asset. Flink's ambition is to produce good work that speaks for itself.

TITLE // The Flink Paper
TYPE OF WORK // Promotional publication
CLIENT // Flink
YEAR PRODUCED // 2003
ART DIRECTION // Fanny Khoo
DESIGNER/ILLUSTRATOR // Tom Merckx
PHOTOGRAPHER // Raf Coolen

DESCRIPTION OF WORK //
The Flink Paper is a one-off publication published to coincide with the new Flink launch. A poster 'Flink for a change' comes attached with it.

The Flink Paper brings together several prominent industries and examines the impact of change: a time to change old mentalities and how the design and advertising industry can help inject humanism back into our everyday lives.

While the articles featured capture a moment in time, the paper serves more as a visual representation and statement of the new creative spirit.

Contributors include *The Guardian*, KesselsKramer, The Designers Republic, D&AD (British Design & Art Direction) and *Creative Review*, etc.

It is now being circulated around the world for selective audiences.

Time for ZZZ

a Flink PUBLICATION

Energieën-Oogst-Machine

Where do you live now and where are you from?
I've been based in Antwerp (Belgium) for the last four years but am originally from Singapore.

Flink is Belgian though.

Where and what did you study?
I studied at LaSalle College of the Arts in Singapore and majored in Advertising and Visual Communications (which is probably what's called 'Integrated Communications' today).

When did you set up your design firm? And why?
Flink was previously named Bizart, which was founded by Jean, Thierry and Stephan (my bosses) in '97.

Tom Merckx is the reason I'm here in Belgium (when we got married), as he worked for Bizart. I only arrived last year.

Tom and I always had big visions and we wanted to be more than what we were. Flink offered a lot of potential with better content and a depth that we couldn't achieve with Bizart. However, making that leap to Flink was only possible with the partners' blessings. They were incredibly supportive and believed in us even when things got rough.

I just became a huge catalyst in the story.

What services does your company provide and what is your aim/vision?
Flink offers a complete range of creative services, from brand development to print and interactive media. Our vision is very simple: that is to do great work for good people.

Quite appropriate as Flink means 'good' or 'be good' in Dutch and we love the idea of doing better each time – thinking outside the box and looking at things differently.

What was your dream work when you were young?
As a child, I wanted to change the world. To become a missionary or a social worker, all of which has to do with changing people and society.

That hasn't changed much, though... I just learned to become more realistic. Unfortunately, I still much too idealistic for the modern world.

Could you describe about The Flink Paper?
The Flink paper is a one-off publication on change and revolution. It was published to coincide with the new Flink launch, 'Flink for a change'. It serves more as a visual representation and statement of the new creative spirit rather than a vacuous self-promotional piece.

All the articles featured have a direct correlation with the idea of change. As we wanted this to be a qualitative, not to mention inspiring read, we involved creative minds and writers of varied disciplines to exchange ideas and be part of the bigger picture. Contributors include *The Guardian*, KesselsKramer, The Designers Republic, D&AD (British Design & Art Direction), *Creative Review* and *Shift Japan*, with photography by Raf Coolen.

What inspired you to do The Flink Paper?
Like many others, I think that the biggest cultural revolution we are going to see is going to come about from a move to a more intuitive, personal age. Away from mass-production, away from overt consumerism. Everything is moving too fast with everyone going up in flames. The world has become a much colder place, filled with faceless brands. Individualism has run off and joined the circus.

What is your aim in doing The Flink Paper and what do you expect in return?
'Time for a revolution' also implies a time to change old mentalities, which is something I've always wanted to do – though essentially, one probably can't. We can only inform and hope to inspire? We really didn't know what to expect because we had never done anything like this before. It was like we went into the laboratory, tried concocting some strange experiment and then waited to see if it takes off. What's really gratifying though, is all the positive reactions we receive from all over. That makes the whole experience really worthwhile!

tion
dgements
& science
ation & architecture
on
tomy & technology
vertising & design
nk culture

Interview#04 // Flink
Page 106/107

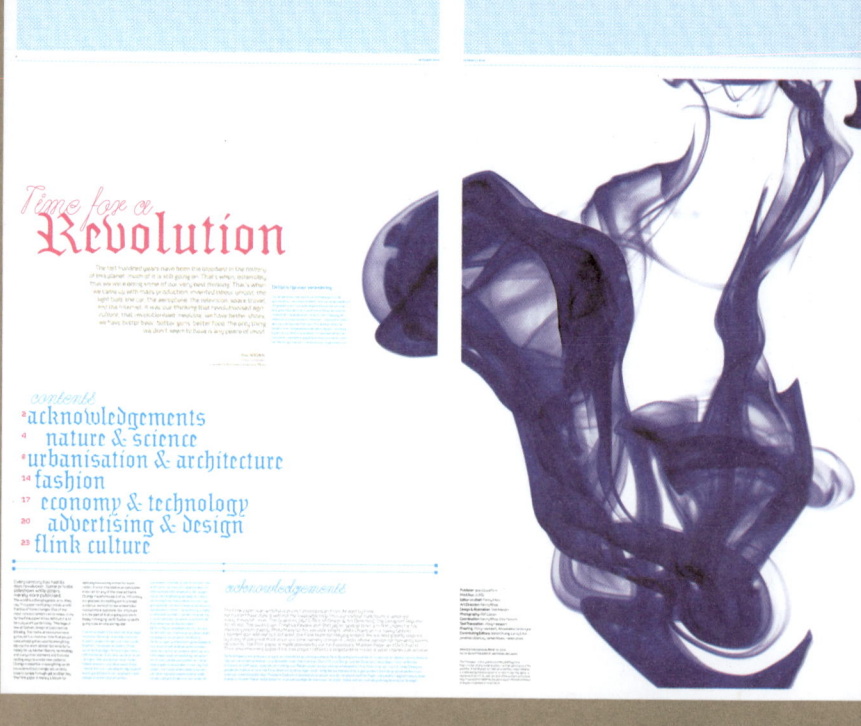

Evolution is
in our hands
say scientists

Energieën-Oogst-Machine
WERKENDE VREDESENERGIEËN
OOGST KUNST WERKEN

Change but hardly
a revolution
Empower the individual

Did you set any grids, style or particular elements for the layouts of *The Flink Paper*? Do you think it is important for a publication?

I provided the initial art direction for the design but it was really Tom who put everything together so beautifully. He also made those fantastic illustrations.

The large format of the paper meant that optimal legibility was an important consideration. Tom formed a simple grid system, made up of pixel patterns (as it was a big part of our identity) and the right fonts and basic frames that surround the titles. Most designers think that grids are stifling but we think it's really useful when it comes to designing difficult layouts. Without that grid, it would have been hell to fit in all those articles, translations, images and illustrations. Of course, our priority was still making sure that it looked innovative and awe-inspiring.

Have you experienced any difficulties in doing this project during the whole process?

This may come as a surprise, but with *The Flink Paper*, the hardest thing I had to overcome was the skepticism at Flink itself. Hard to believe, but it's difficult enough to change what others once thought, but truly unimaginable if you have to change existing mentalities. It is a difficult process, but not one without progress, even if it means we still have a long way to go.

It was also not easy making that language switch from English to Dutch but Vicky Haesaert, who did all the translations pulled it off admirably.

The deadline was another big issue because we did *The Flink Paper* in between all the client work. It took like, forever to finally deliver it. Nine months to be exact:)

So far, what has happened to impress you most during the project?

The overwhelming response we have had from a cross-section of different people and fantastic support shown by the contributors, especially KesselsKramer, *The Guardian* and the D&AD. They're extremely intelligent people and have been so very inspiring. Also when Raf (the photographer), who was initially dead against the idea of change, actually said that while working on this project he believed that we all needed a change.

I'm still amazed that our sponsors Munken Paper and De Schutter made it possible for us to produce such a beautiful piece of legacy. Thank you!

Do you have any favourite artists or designers? What is it you like about them?

I don't know if this is cliché but my favourite artist and designer is actually Amy Francescini (Futurefarmers). She's incredibly talented and also extremely down-to-earth. But really, I have immense respect for so many people in this industry and for people who have the ability to think differently and do what they believe in, not at anyone else's expense.

I have to quote Gerard Saint (Big Active) on this: 'Next time you walk past Gap, Prada or Top Shop, do the world a favour – throw a brick through the window and think for yourself.'

Following the question above, do you think that you have been influenced by them? If not, what are your strongest influences and where/what is your inspiration?

Like so many creative people, I have been touched and inspired by so many influences – nature, my mother, Tom – but Tibor Kalman has been one of my strongest influences. He was wildly passionate about his beliefs and was also extremely committed to social causes. His desire to break new ground was expressed everyday in his life, no matter what he did.

At last, what kind of publications do you usually read? Do you have any book recommendations to our readers?

I read a lot, but love my share of graphic publications like *CR, Grafik, Archive, IdN*, and magazines like *Dazed, Wallpaper, The Face* – the whole lot… However, the *Colors Magazine*, which Tibor Kalman created, holds a special place in my heart because it has such great context. I personally think Fernado Gutiérrez has done a great job by taking it to another level.

I have been reading this life-changing book called *Leadership & the New Science* by Margaret J Wheatley. It was written primarily for leaders in organizations but has relevance to anyone seeking to understand the world he lives in. What an eye opener! I couldn't sleep for days after reading it. I strongly recommend it!

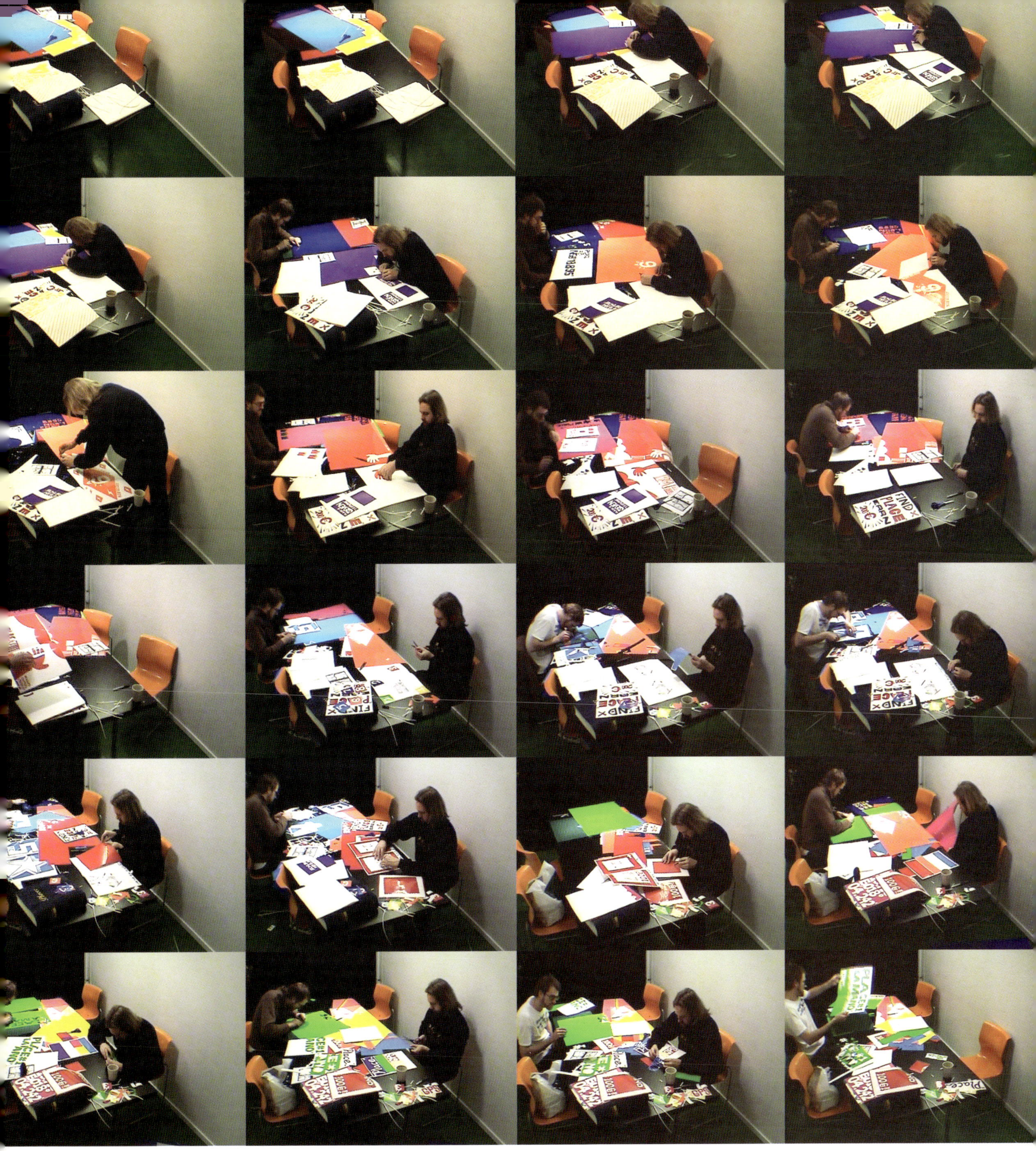

+ Sweden Graphics

Page
110

Client
Place/Vasava

Title of work
Place: Sweden's 200 euro
GPS Treasure Hunt

Art Director
Sweden Graphics

Type of work
Book

Designer
Sweden Graphics

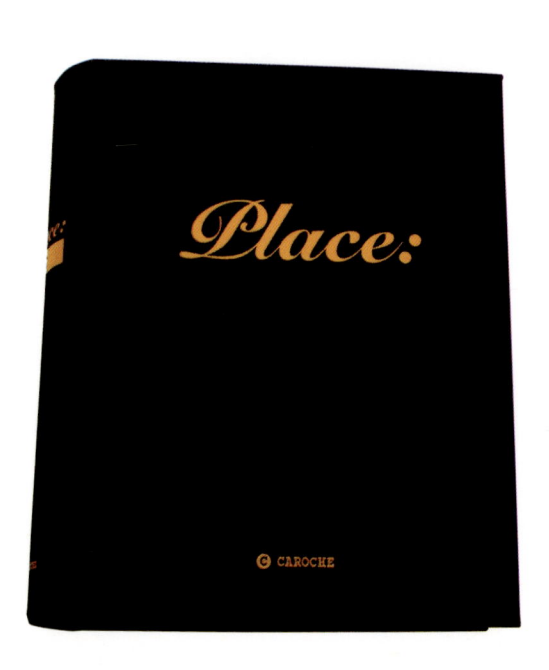

Origin
Stockholm, Sweden

Year produced
2003

Description
A collection of loose pages made from cut-out coloured adhesive plastic.

N59°
19.715'
E018°
04.242'
Place 3

PLACE
6
N59°20.089'
E018°07.599'

G★P★S
N 59°19.504'
E018°05.043'
NIKI
PLACE
4

PLACE #
SEVEN
"STUDIO"
N59°18.654'
E018°04.701'

5
PLACE
N59°20.297'
E018°06.260'

N
59°21.539
E
018° 07.247
PLACE VIII
MILLES:
GENIUS,
FASCIST

+ Anthony Burrill

Page
112

Client
FAT (Architects)

Origin
London, UK

Title of work
The Brindley Estate Public Works Programme

Art Director
—

Year produced
2003

Type of work
Book

Designer
Anthony Burrill

Description
This book was made as part of an art commission, in consultation with residents of an inner city housing estate. The residents were given a number of options for an artwork that would be installed in the estate. The book includes proposals by the architects and the residents, who were also asked to make suggestions. A voting card was included with the book that residents could post back to the architects. The results showed the fountain earned the most votes.

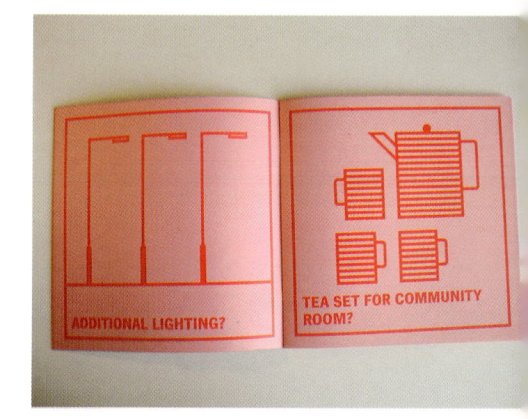

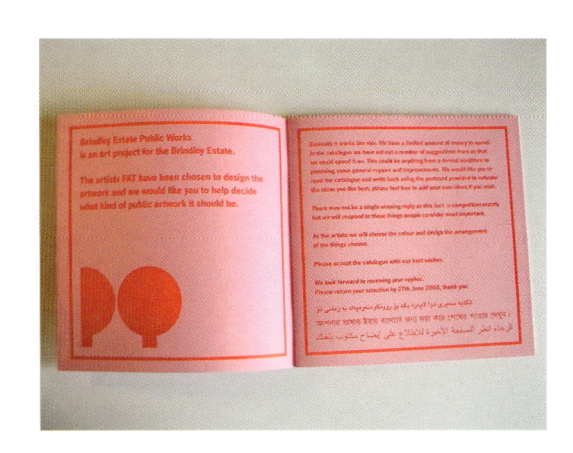

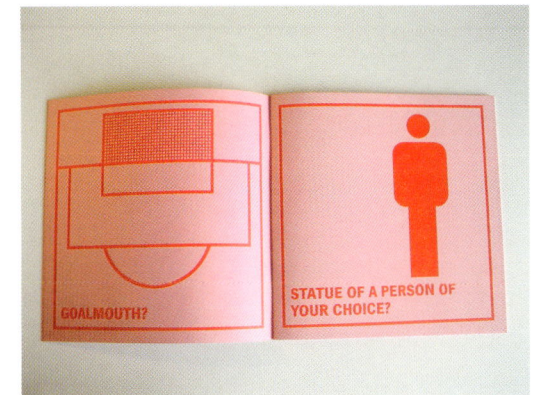

GOALMOUTH? — STATUE OF A PERSON OF YOUR CHOICE?

GENERAL REPAIRS? — FLOWER BED?

NEW SECURITY GATES? — PLAYGROUND EQUIPMENT?

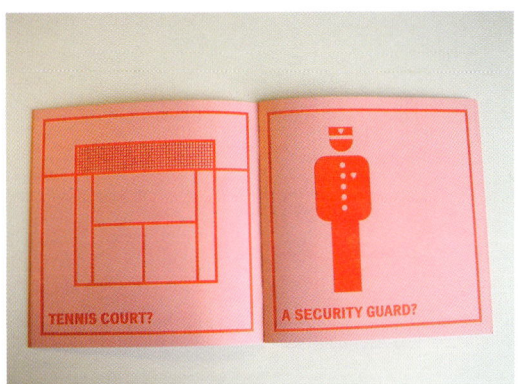

TENNIS COURT? — A SECURITY GUARD?

COMMUNITY ROOM PLAYSTATION? — PLANT SOME TREES?

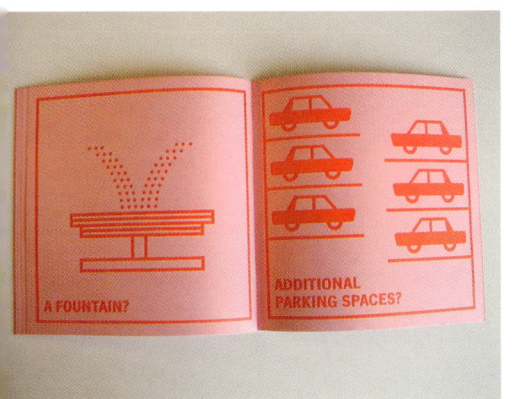

A FOUNTAIN? — ADDITIONAL PARKING SPACES?

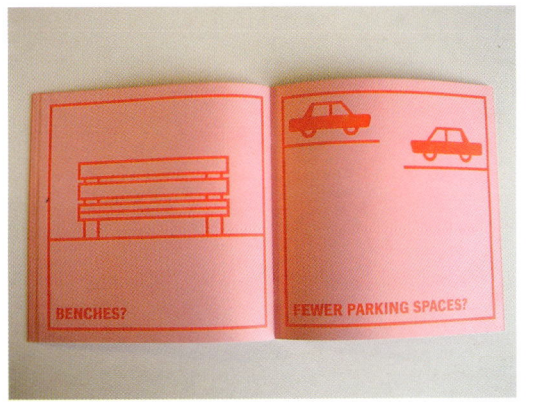

BENCHES? — FEWER PARKING SPACES?

+ Dainippon Type Organization

Page
114

Client
Actar, Barcelona

Origin
Tokyo, Japan

Title of work
Type Card Play Book

Art Director
Dainippon Type Organization

Year produced
2003

Type of work
Book

Designer
Dainippon Type Organization

Description
The team of Japanese experimental graphic designers called Dainippon Type Organization continually reinvents the art of typography beyond its practical dimension, turning it into an active and essentially playful experience. Here they give you a big blow: a retrospective from ten years of font and graphic production presented in a manner where you can look, play, think and enjoy the letters at your own will.

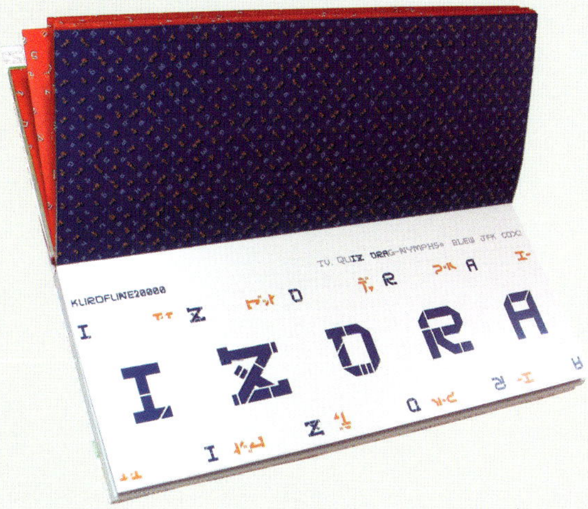
IZDRA

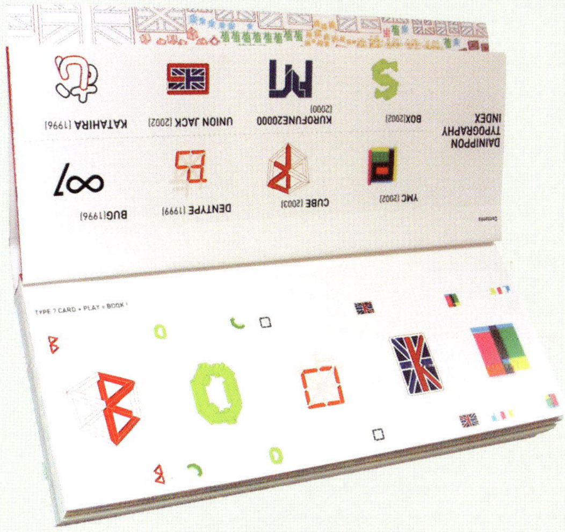

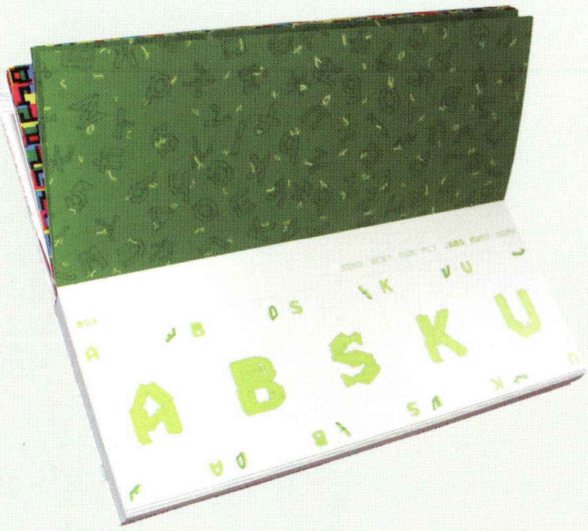
ABSKU

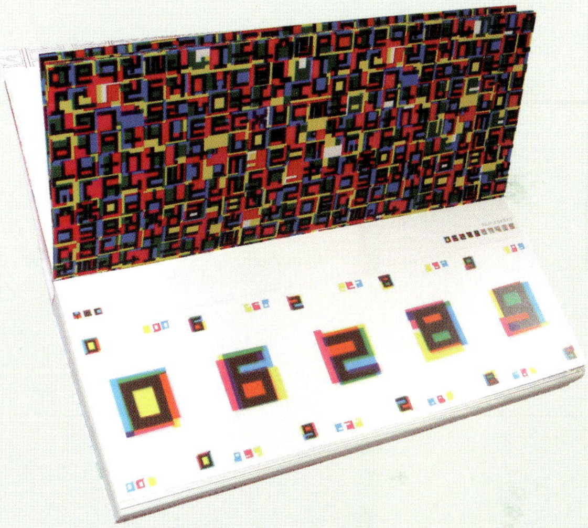

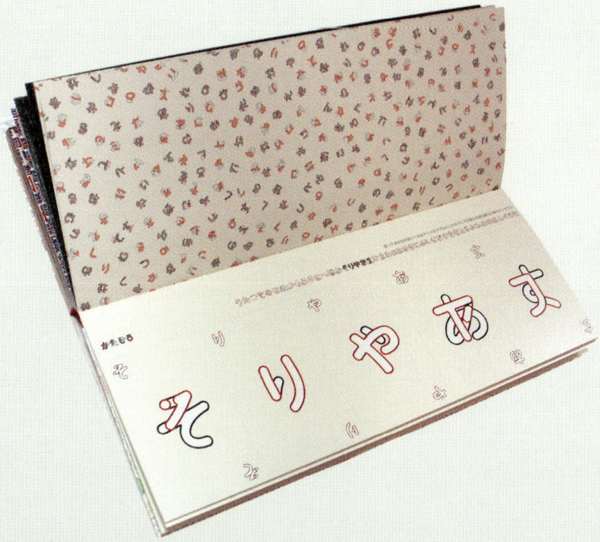

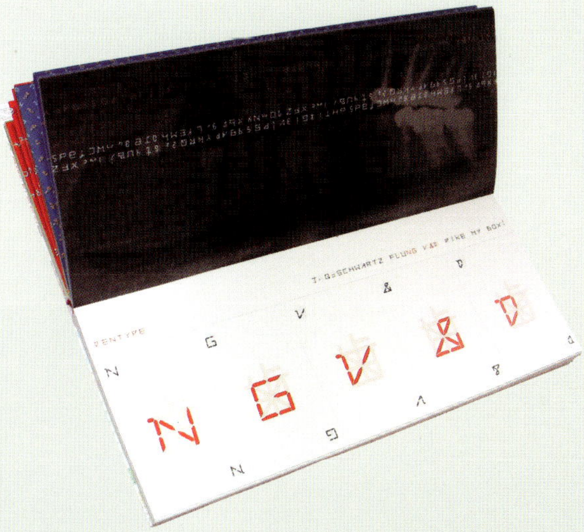
NGV&D

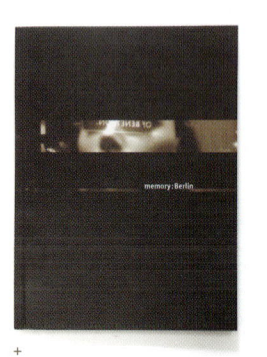

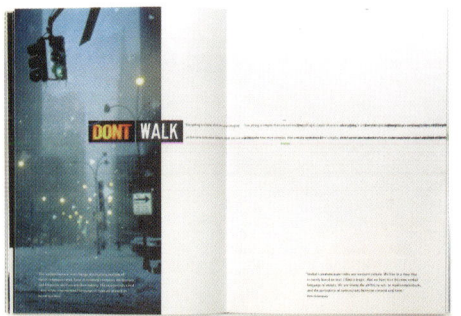

+ Envision +

Page
116

Title of work
Memory City
+ Memory: Berlin
++ Memory: London
+++ Memory: Tokyo

Type of work
Book

Client
–

Origin
Bühlertal, Germany

Art Director
Esther Mildenberger

Year produced
2001

Designer
Esther Mildenberger, Brian Switzer

Description
This publishing project investigates our perception of cities: their chaos and relationship to cultural and architectural theory.
+ *Memory: Berlin* reflects upon the tendencies in experimental typography, language and signs.
++ *Memory: London* relates architectural theories to our perception of everyday experience with urban spaces.
+++ *Memory: Tokyo* journeys through the culture of Tokyo, with texts from *Empire of Signs* by Roland Barthes.

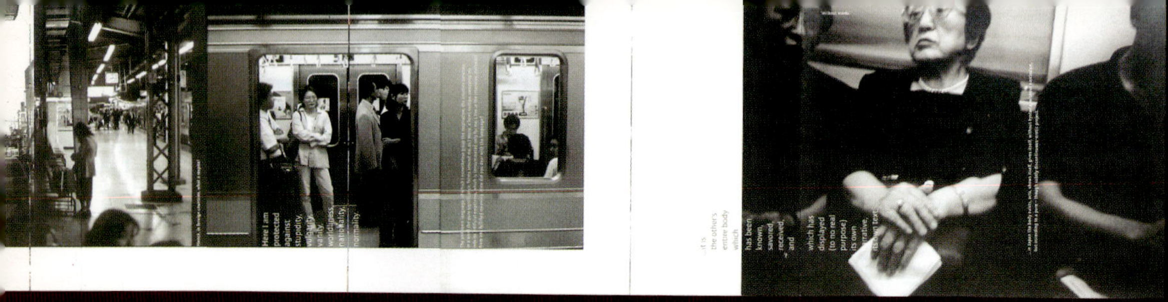

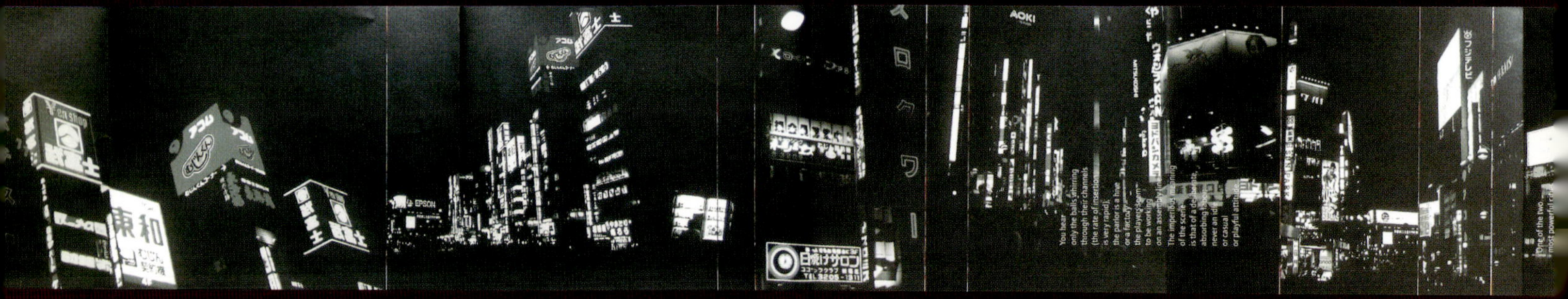
EPSON
AOKI

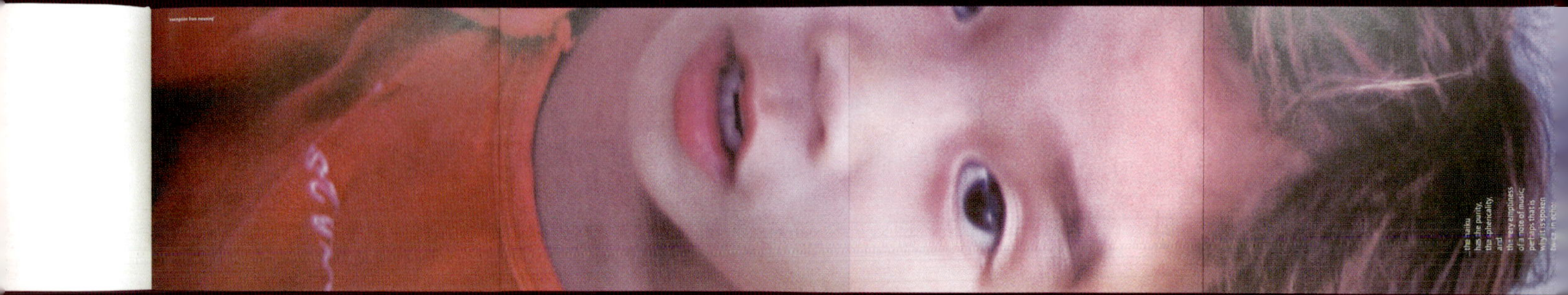

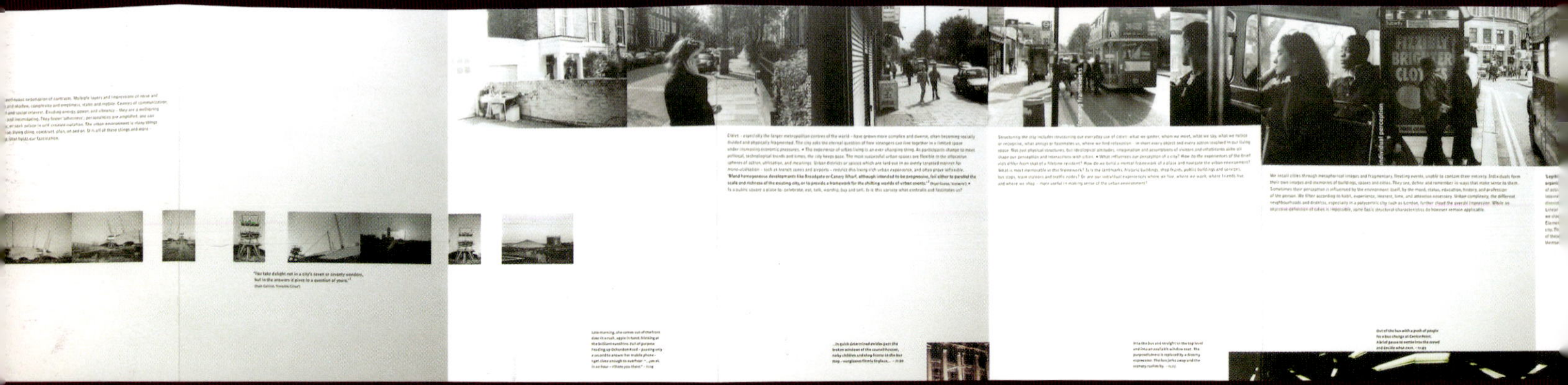

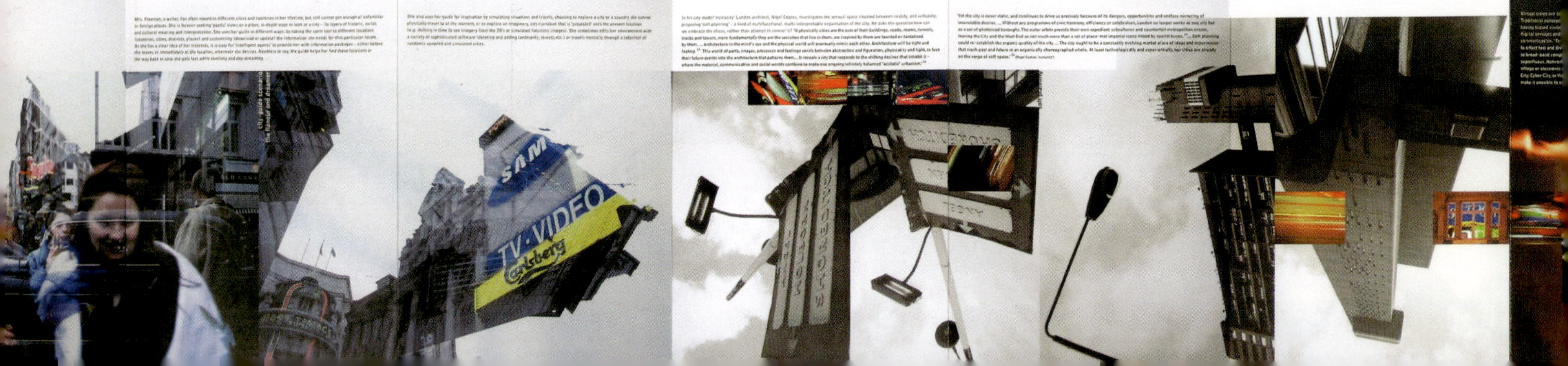
TV-VIDEO
Carlsberg

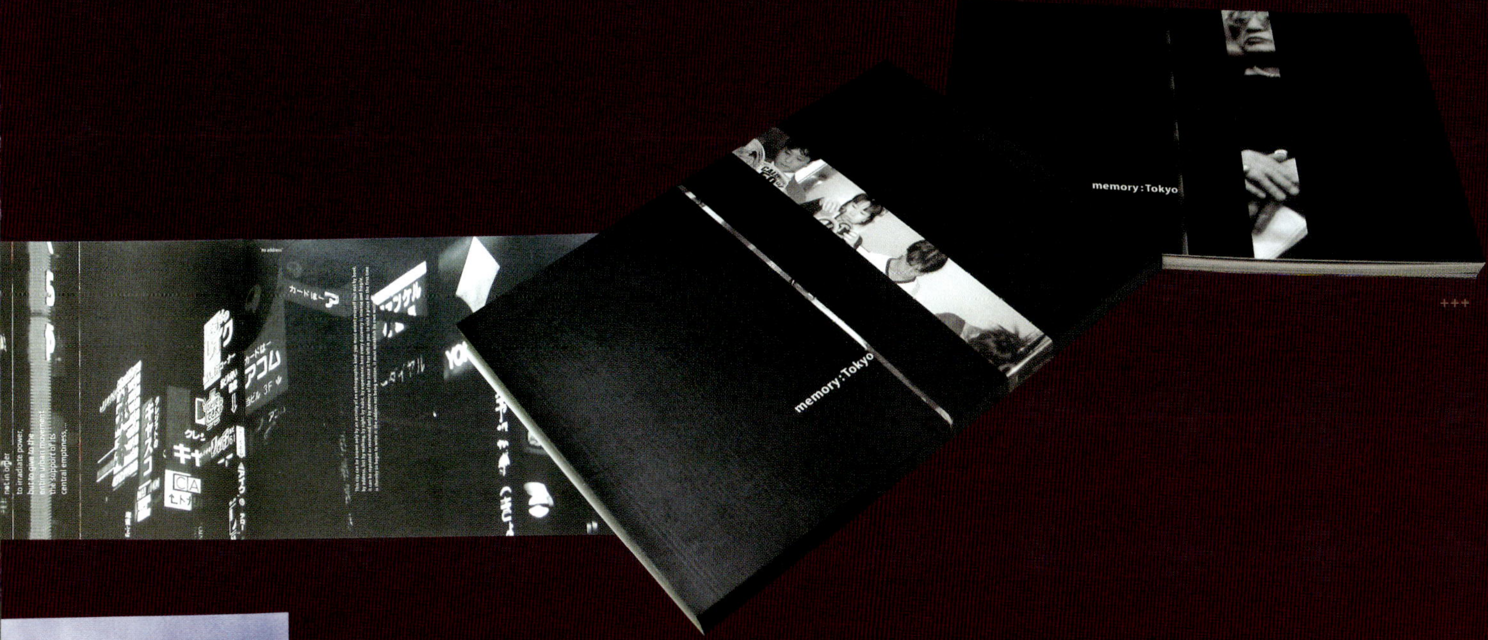
memory:Tokyo
memory:Tokyo

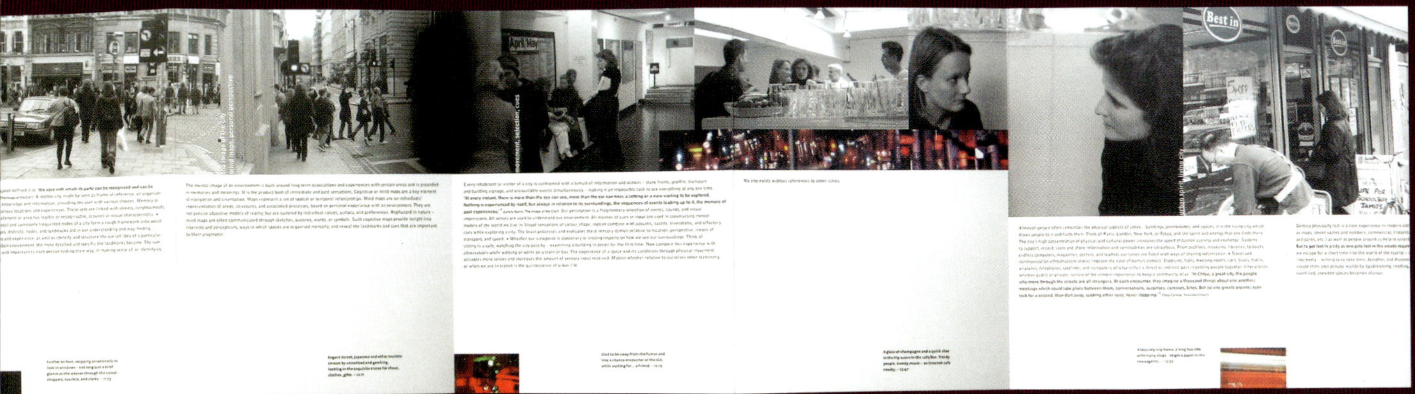

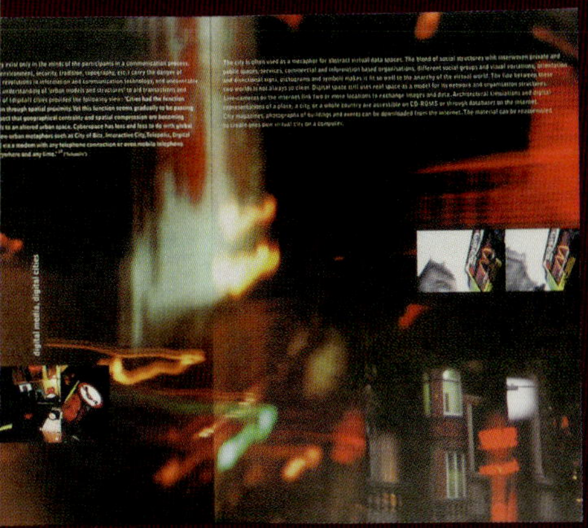

+ Büro International London

Page
126

Client
Akademisk Forlag, Copenhagen

Origin
Germany / UK

Title of work
Kryds

Art Director
Büro International London /
Copenhagen

Year produced
2003

Type of work
School book

Designer
Oliver Klimpel, Svend Wennick

Description
Büro International London + Copenhagen
has developed a new workbook for the
Danish publisher Akademisk Forlag.
The image of the book is plain, drawn
by introducing a range of graphic
and tactile devices into the working
experience, the book design engages
and guides the user. Various
chapters make use of various visual
vocabularies, materials and special
inks. Besides having to fill in pages
with your own personal handwriting,
perforated sections and a DIY thumb
index customize the workbooks and
give an indication of the tasks still ahead.
The set includes a VHS and audiotape.

KRYDS
KRYDS
KRYDS
5

Opgave #17 Grethe Buch i tv
KASSE
Opgave #18

Navn
Dato
08 10 2002
Andet
Lærebog i dansk som andetsprog

Opgave #9

+ Hyperkit

Page
122 - 125

Title of work
Life Size

Type of work
Book

Client
viction:workshop

Art Director
Tim Balaam
Kate Sclater

Designer
Tim Balaam
Kate Sclater

Origin
London, UK

Year produced
2004

Description
Life Size was conceived of as a site-specific project with the content being formatted according to two primary themes: the alternative functions and the spatial constraints of a book. Using clever production techniques, the book can also be used as a photo album, a ruler and even a desk organiser. Also explored are representations of size – objects are displayed across a series of pages, true to life size. The aim is to change the reader's perception of what a book is and how it can behave.

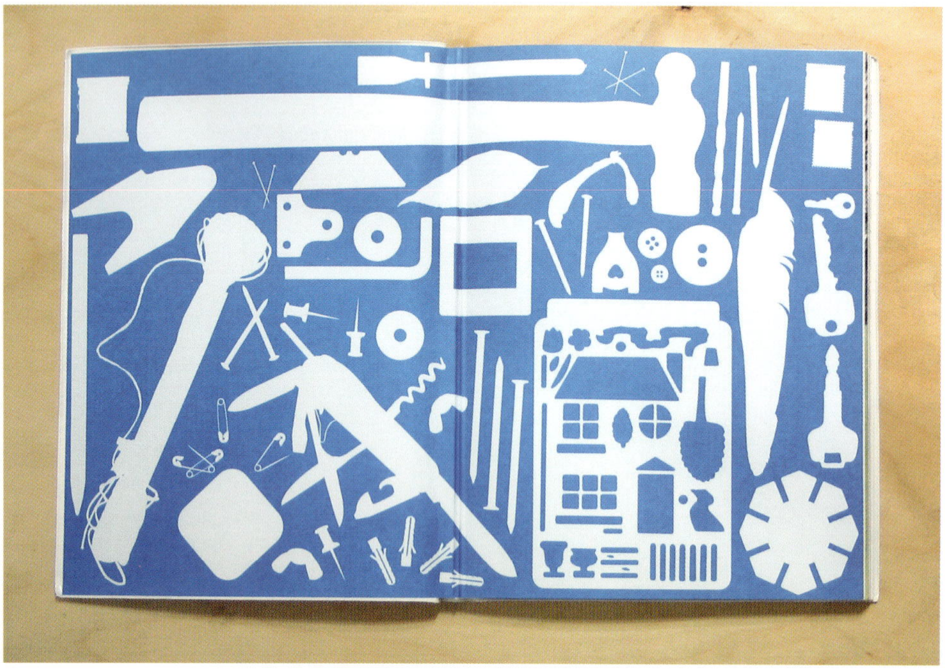

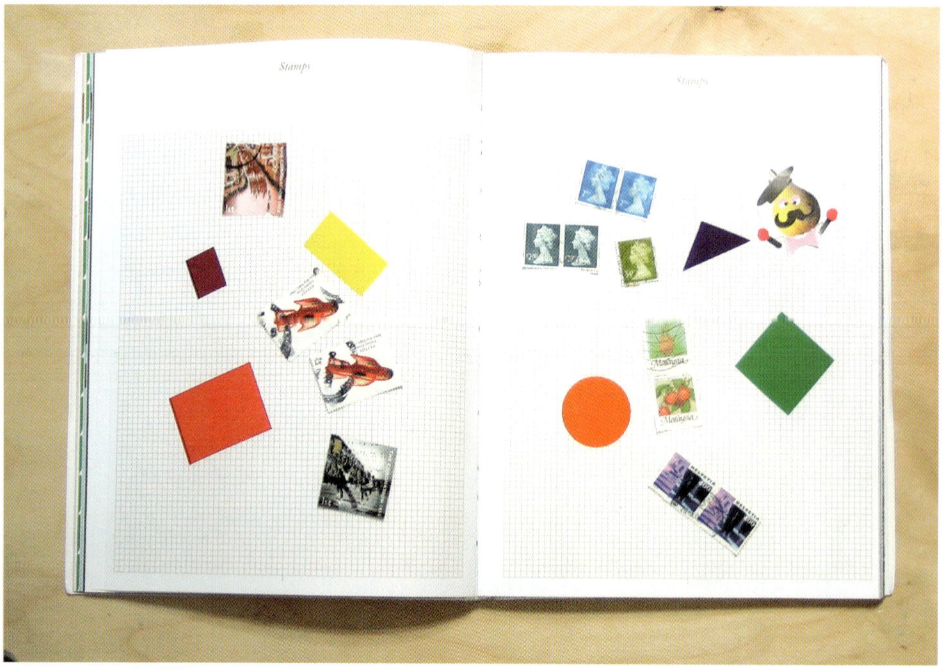
Stamps
Stamps

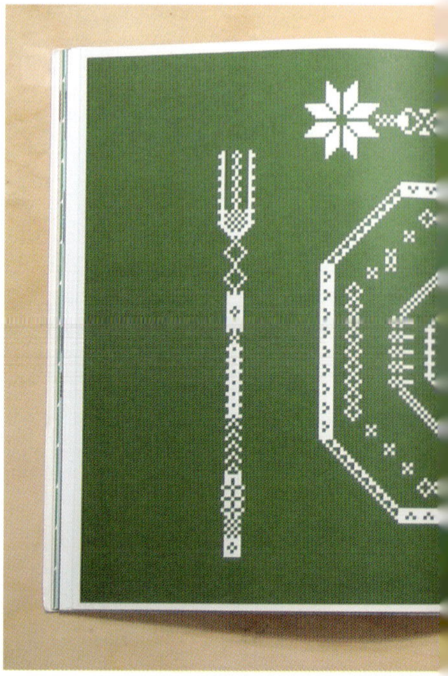

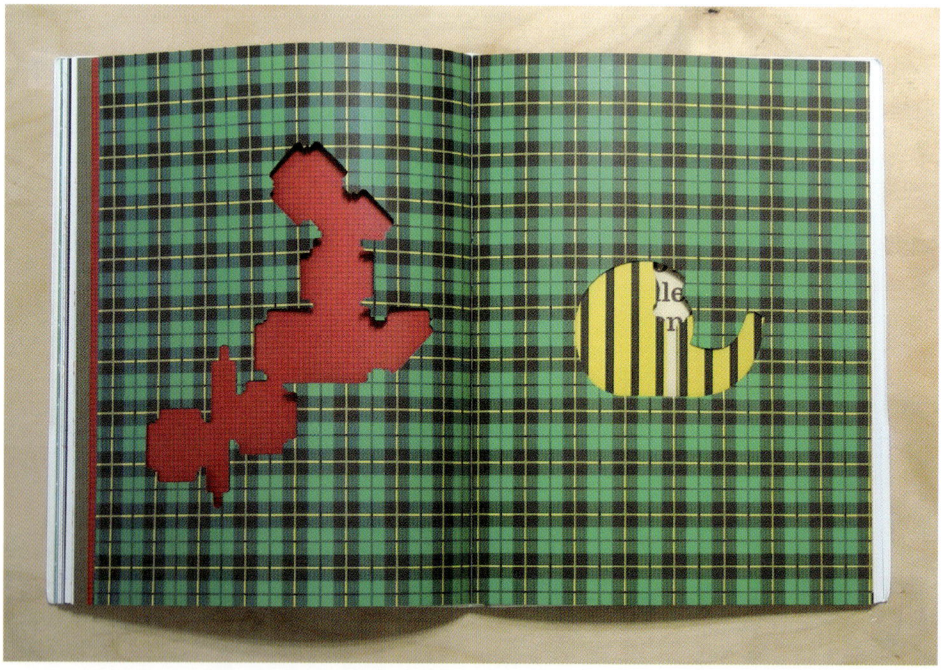

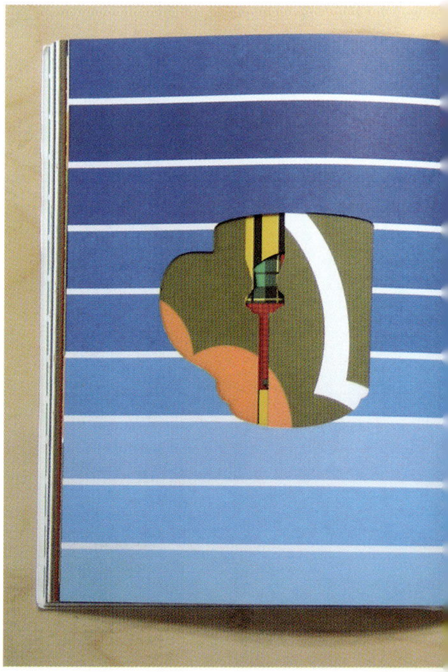

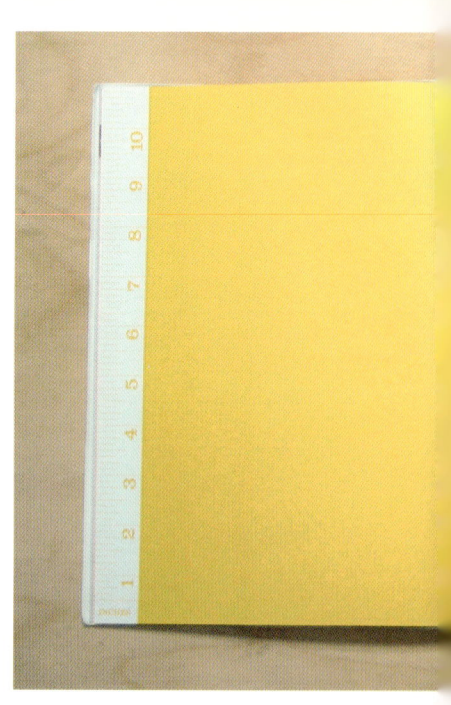

You are 0.0157238 miles from the front cover

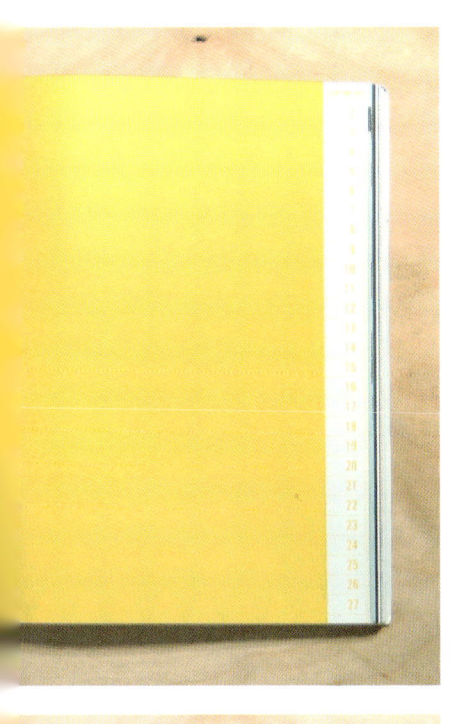

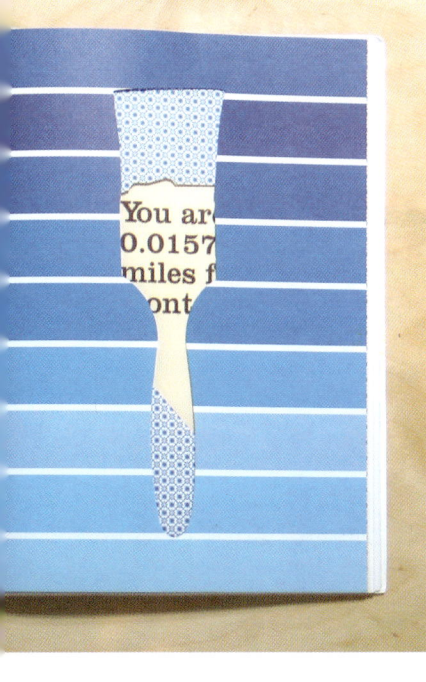

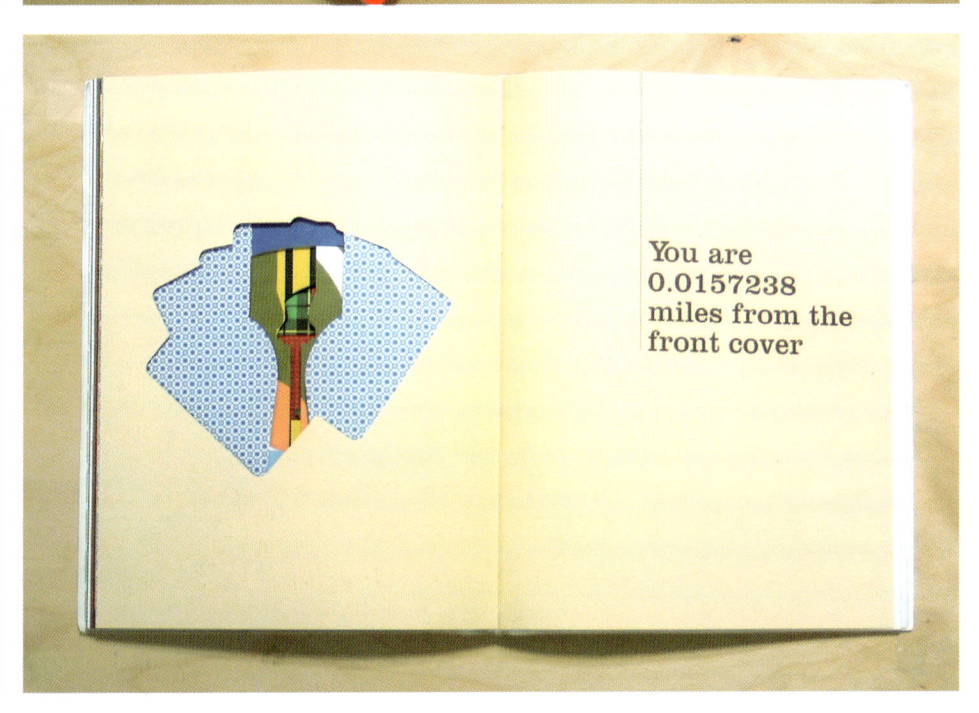

+ Milkxhake

Page
126

Client
Hong Kong

Origin
Hong Kong, China

Title of work
HK:Hug&Kiss

Art Director
Milkxhake

Year produced
2003

Type of work
Book

Designer
Milkxhake

Description
HK:Hug&Kiss was a self-initiated project in response to the SARS disease in Hong Kong last year. It was a self-expression towards the place the designers lived. Milkxhake created a 'sweet' identity for Hong Kong and offered a new meaning to it. 'Hug' & 'Kiss' using snaps of different times, places and people to express their love and memories toward HK, they designed a handmade booklet and put it on their website www.milkxhake.org to share their vision with others. To hug & kiss our city more than ever!

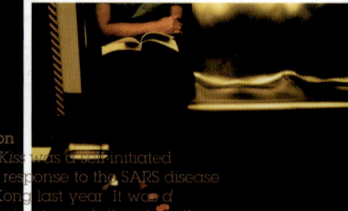

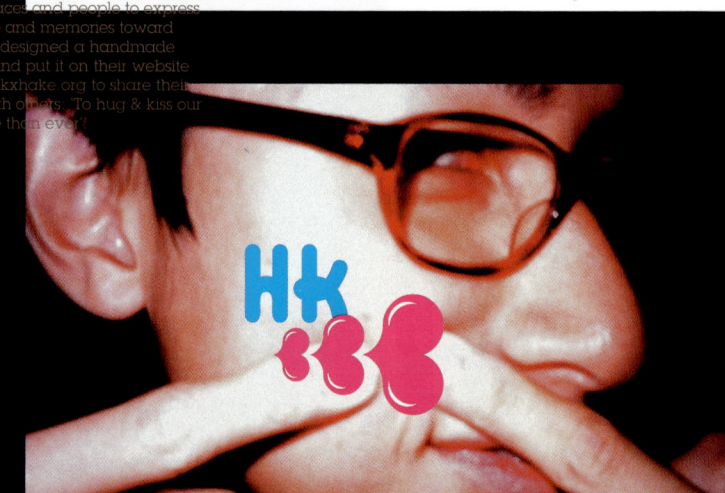

Just talk less,
it's time to **hug & kiss** our home
more than ever.

March-June_03@hong kong

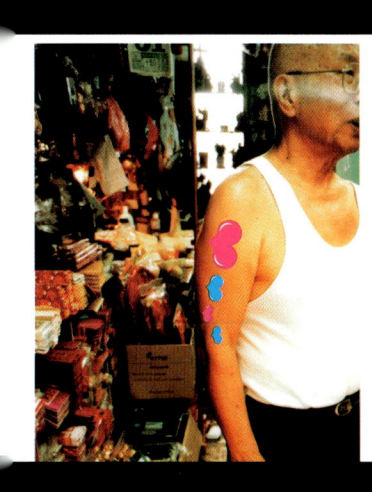

↘112

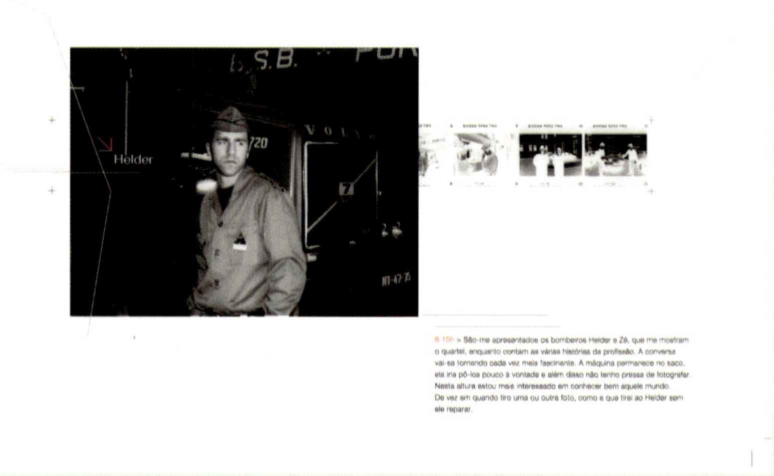

Page	**Client**
128	FBAUP
Title of work	**Art Director**
112	Nuno Martins
Type of work	**Designer**
Book	Nuno Martins

Year produced
2002

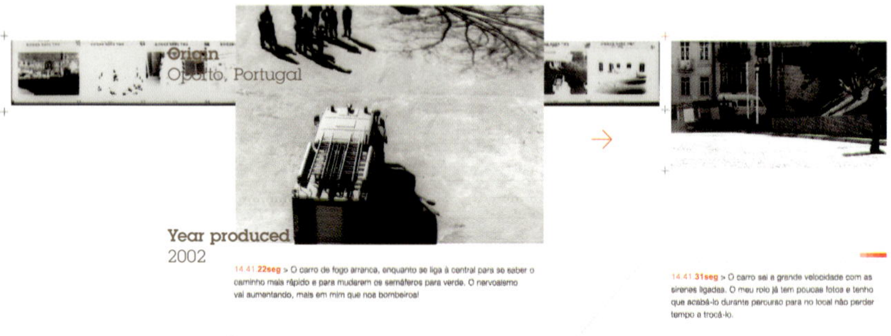

Description
Portuguese firemen have a negative image that is perpetuated by society: unprofessional people with inadequate training who occasionally carry out a heroic act.
By carefully relating work in photography and graphic design, this book intends to reverse that public perception. Through a photographic narrative supported with small texts, the aim is to illustrate the real image of Portuguese firemen: modern, respected and professional. This project was instigated by FBAUP.

+ Sweden Graphics

Page
129

Title of work
"Pocky' Book Design

Type of work
Book

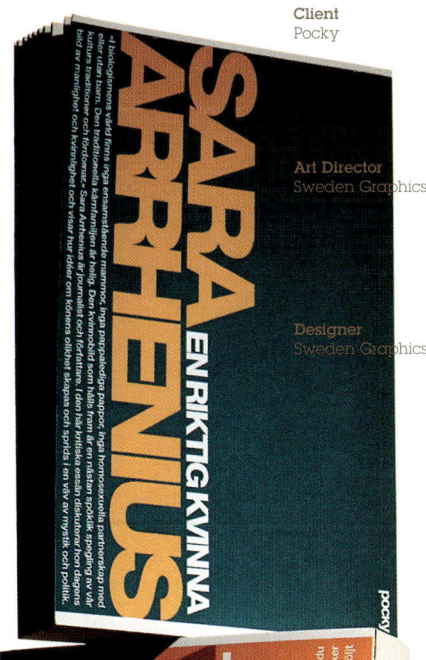

Client
Pocky

Art Director
Sweden Graphics

Designer
Sweden Graphics

Origin
Stockholm, Sweden

Year produced
2000 - 2002

Description
--

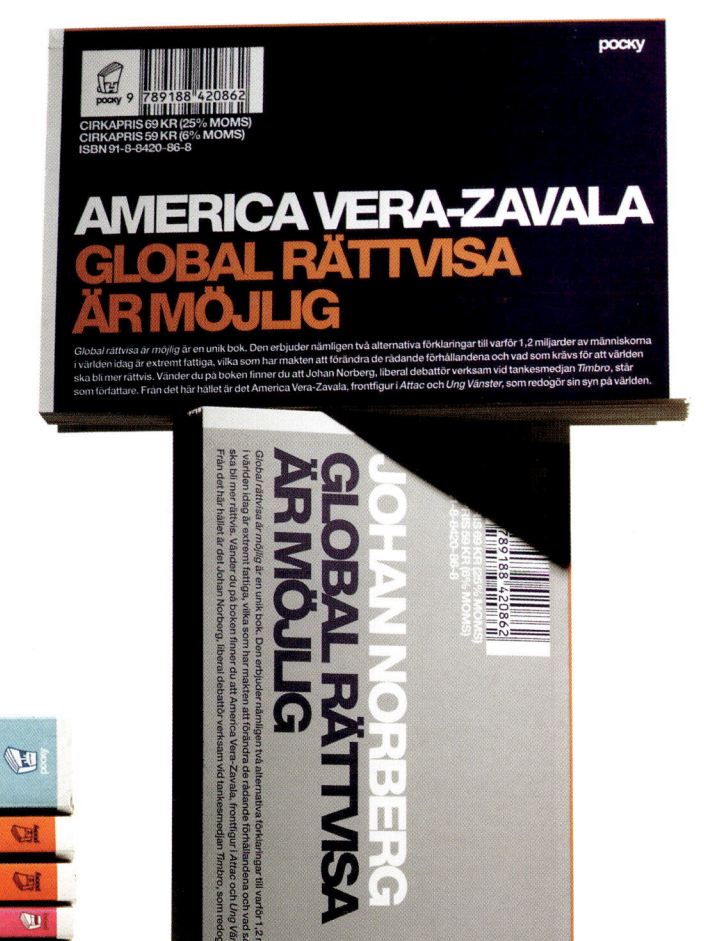

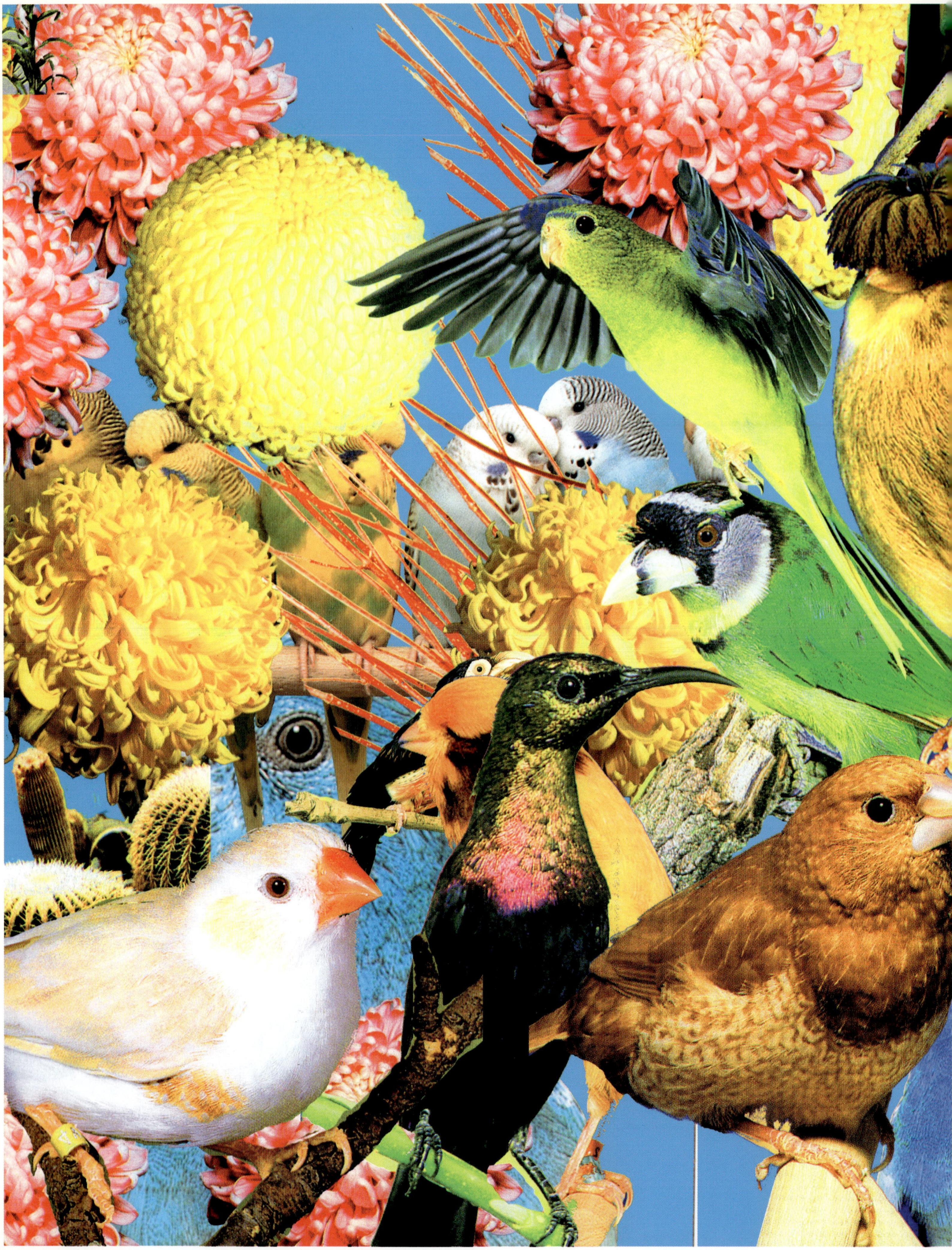

+ Bleed

Page
131

Client
Bleed

Origin
Oslo, Norway

Title of work
YoungBlood

Art Director
Erik Hedberg

Year produced
2004

Type of work
Book

Designer
Erik Hedberg

Description
Youngblood is a book containing artwork and design made by Nordic designers and art students. Bleed invited 40 schools to participate in the project. They wanted to highlight Nordic students because it's not always easy to get your name out there when you're a student. The book itself is clean and simple so that it will not steal too much attention from the contributions.

THE GREAT COMMUNICATOR

CAMEL

SHERYL 12.00
PAINA LOPUT
KORJAUSLUKUTENTTI JH KLO 10
EVE.
TULOSTA!
GIRLS
NIGHT
OUT
VILLE 26
DESIGN4ALL!
A3-VALKOSET
DESIGN MANIFESTO-KIRJA HIMASTA

TANGO KABAREE TV1
EVE
NOUSU
MINTTU.
ESSEET
OMPELE!
LEFFAKERHO PULP FICTION

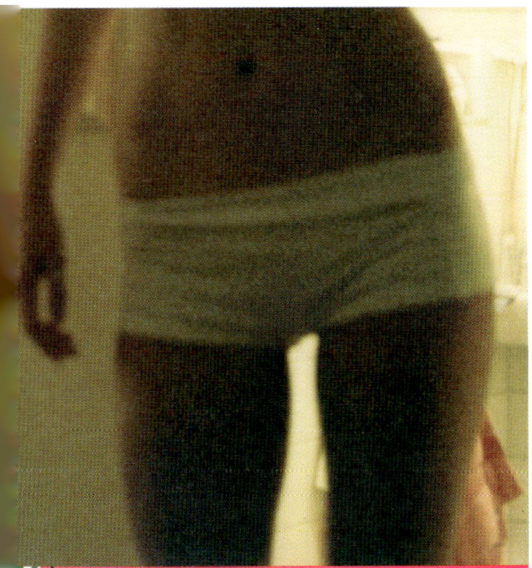

MAP OF SKANDINAVIA.

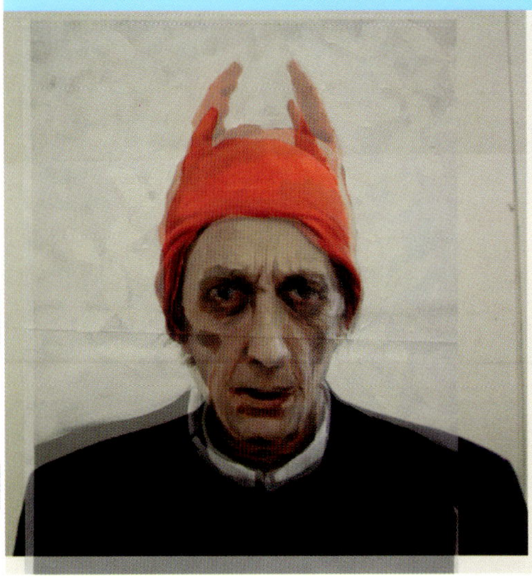

Peter
Peter
flackande blick och handsvett
Fan jag vill känna närhet
Lite vanlig, riktig jävla hud
Håll käften nu!
Jag har fått spon

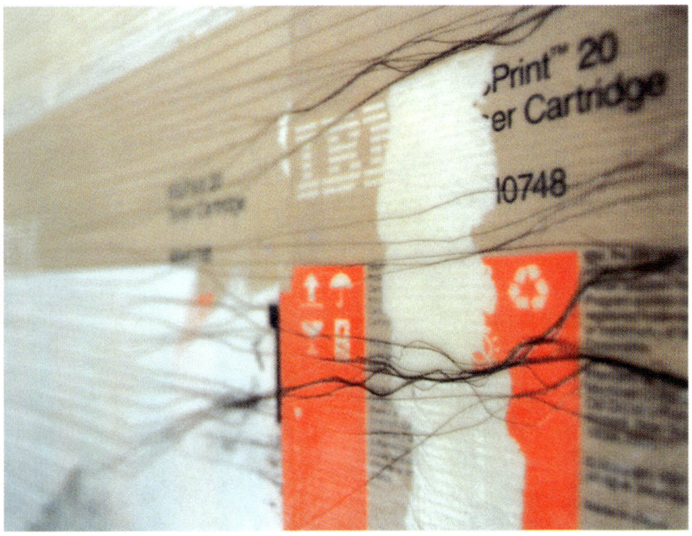
Print™ 20
er Cartridge
0748

+ Benjamin Güedel

Page
134

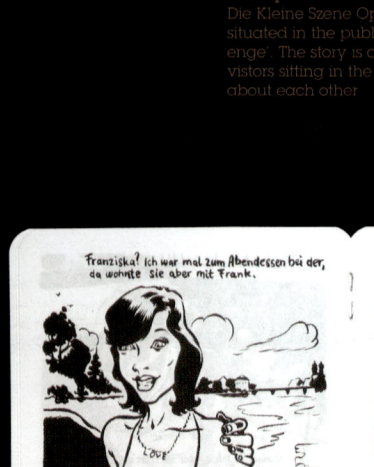

Client
Seebad Enge, Switzerland

Origin
Zurich, Switzerland

Title of work
Die Kleine Szene Oper

Art Director
Benjamin Güedel

Year produced
2002

Type of work
Comic

Designer
Benjamin Güedel

Description
Die Kleine Szene Oper is a short comic, situated in the public bath 'seebad enge'. The story is about the young vistors sitting in the sun and gossiping about each other

s Brumnjak

Client
Boris Brumnjak

Art Director
Boris Brumnjak

Designer
Boris Brumnjak

typo
grafie
lebt

Page
136

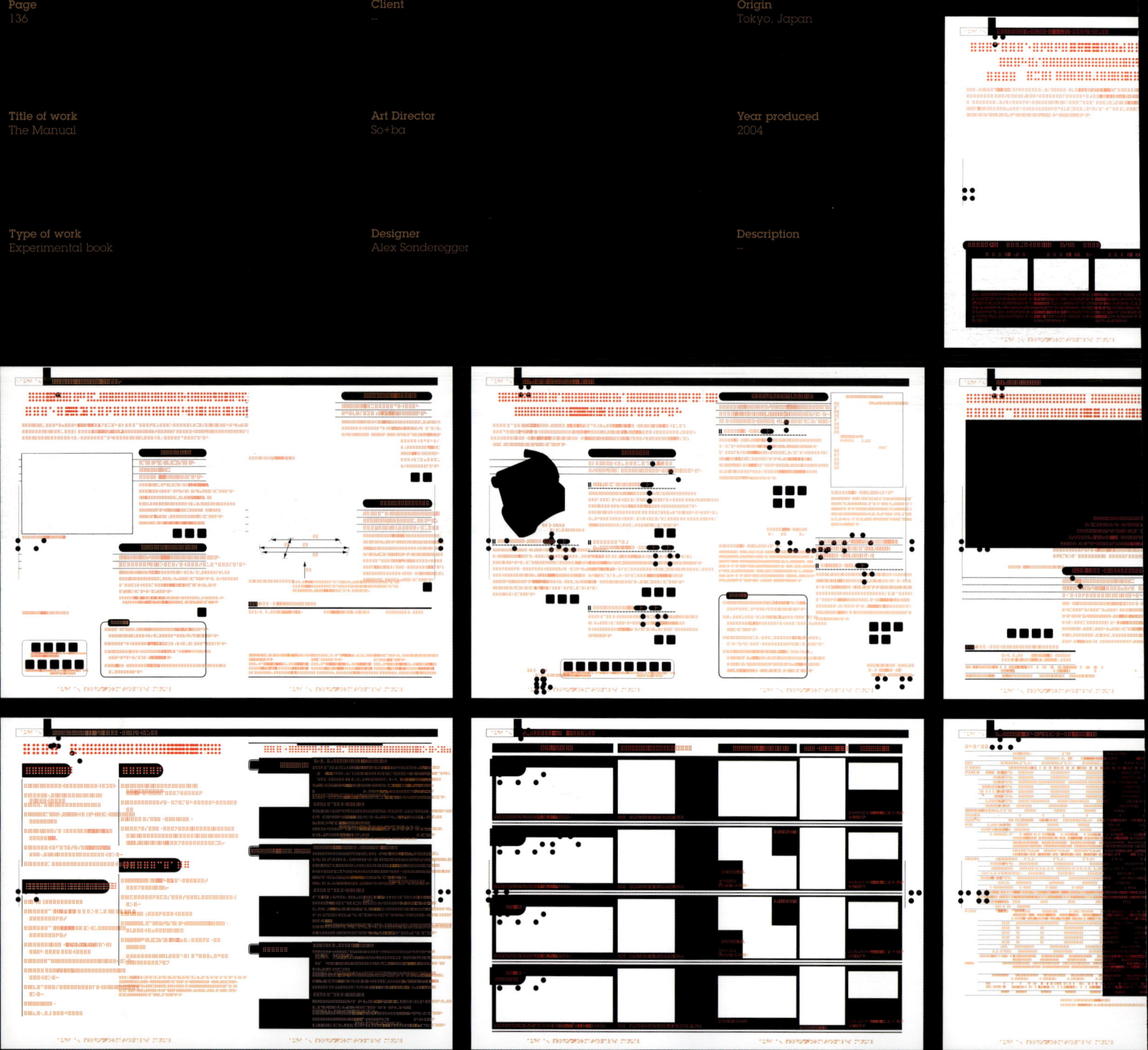

Client
--

Origin
Tokyo, Japan

Title of work
The Manual

Art Director
So+ba

Year produced
2004

Type of work
Experimental book

Designer
Alex Sonderegger

Description
--

Product Information
& Sales Manual

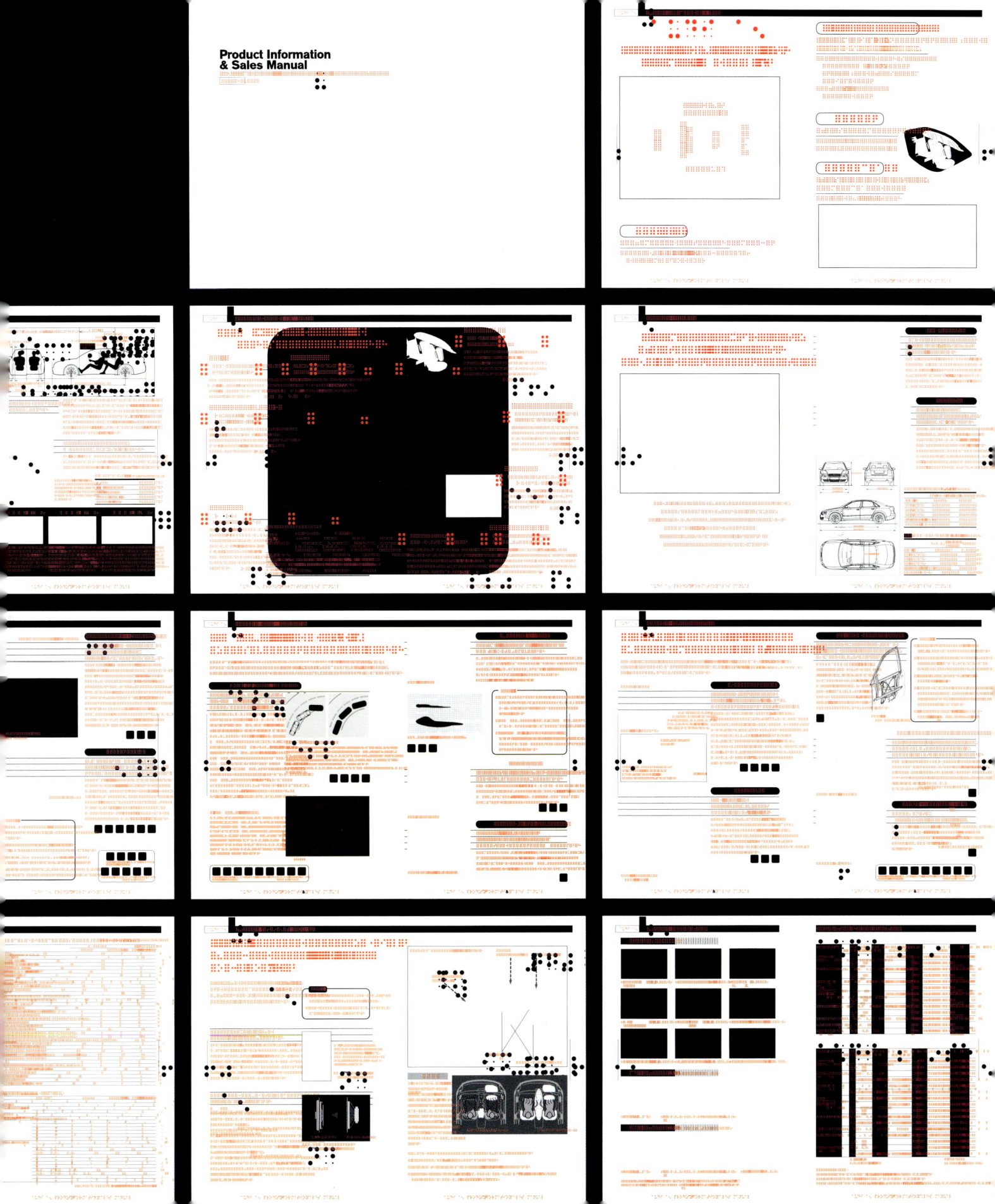

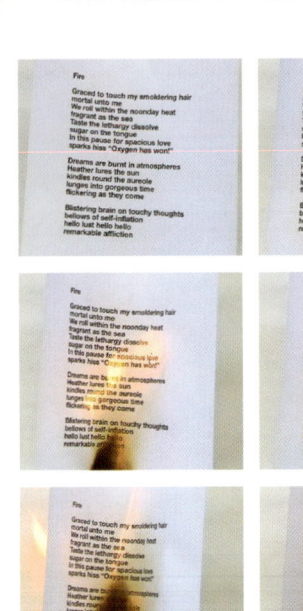

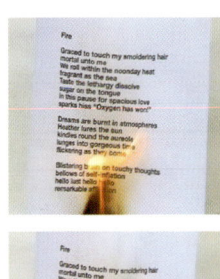

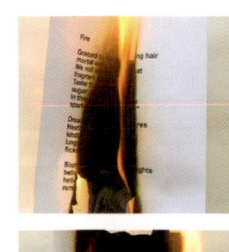

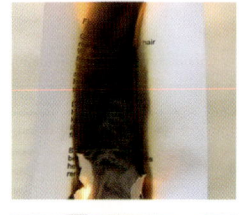

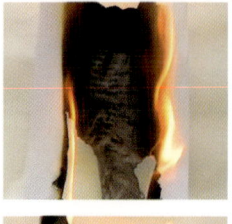

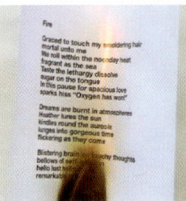

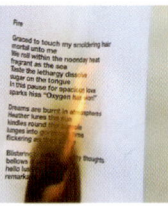

+ WIG-01™

Title: **Fire** Graphic: **WIG-01** Poetry: **Kaethe Fine**

Page
138

Client
WIG-01

Origin
Doncaster, UK.

Title of work
Graphic Poetry - A WIG-01 Project

Art Director
Andrew Townsend

Year produced
2003 - 2004

Graphic Poetry

A Wig-01 Project

Foreword
By Paula Carson

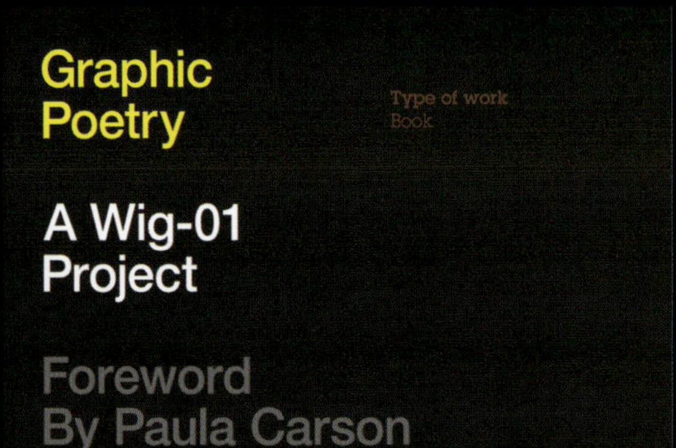

Type of work
Book

Designer
Andrew Townsend
Contributors: Illustrator/poet
+ WIG-01/Kaethe Fine
++ Alan Kitching/Maureen McManus
+++ Michael C. Place, Build/ Conner Kilmer
++++ Happypets/Christine Boyka Kluge
+++++ House Intro/Barbara Jane Reyes
++++++ WIG-01/Brian Burch
+++++++ Michael Gillette/Barbara Jane Reyes
++++++++ Rinzen/Maureen MaManus
+++++++++ Michelle Thompson/Catherine Simmonds

Description
Graphic Poetry contains contemporary poetry illustrated by the world's leading designers, illustrators and image-makers. Thirty poets and fifty designers/illustrators have contributed to the project. Visual contributors include: Big Active, Blue Source, Marc Boutavant, Build, Delaware, Marion Deuchars, Eboy, Michael Gillette, Happypets, Angus Hyland, Intro, Alan Kitching, Norm, Phunk Studio, Power Graphixx, Rinzen, Tomato and Why Not Associates.

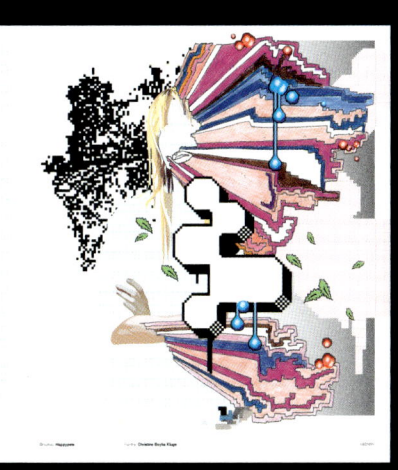

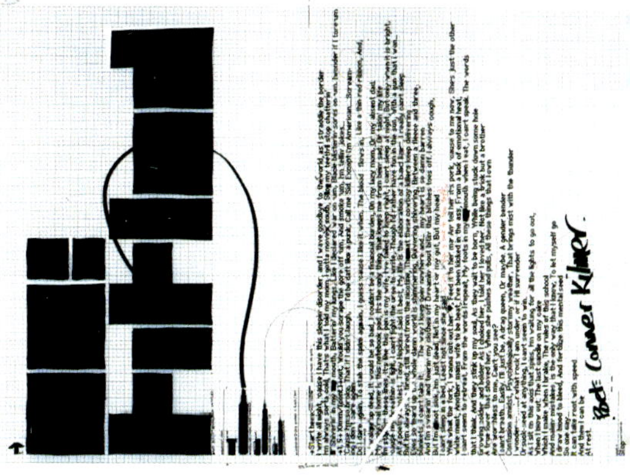

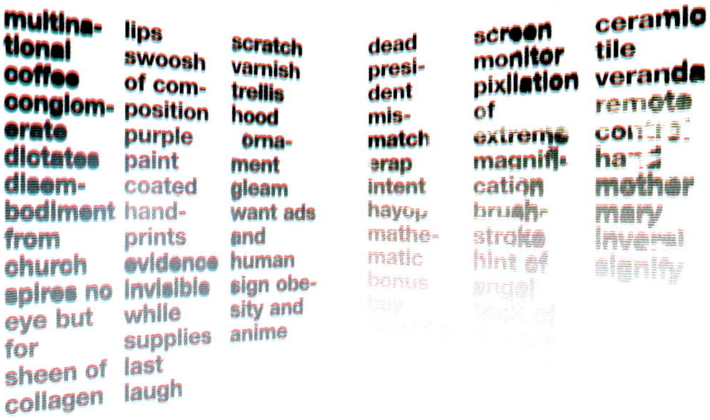

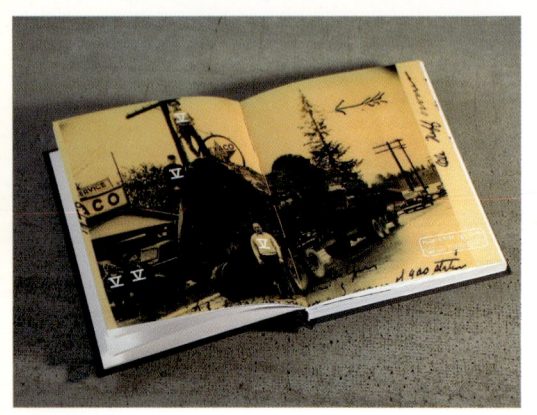

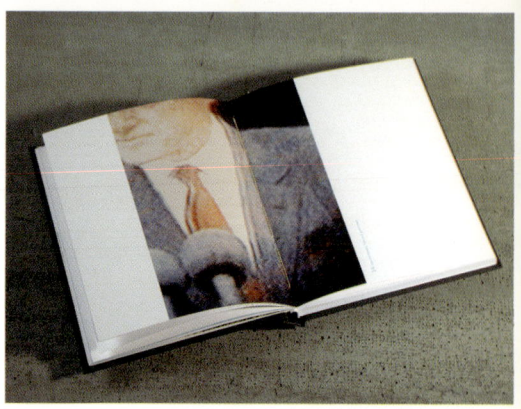

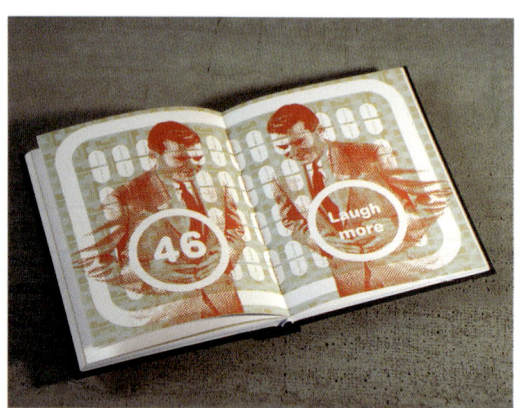

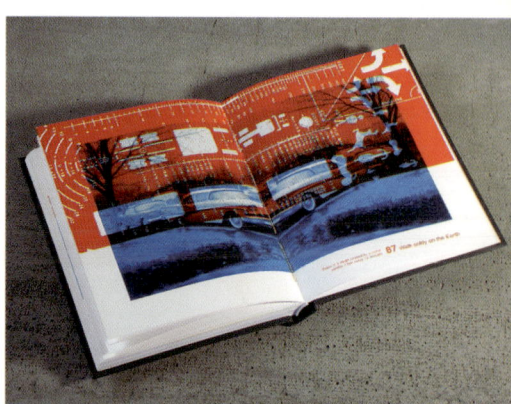

+ Chen Design Associates

Page
140

Client
Chen design Associates

Origin
California, USA

Title of work
Peace: 100 Ideas

Art Director
Joshua Chen

Year produced
2004

Type of work
Book

Designer
Joshua Chen

Description
Peace: 100 Ideas is an innovative pairing of text and 200 pages of original, full-color illustrations and photographic imagery. This ambitious volume provides 100 simple solutions for promoting peace that will challenge readers to rethink previous perceptions and reexamine their roles as members of an extended community.

+ Supershapes

Page
141

Title of work
55 Degrees North: Contemporary
Scandinavian Graphic Design

Type of work
Book

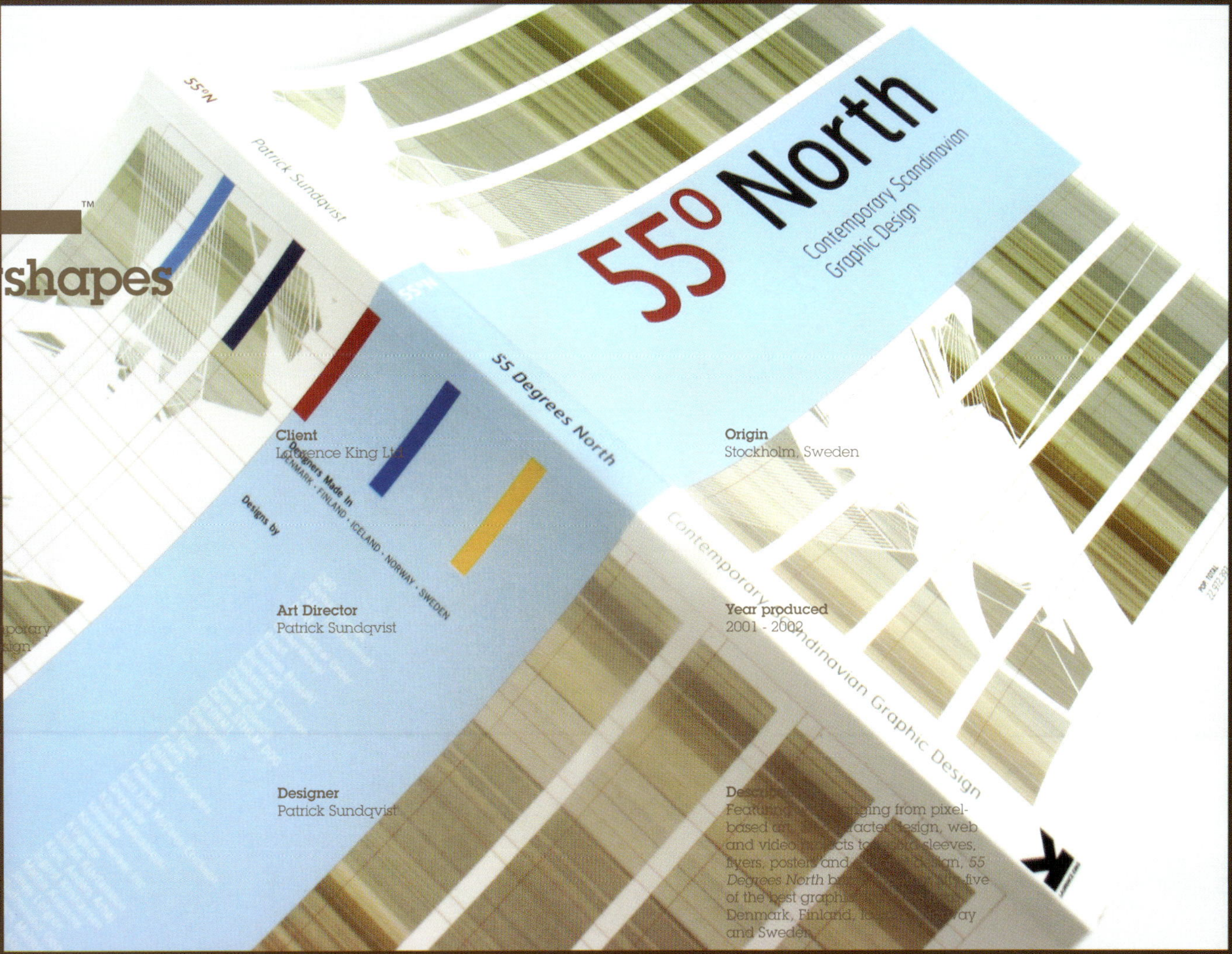

Client
Laurence King Ltd

Designs by
DENMARK · FINLAND · ICELAND · NORWAY · SWEDEN

Art Director
Patrick Sundqvist

Designer
Patrick Sundqvist

Origin
Stockholm, Sweden

Year produced
2001 – 2002

Description
Featuring work ranging from pixel-based on-screen character design, web and video projects to record sleeves, flyers, posters and book design, 55 Degrees North brings together five of the best graphic designers from Denmark, Finland, Iceland, Norway and Sweden.

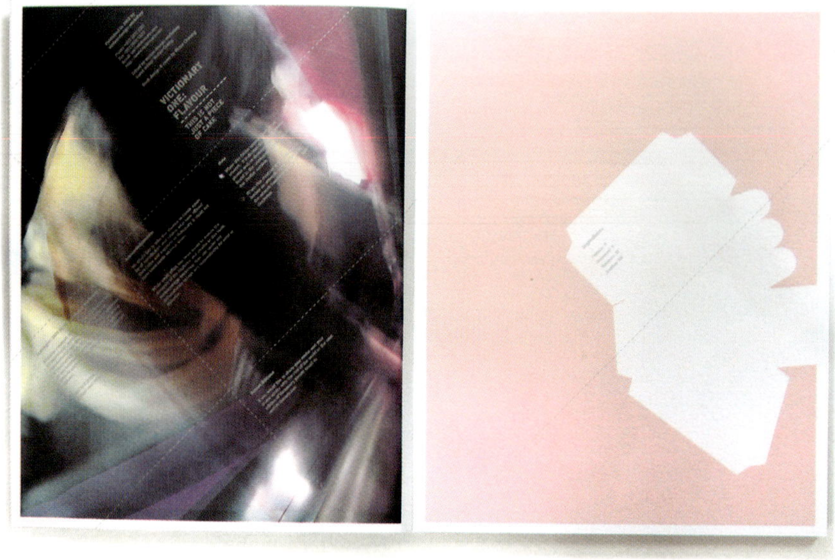

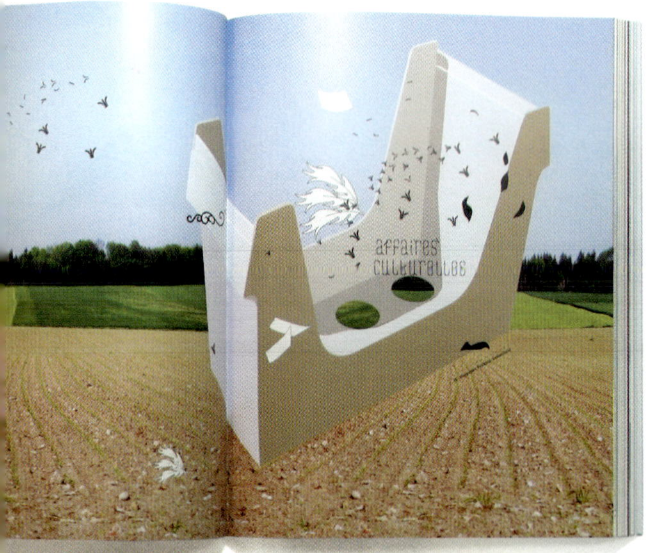
affaires culturelles

+

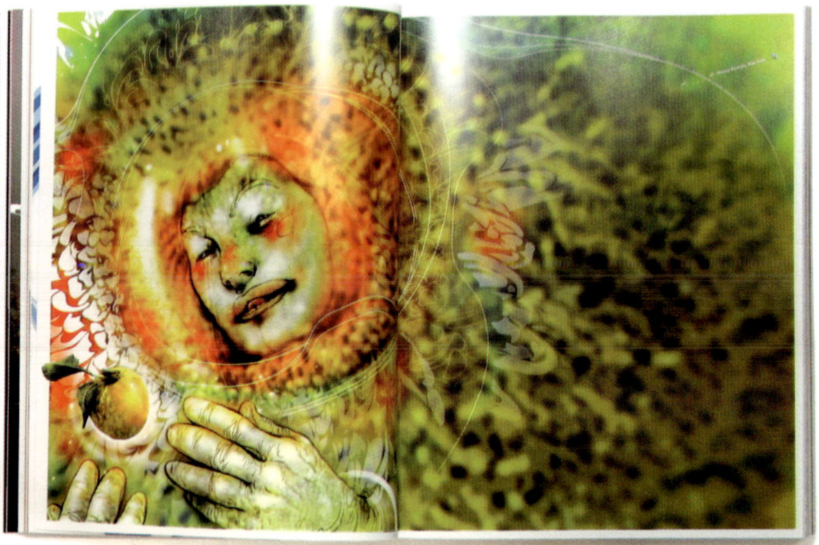

+++

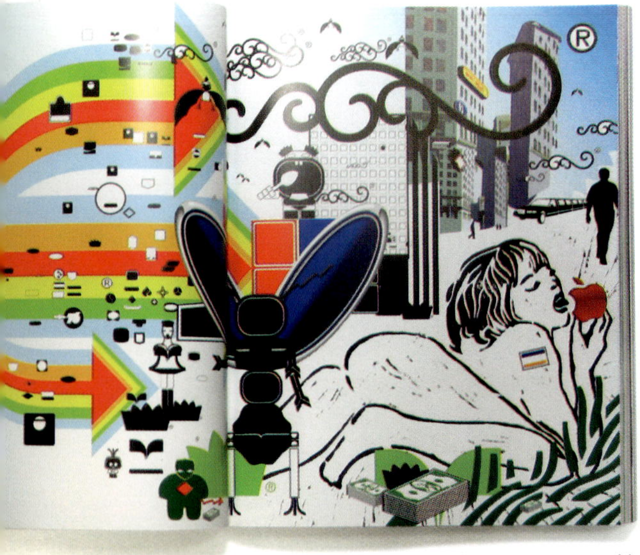

++

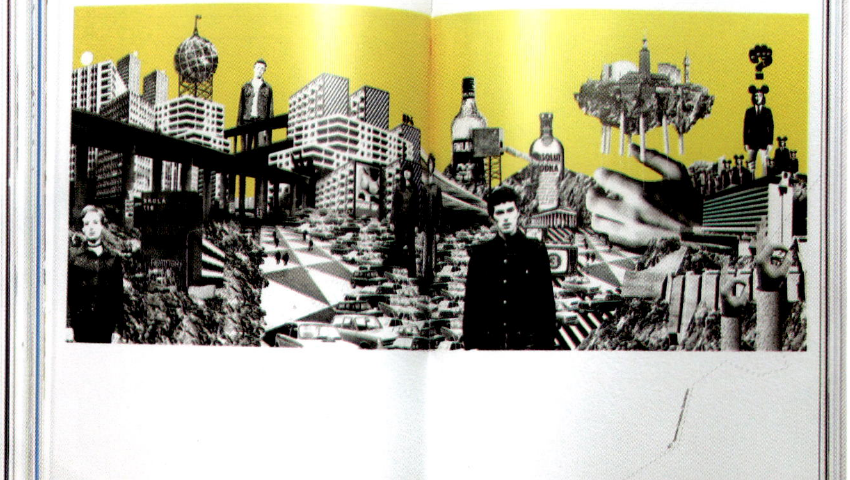

++++

+ viction:design workshop

Page
143

Client
viction:workshop

Origin
Hong Kong, China

Title of work
Victionary.one: Flavour

Art Director
Victor Cheung

Year produced
2002

Type of work
Book

Description
This book explores the unique flavour and signature style in design through the use of photography. It showcases various edgy artworks of 44 distinctive creators and artists from around the world. With the above perspective in mind, each of them has created artworks that represent their personal taste, style and commentary about their creative lives.

+++++

Design For Kids

THERE ARE NO LULLABYES
NO CHAIRS WITHOUT ARM RESTRAINTS
NO VISIBLE EXITS
IN MY DREAMS
I SAW IN HALF GLANCE A BILLBOARD
THAT OFFERED DONKEY RIDES TO HEAVEN
THEN THEY KICKED US OUT OF THE TOY STORE.

+

RPSONC

++

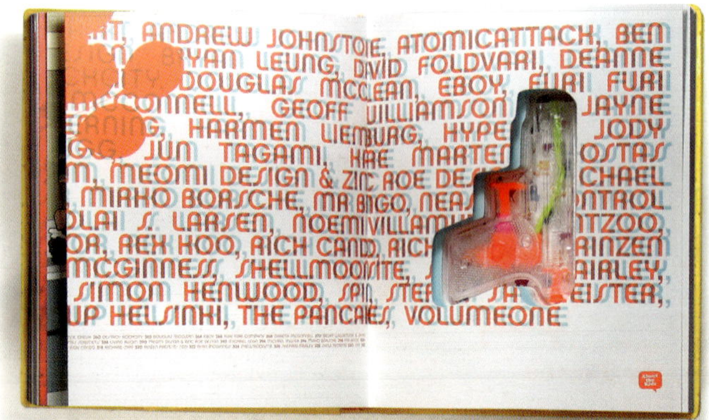

Printzoo
Pp

Simon Henwood
Ss

Design For Kids

+ viction:design workshop

Page
145

Client
viction:workshop

Origin
Hong Kong, China

Title of work
Design for Kids®
from Victionary Two

Art Director
Victor Cheung

Type of work
Book

Designer
Victor Cheung
Contributors:
+ Ben Frost
++ Syrup Helsinki

Description
DFK is a collaboration of artwork from over 50 artists and designers from around the world. It inspires to reach the kid within us and to tap into the fun, silly and imaginative world presently suppressed by social norms and financial obligations.

+ RMAC

Page
146

Title of work
+ Fashion Note
++ VOYAGER-03

Type of work
--

++

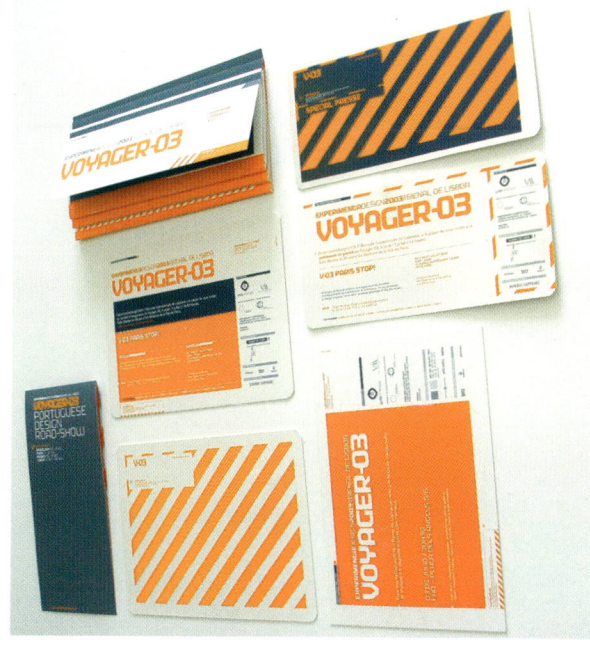

Client
RMAC Design

Origin
Lisbon, Portugal

Art Director
Ricardo Mealha and Ana Cunha

Year produced
+ 2002
++ 2003

Designer
+ Ricardo Mealha (designer, photographer)
Ana Cunha (illustrator)
++ Ricardo Mealha
Ricardo Matos

Description
+ Fashion Notes is an object of design to be used as a daily notebook to keep all important moments fresh in the memory and ready to use. The presentation of these fashion notes is inspired by the fresh-produce packaging one finds in supermarkets.
++ VOYAGER-03 is a transportable container that parks in public spaces in different countries. It shows Portuguese modern design in different areas. This container has a unique design that interacts with each city's urban style, such as Lisbon, Madrid, Barcelona and Paris.
For this client they created the visual identity and the graphic design for several communication supports.

+ RMAC

Page
148

Title of work
Shopwindow

Type of work
Exhibition Catalogue

Client
Portuguese Presidency of
the Republic

Art Director
Ricardo Mealha and Ana Cunha

Designer
Ana Cunha

Origin
Lisbon, Portugal

Year produced
2002

Description
RMAC was invited by the Presidency of the Republic to do this work for the Portuguese Contemporary Design Exhibit, which took place in Finland in October 2002 under the subject *Shopwindow*. Among the various effects RMAC used, the cover of the catalogue has an open stencil allowing the reader to see through the objects that lie inside, a direct connection to the 'shopwindow' concept of the exhibit.

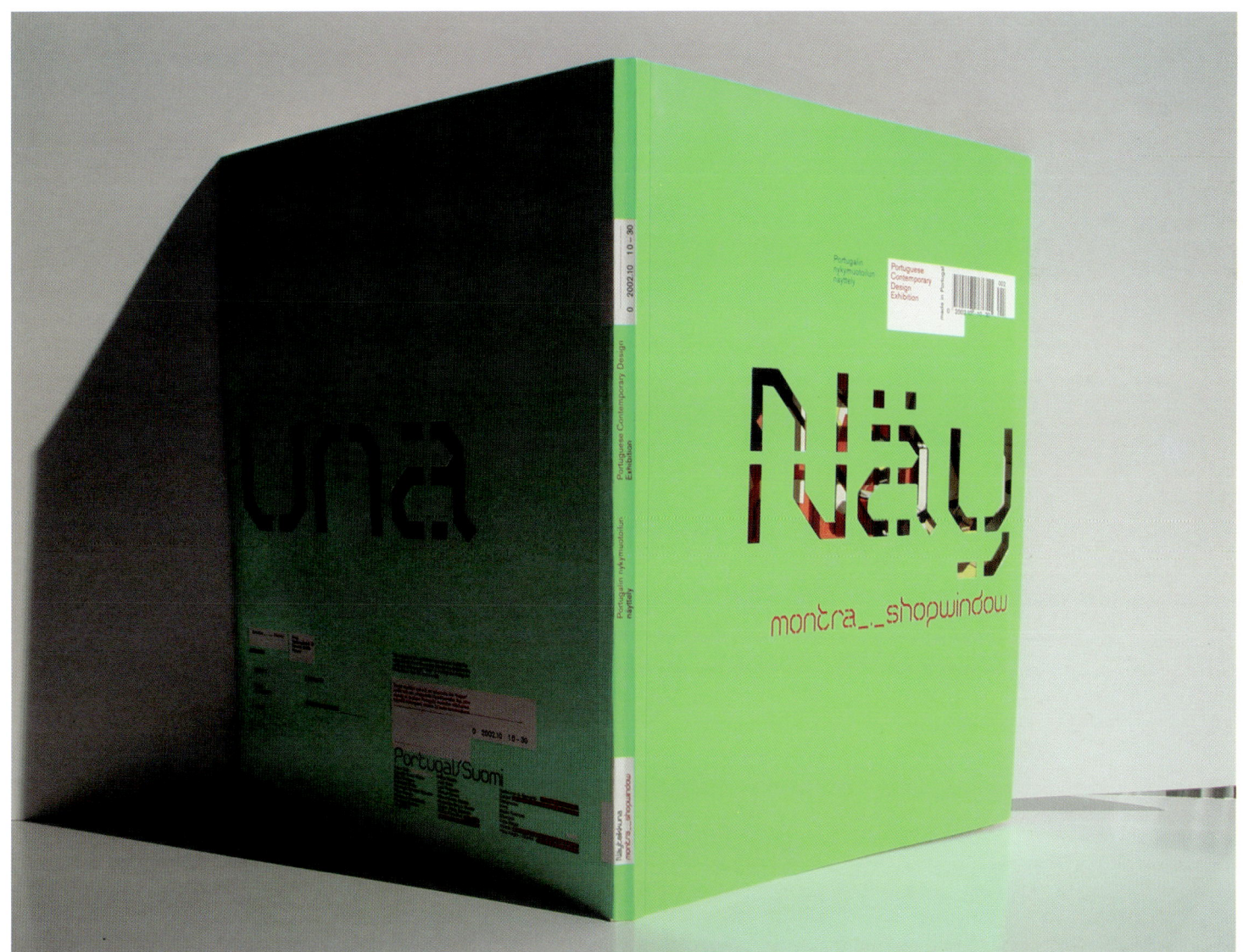

+ Mirko Ilic Corp

Page
150

Client
The Cooper Union School of Art & Future-flair

Origin
New York, USA

Title of work
Massin: In Continuo Poster

Art Director
Mirko Ilic

Year produced
2001

Type of work
Poster/book

Designer
Mirko Ilic & Heath Hinegardner

Description
A poster that you can cut and make a small copy of Massin's rare book *La Cantatrice Chauve*.

MASSIN

Massin in Continuo: A Dictionary ▸ December 17, 2001–March 2, 2002 ▸ The Herb Lubalin Study Center of Design and Typography ▸ The Cooper Union School of Art, New York

The Cooper Union School of Art ▸ East 7th Street at Third Avenue, lower floor ▸ **Reception** ▸ Monday, January 28, 2002, 8–10 p.m.

Echocolates, NYC ▸ Exhibition organized at The Herb Lubalin Study Center of Design and Typography, The Cooper Union School of Art, by Philippe Apeloig and Ann Holcomb

Poster designed by Mirko Ilić

Massin and Milton Glaser in Conversation ▸ Great Hall, The Foundation Building ▸ Arti Grafiche E. Gajani printing, Italy ▸ Corp. Job Parilux Paper ▸ Scheufelen ▸ Gallimard Editions, Paris ▸ Cultural Services, The French Embassy, NYC ▸ **Sponsors:**

Third Avenue, 2nd floor ▸ East 7th Street at ▸ The Herb Lubalin Study Center of Design and Typography ▸ Exhibition hours ▸ 11 a.m.–7 p.m. weekdays ▸ 12:00 p.m.–5:00 p.m. Saturdays ▸ Closed Sundays and holidays ▸ For information: (212) 353 4207 ▸ Exhibition curated by Laetitia Wolff ▸ **Lecture** ▸ Monday, January 28, 2002 at 6:30 p.m.

Page
152

Title of work
+ Brochure for Ben Kelly Design
++ D&AD Booklet

Type of work
+ Brochure
++ Booklet

Client
+ Ben Kelly Design
++ D&AD

Art Director
+ Harry Pearce
++ Domenic Lippa

Designer
+ Harry Pearce
Jeremy Roots
++ Domenic Lippa

Origin
London, UK

Year produced
+ 2001
++ 1998

Description
+ This is the brochure designed for 3D/environmental designer Ben Kelly
++ This is the booklet designed for D&AD, the professional association and charity that represents the thriving design and advertising communities.

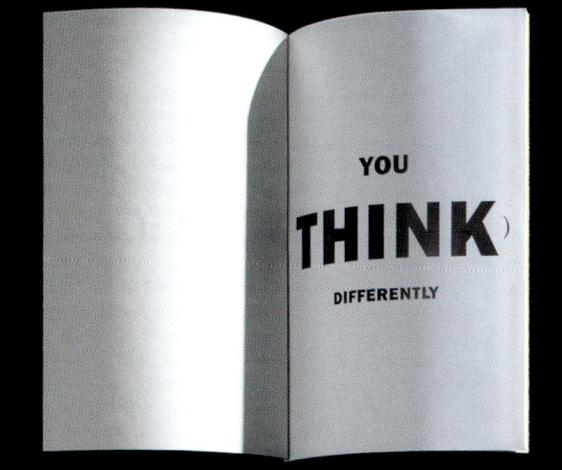

++

+ Blokes

Client
[Plugin] and Tilman Baumgärtel

Origin
Lucerne, Switzerland

Title of work
Install.exe - Jodi

Art Director
Rafael Koch & Jodi
INSTALL.EXE
JODI

Year produced
2002

Type of work
Book

Description
install.exe is the first com...

+ Époxy

Page
155

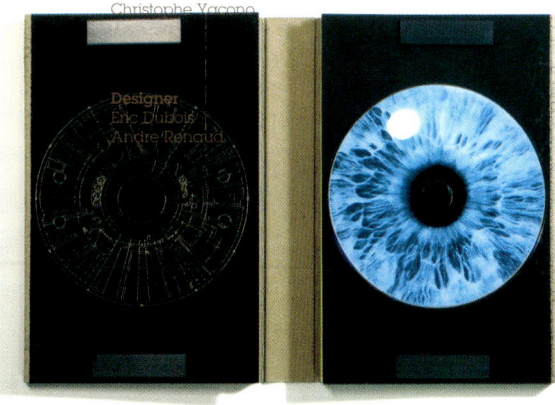

Client
Époxy Communications Inc.
La Fondation

Origin
Québec, Canada

Title of work
Digital Snow

Art Director
Jean-Christophe Yacono, Éric Dubois
Daniel Fortin, George Fok, Jean-Christophe Yacono

Year produced
2002

Type of work
Educational DVD/book

Description
The paper required two weeks to prepare and consisted of finding and recycling old plates in an industrial print shop; using treated blankets to exploit their 'materiality'; and then randomly feeding the sheets, ream by ream, through a six-colour press, whose six rollers carried only yellow and cyan inks. Then the project was printed in black and blue on those sheets. This method created a random book, where each of the 3000 copies is unique.

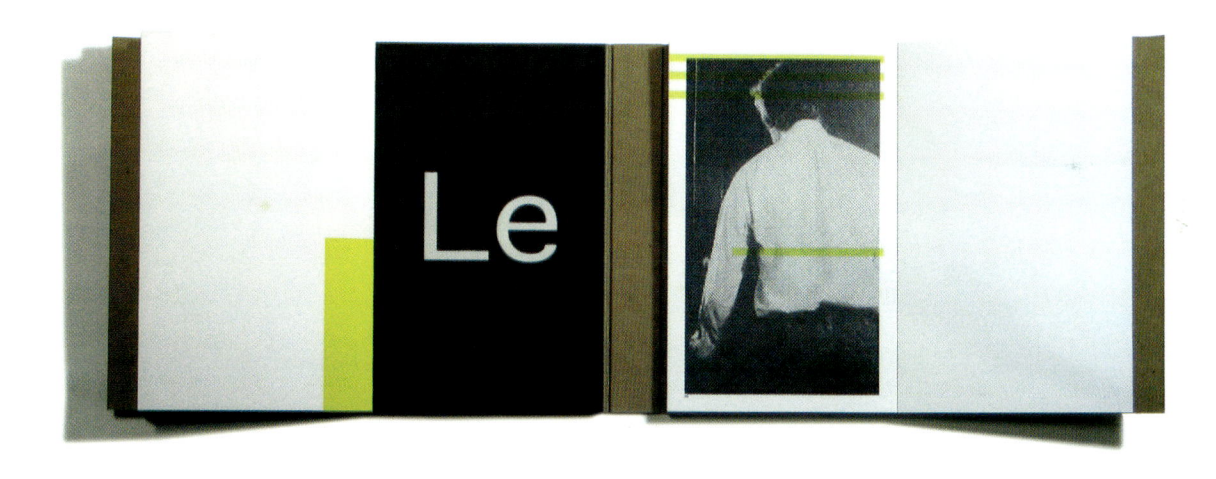

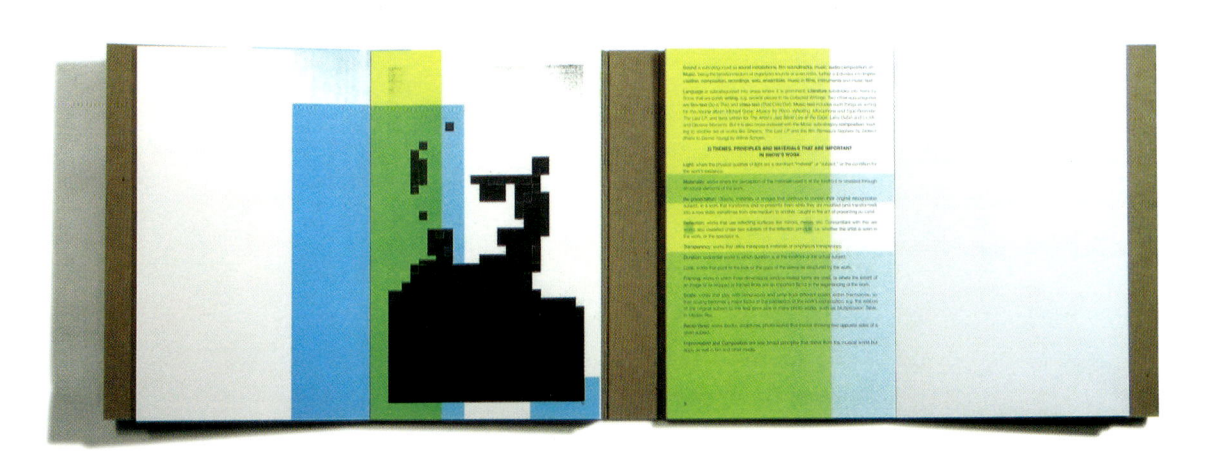

Designer
Deirdre O'Callaghan (photographer)

Description

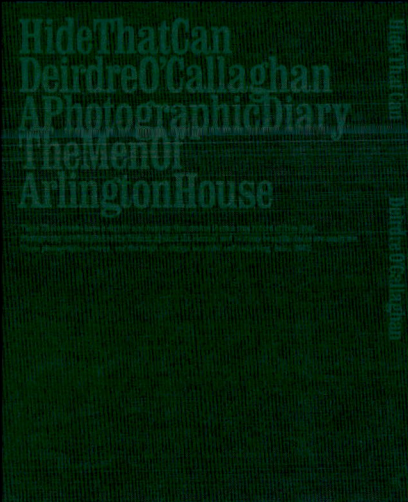

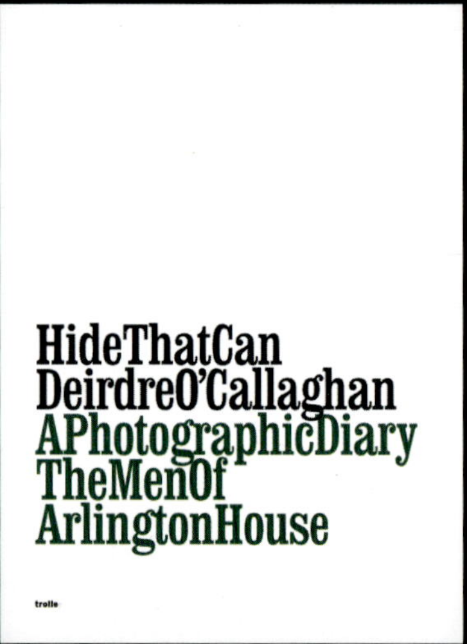

HideThatCan
DeirdreO'Callaghan
APhotographicDiary
TheMenOf
ArlingtonHouse

They'll tell you my equal was ne'er to be seen
They called me The Horse and The Digging Machine
The gangerman loved me
The agent would stare
All admiring the strength of the Rambler from Clare.

But now I am bent and me fire has turned cold,
In another four years I'll be fifty years old
So now I'm worn out and finished
But what do they care
For they've had all they want from the Rambler from Clare.

THE RAMBLER FROM CLARE, Barry Finnott, With thanks to Onnon Publications

HideThatCan
DeirdreO'Callaghan
APhotographicDiary
TheMenOf
ArlingtonHouse

trolle

"Are those real pearls?"

"I wouldn't be feckin wearing them if they weren't."

"The best way to test poteen is you get a saucer and put a little bit of poteen on it. You put out a match to it and if it goes blue then it is poteen but if it goes out or if it bubbles then you throw it out the window"

"With the first glass of poteen you pour, you throw it over your shoulder. It's for the fairies. It's called the Ballymaguigan"
"Well if I say that fairy didn't hang around for long the amount he'd get from you"

"He'd have no headache in the morning with the drop you'd give him!"
"If you drink enough poteen you'd end up seeing fairies"
"If you drink enough of anything you'd see fairies and elephants"

"I came to London looking for the Rolling Stones"

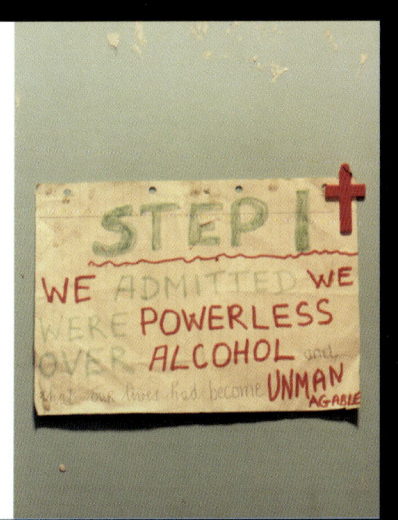

"I wasn't drunk when this happened, but I was on the way to the offie"
"Lend me a fiver till Nelson gets his eye back"

STEP 1
WE ADMITTED WE WERE POWERLESS OVER ALCOHOL and that our lives had become UNMANAGABLE

+ A2-Graphics/SW/HK

Page
158

Client
ISTD, The International Society of Typographic Designers

Origin
London, UK

Title of work
TypoGraphic 60

Art Director
Scott Williams, Henrick Kubel

Year produced
2003

Type of work
Typographic journal

Designer
Scott Williams, Henrick Kubel

Description
TypoGraphic 60 was inspired by 'Primal Typography' and consists of eight interleaved 8-page sections of coated and uncoated papers, printed offset litho by FS Moore printers in London and then transported to Gloucester to be over-printed in letterpress (both wood and metal) by Stan Lane at Gloucester Typesetting Services. TypoGraphic 60 includes three typefaces specifically designed and developed by A2-GRAPHICS/SW/HK: FY-Typographic Regular & Italic, FY-Typewriter and FY-Merlin Carpenter.

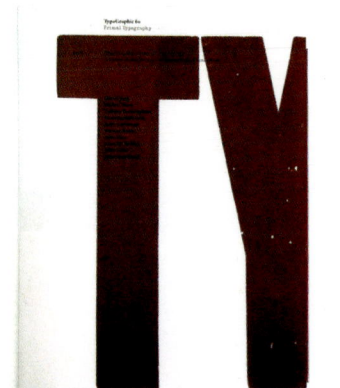

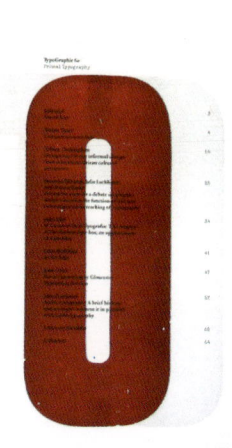

CUT

John Allen
El Carnaval de la Tipografía. The enigma of the Havana cigar box, an appreciation of a paradise.

Cuba, or Juana as it was originally called by Christopher Columbus (in honour of Prince Juan of Spain) when he landed there in 1492, is still an island with a rich ecology of pine and tropical rain forests and stately palm trees, particularly the royal palm which features as one of Cuba's emblems. Curiously relevant to this palm-strewn paradise, with its turquoise blue waters, home of the cigar and its famous marques, is a list of names which ran, more or less, parallel with the establishment of the early cigar businesses in Havana. Names of the great type founders that spanned most of the nineteenth century: Figgins, Thorowgood, Caslon and Catherwood, Stephenson and Blake, Wilson, Austin Wood, Harrild and others.

Like the owners of the cigar factories who created exotic, seductive and romantic brand names, these British and American typefounders also imbued many of their new founts and display faces with similarly evocative names: Egyptian, Etruscan, Rustic, Corinthian, Holbein, Renaissance, Phantom, Skeleton, which in their turn, carried numerous formal variations such as Reversed Egyptian, Egyptian Ornamented, Grotesque Outline, Half Skeleton, German Text Ornamented, and so on.

AT THE EDGE

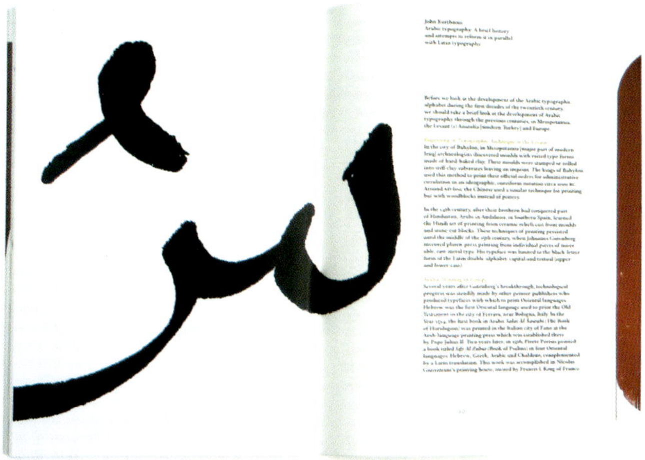

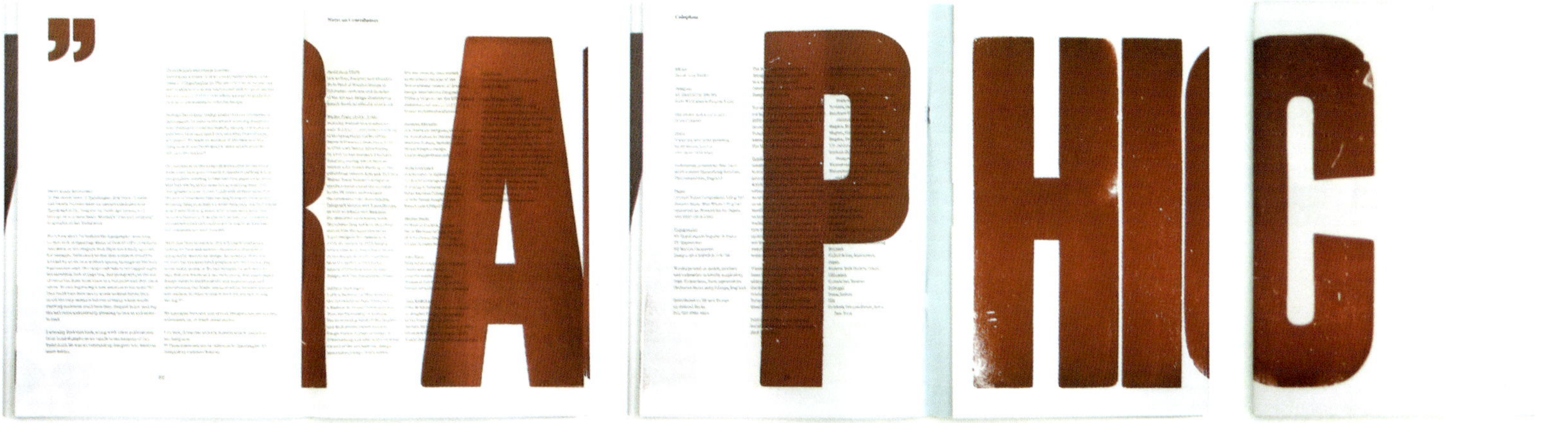

John Trenhouse
Arabic typography. A brief history and attempts to reform it in parallel with Latin typography.

'RAPHIC

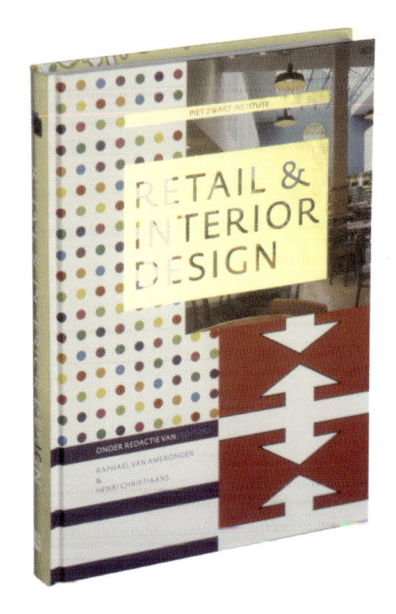

+ Lonne Wennekendonk

Page
160

Client
Piet Zwart Institute

Title of work
Retail & Interior Design

Art Director
Lonne Wennekendonk

Type of work
Book

Designer
Lonne Wennekendonk

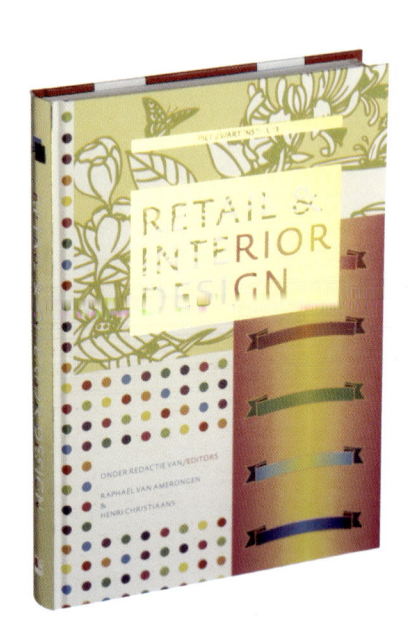

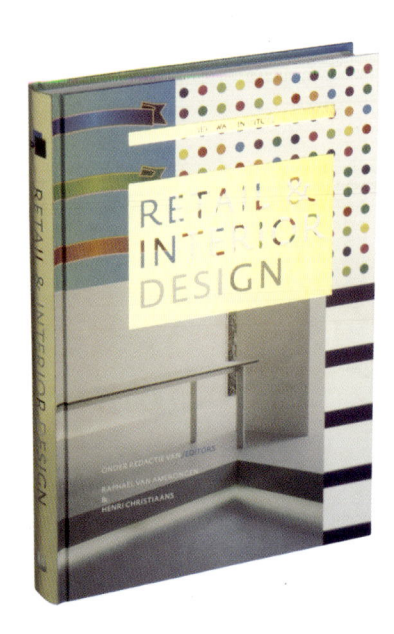

Origin
Rotterdam, Netherlands

Year produced
2004

Description
Retail & Interior Design is about branding, design, experience, emotion, drama, continuity and sustainability. It conveys the gripping and diverse developments in these fields over the last decade.
Included are eight essays reflective of this diversity and each corresponds to a section of the book with a totally different look. Because the content of every essay varies, the design also varies.

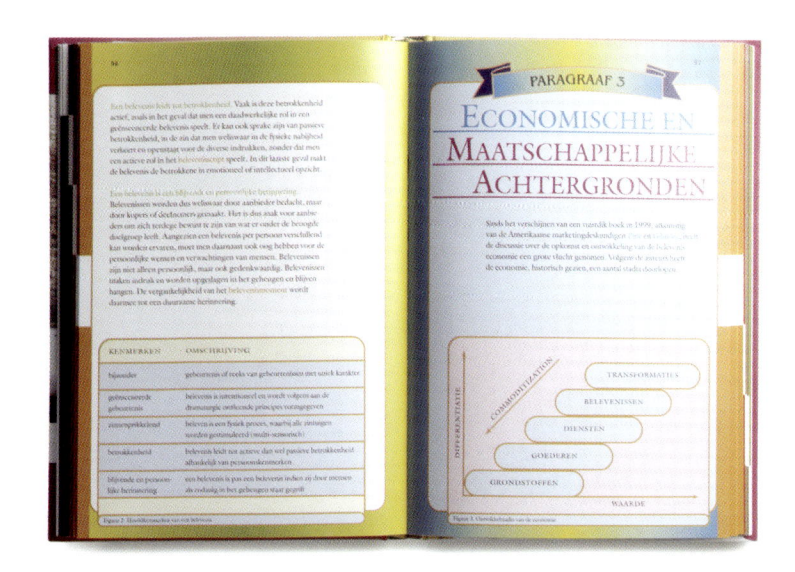

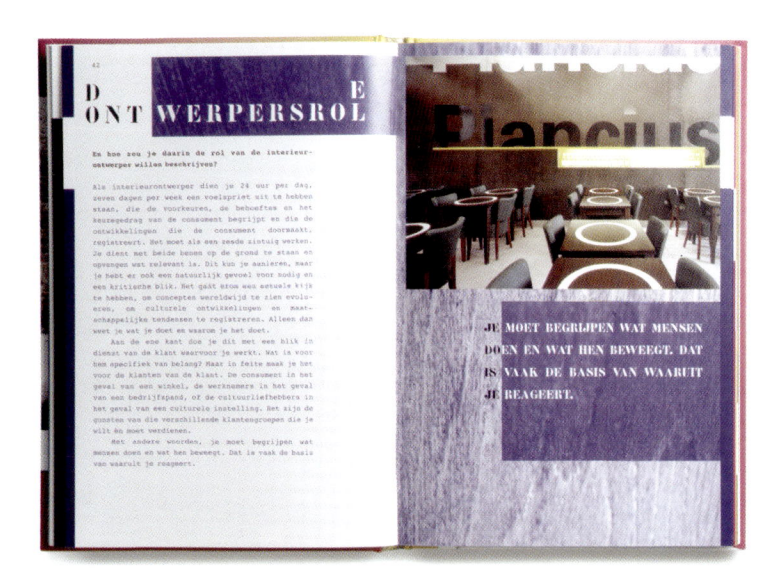

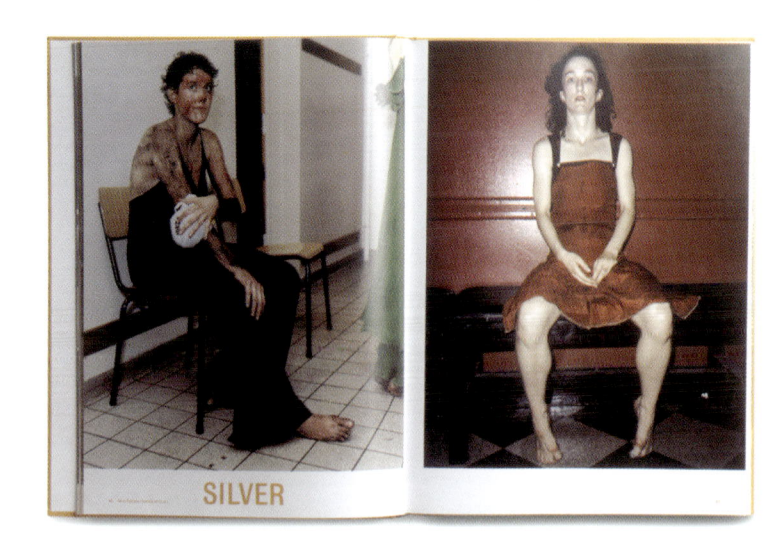

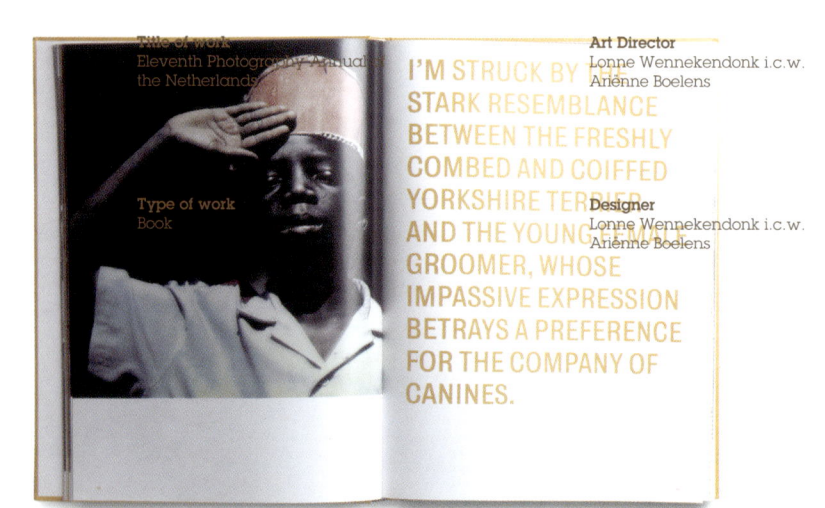

Title of work
Eleventh Photography Annual of the Netherlands

Type of work
Book

Art Director
Lonne Wennekendonk i.c.w. Ariënne Boelens

Designer
Lonne Wennekendonk i.c.w. Ariënne Boelens

Client
Photographers Association of the Netherlands (PANL)

Origin
Rotterdam, Netherlands

Year produced
2002

Description
Each year PANL publishes a book featuring nominated and prize-winning photographs selected by an international jury. Through this annual publication, PANL promotes Dutch photography abroad. Lonne Wennekendonk was chosen to design the 11th annual PANL publication, taking the theme 'the seen and unseen'.
In addition to viewing the photographs, you can also read the accompanying texts. When you read these texts you 'see images, in your fantasy, your imagination, your head'. The cover is made of lenticulair material: so depending on the angle from which it is viewed, the reader will see different images.

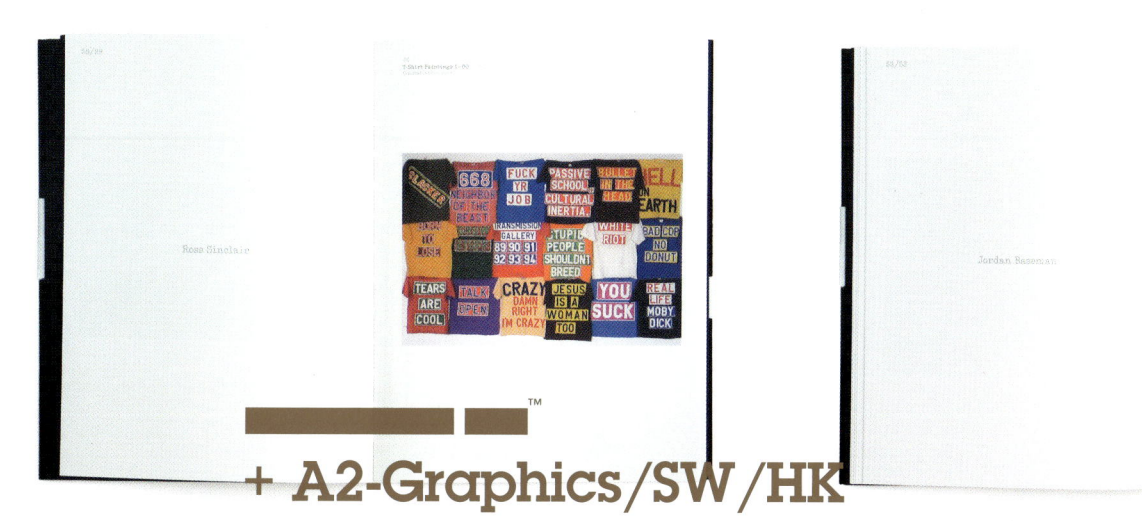

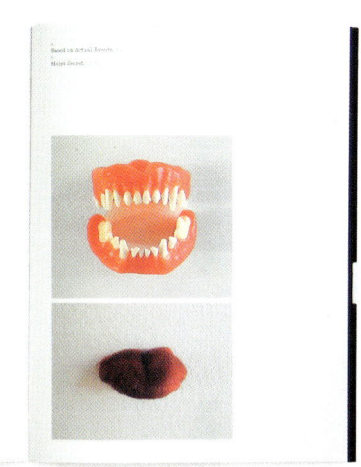

+ A2-Graphics/SW/HK

Page 163	**Client** Hayward Gallery	**Origin** London, UK
Title of work Bad Behaviour	**Art Director** Scott Williams, Henrik Kubel	**Year produced** 2003
Type of work Exhibition catalogue	**Designer** Scott Williams, Henrik Kubel	

Description
Bad Behaviour brings together works of art of a subversive nature, which upend and undermine established conventions. The focus is on Bristish sculpture, installation, photography and video from the 1980's, 1990's and 2000's.
Whether exploring instances of excess and anti-social conduct, sexual taboos or political subversion, the artists featured in *Bad Behaviour* set out to ask questions about the boundaries of acceptable behaviour. The book is divided into three distinct sections: Prelims/Contextual Essay, Artists' Plates and List of Works.

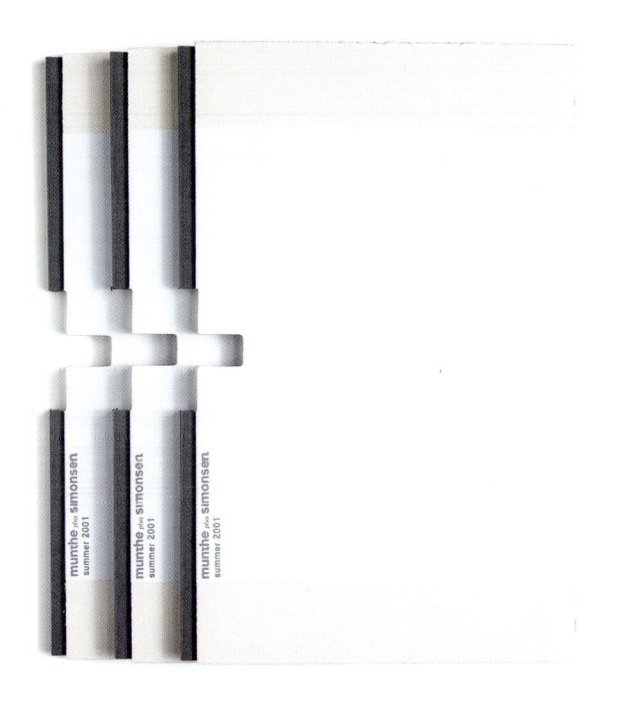

+ e-Type

Page
164

Title of work
MunthePlusSimonsen

Type of work
Corporate Brochure

Client
MunthePlusSimonsen

Art Director
e-Type

Designer
e-Type

Origin
Copenhagen, Denmark

Year produced
2002

Description
--

+ e-Type

Page
166

Client
+ MunthePlusSimonsen
++ Aquascutum

Origin
Copenhagen, Denmark

Title of work
+ MunthePlusSimonsen 2001
++ Aquascutum

Art Director
e-Type

Year produced
+ 2001
++ 2004

Type of work
+ Corporate Brochure
++ Catalogue

Designer
e-Type
++ Casper Sejersen (photographer)

Description
++ The idea was to bring the images and concept in line with the company's core qualities – those of classic, luxurious garments for men and women,' says Rasmus Pefelt, director ... focus the image and concept on the execute detailing and luxurious fabrics of the clothing through the main image and reshoots that have been done in the past.

++

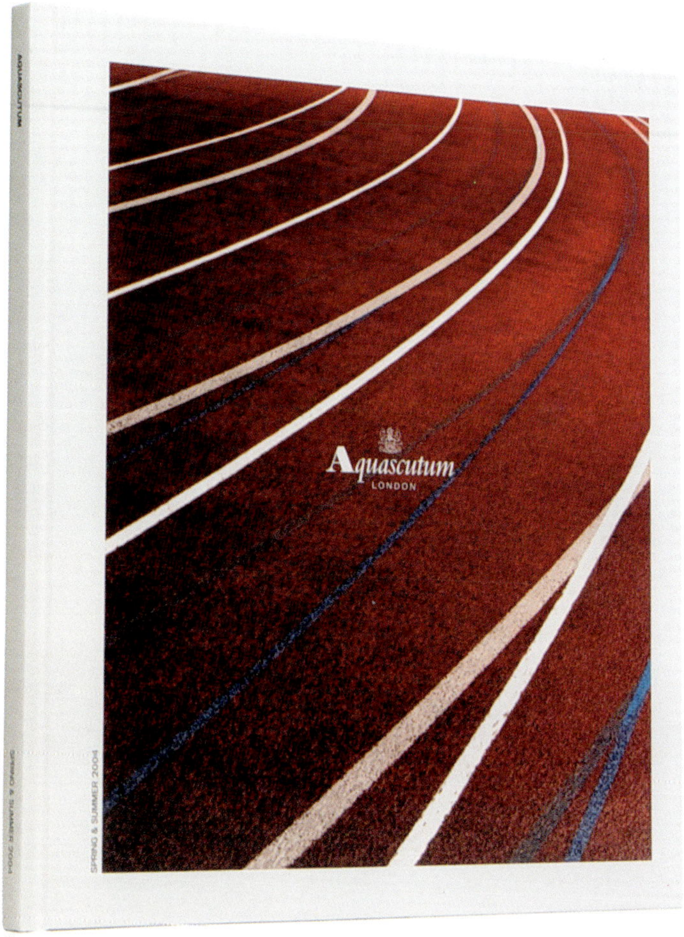
AQUASCUTUM
Aquascutum
LONDON
SPRING & SUMMER 2004

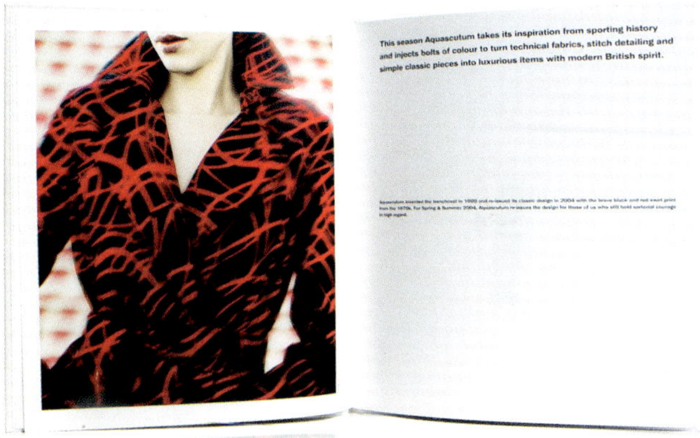
This season Aquascutum takes its inspiration from sporting history and injects bolts of colour to turn technical fabrics, stitch detailing and simple classic pieces into luxurious items with modern British spirit.

3

+ e-Type

Page
168

Client
Framfab

Title of work
Framfab

Art Director
e-Type

Type of work
Corporate Brochure

Designer
e-Type

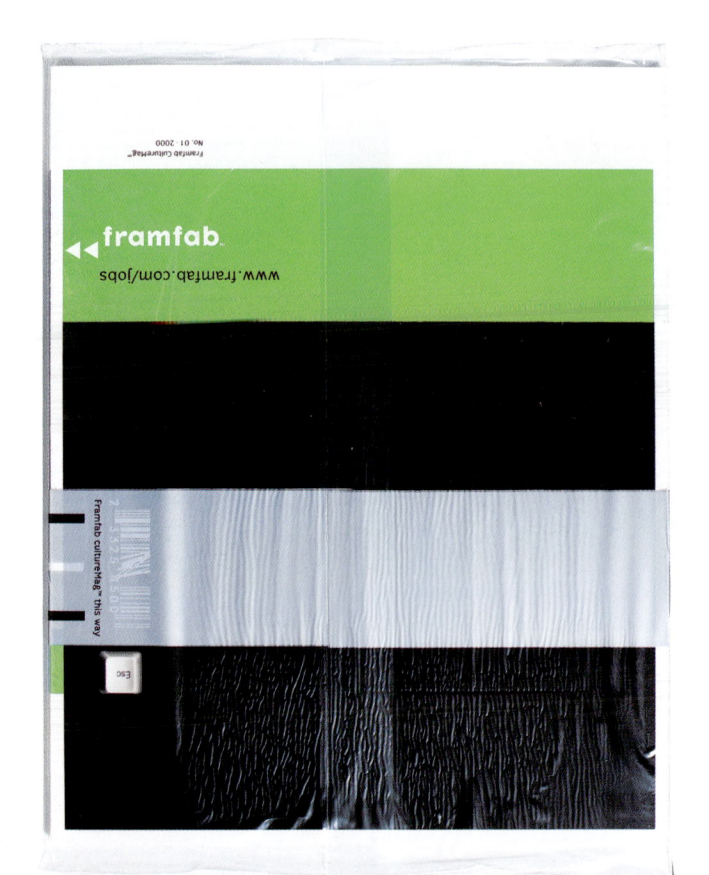

Page 01
CultureMag™

No. 01
May 2000

Origin
Copenhagen, Denmark

Year produced
2000

Description
This design programme is supposed to work as a healing power in turbulent times — a flag for new and long-time employees to rally around when times were changing. The core approach is that a forceful visual expression can create coherence in an ever-changing organisation to avoid confusion for customers, employees and the general public. This design programme embodies Framfab's young energy and "fast forward" attitude.

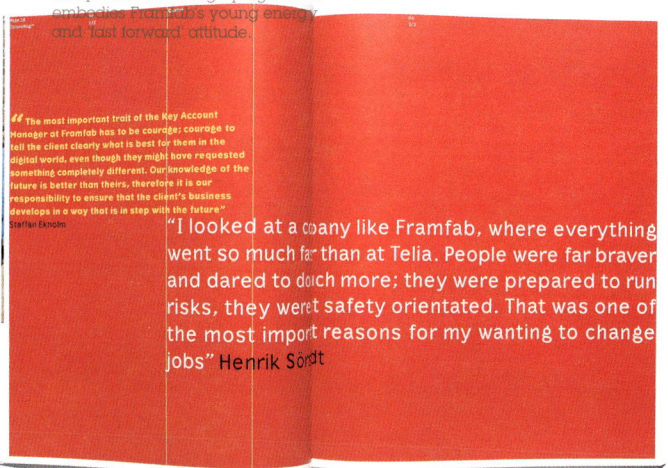

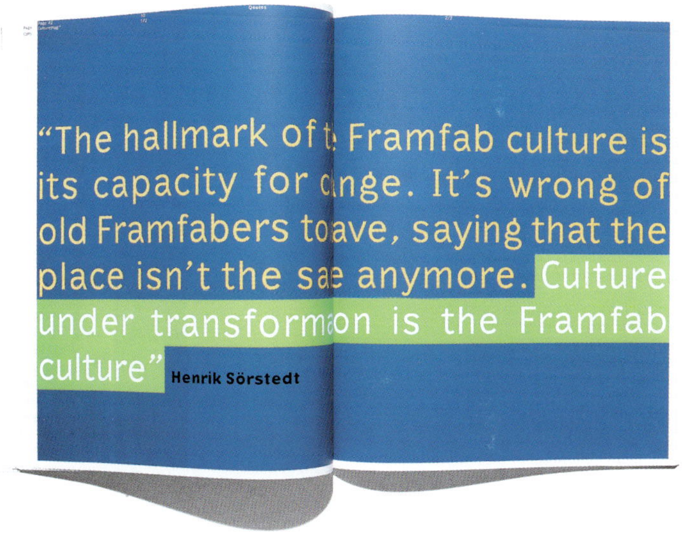

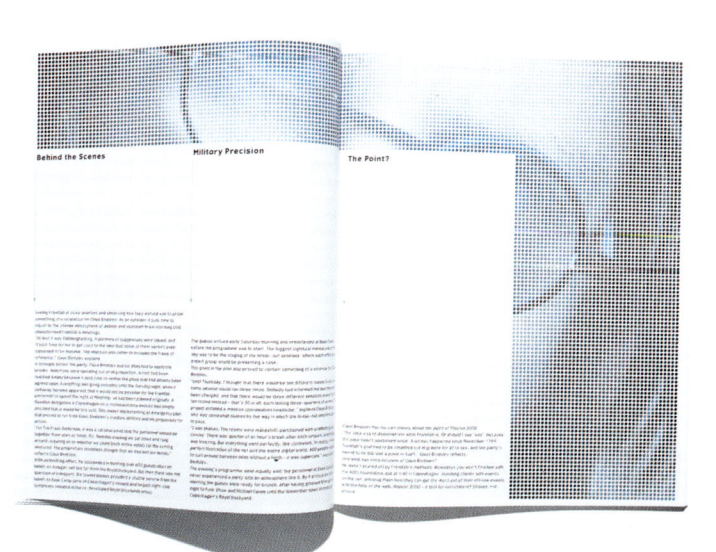

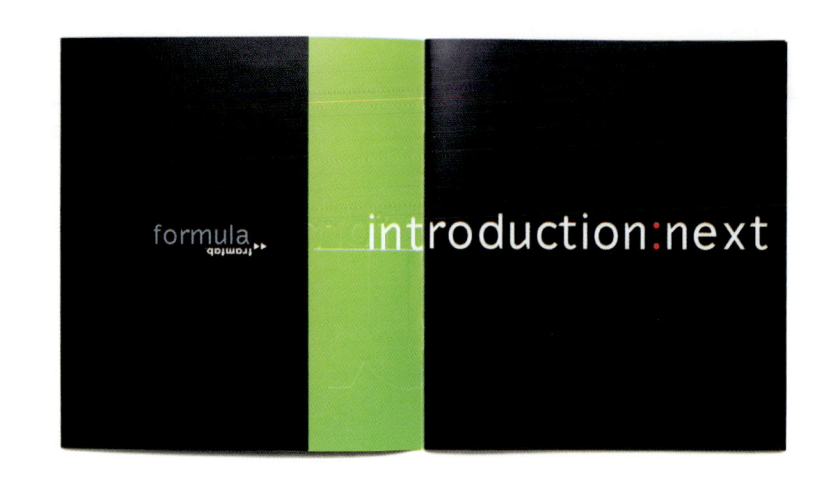

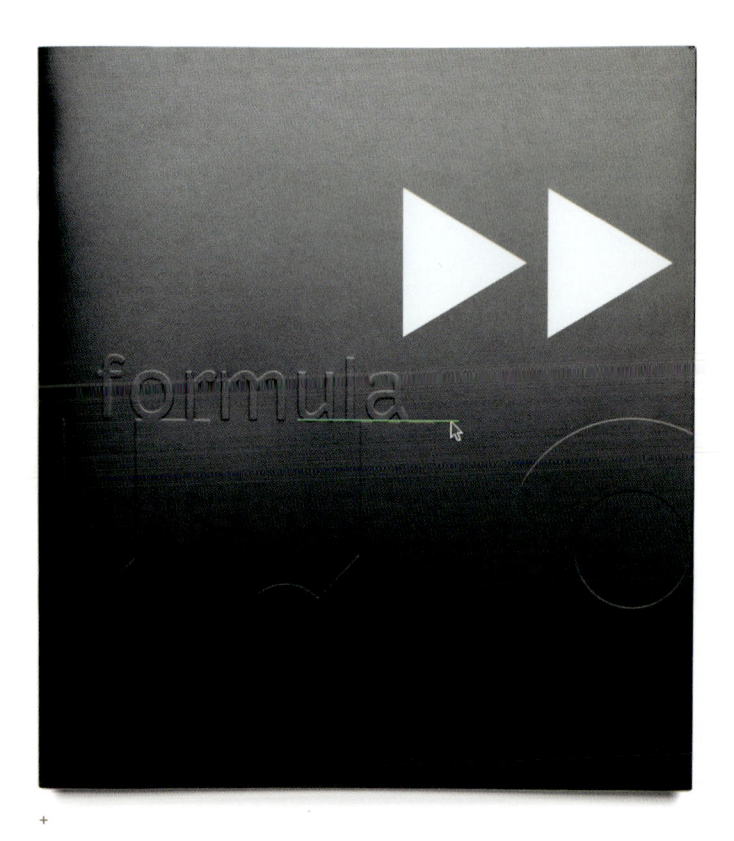

+ e-Type

Page
170

Client
+ Framfab
++ Learning Lab DK

Title of work
+ Framfab
++ Learning Lab DK

Art Director
e-Type

Type of work
+ Corporate Brochure

Designer
e-Type

++

Origin
Copenhagen, Denmark

Year produced
+ 2000
++ 2003/4

Description
++ The core of the design programme is a mutating typeface. The typeface is redesigned annually based on metaphors drawn from the evolving research process and the changes that occur during the life of the organisation.

+ e-Type™

Page
172

Title of work
Learning Lab DK

Type of work

Client
Learning Lab DK

Art Director
e-Type

Designer
e-Type

Origin
Copenhagen, Denmark

Year produced
2003/4

Description

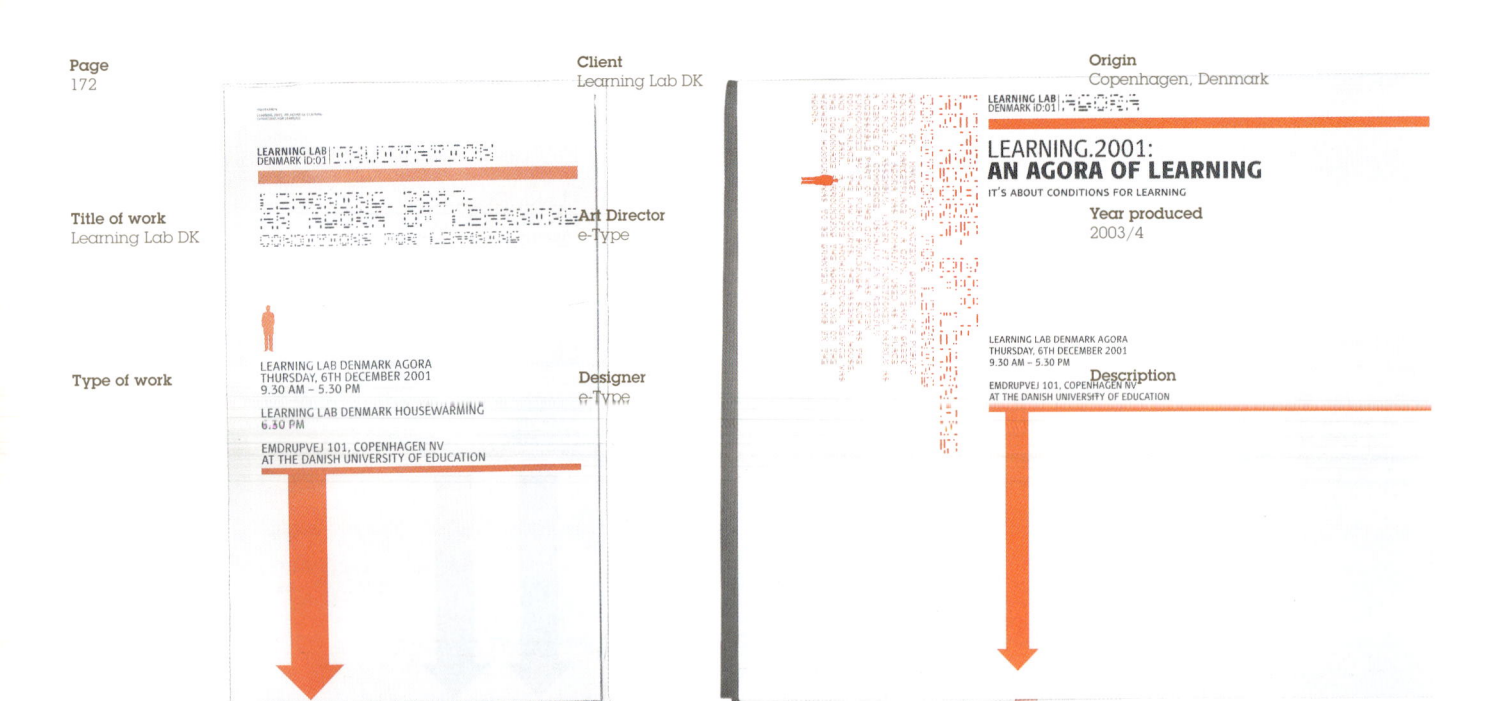

Sølv/Guld

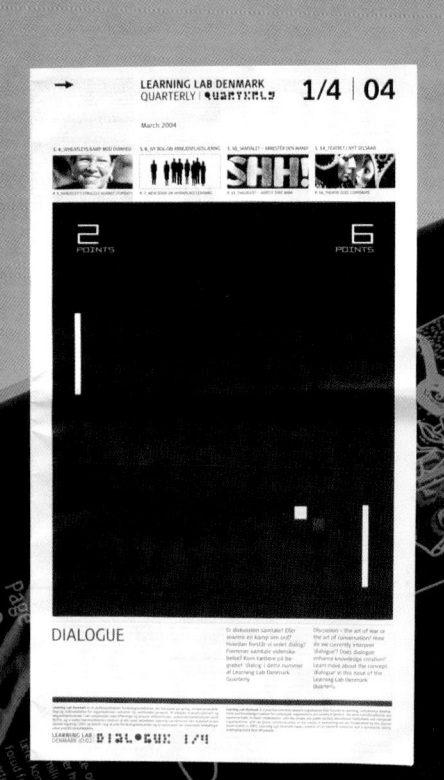

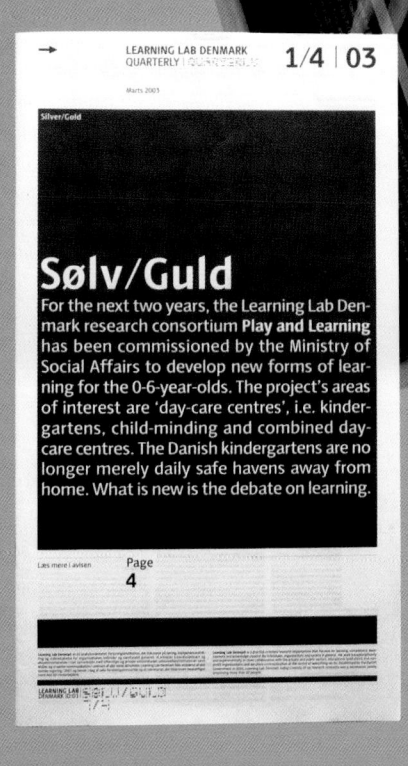

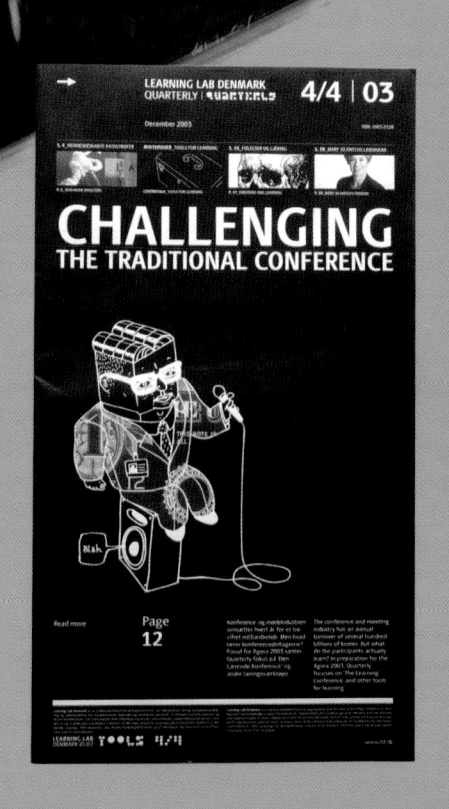

For the next two years, the Learning Lab Denmark research consortium **Play and Learning** has been commissioned by the Ministry of Social Affairs to develop new forms of learning for the 0-6-year-olds. The project's areas of interest are 'day-care centres', i.e. kindergartens, child-minding and combined day-care centres. The Danish kindergartens are no longer merely daily safe havens away from home. What is new is the debate on learning.

CHALLENGING
THE TRADITIONAL CONFERENCE

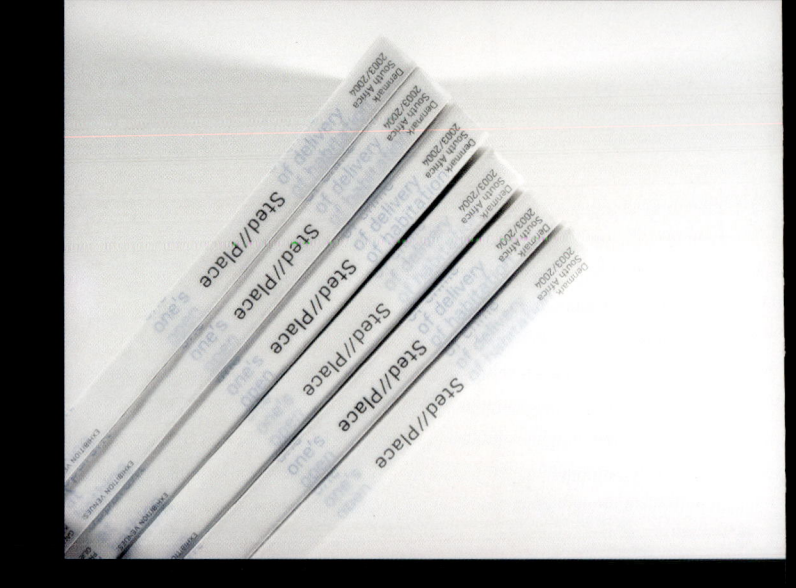

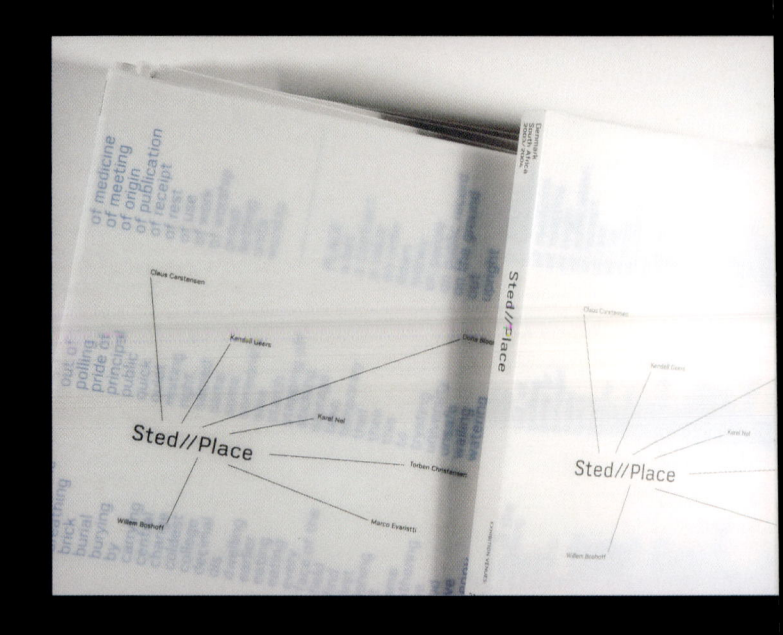

+ e-Types

Page
174

Client
--

Origin
Copenhagen, Denmark

Title of work
Art Book: STED//PLACE

Art Director
e-Types

Year produced
2003

Type of work
Book

Designer
e-Types

Description
Four artists from Denmark: Claus Carstensen, Torben Christensen, Marco Evaristti, and Doris Bloom; and three artists from South Africa: Willem Boshoff, Kendell Geers and Karel Nel explore the nature of memory with a visual expression of cross-cultural perspective.

"Memories rely on places"

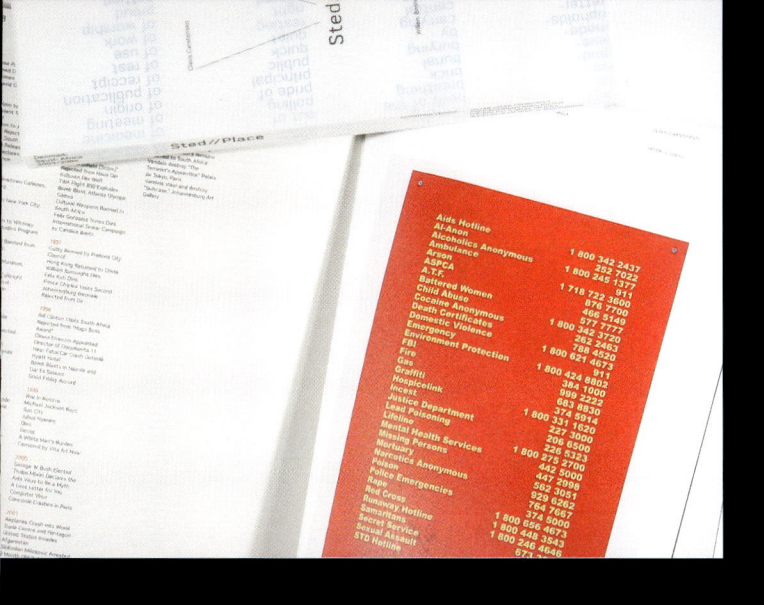

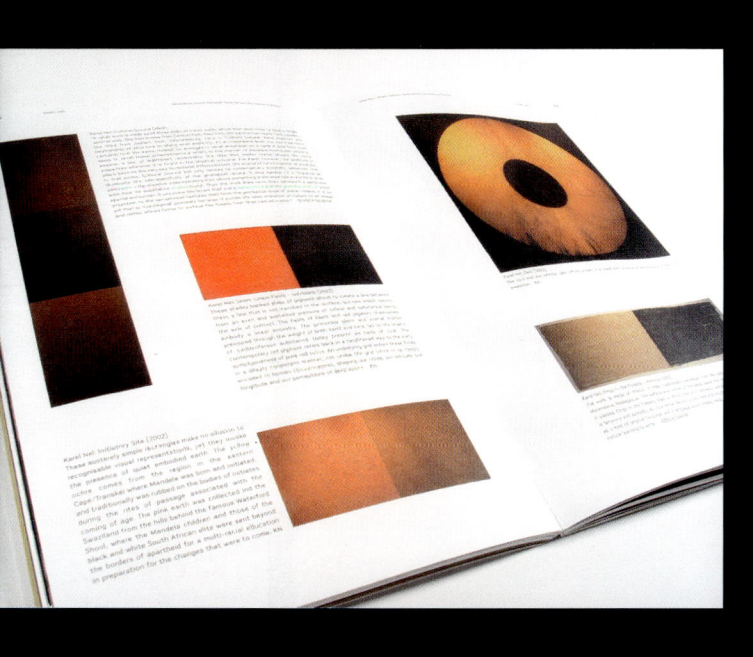

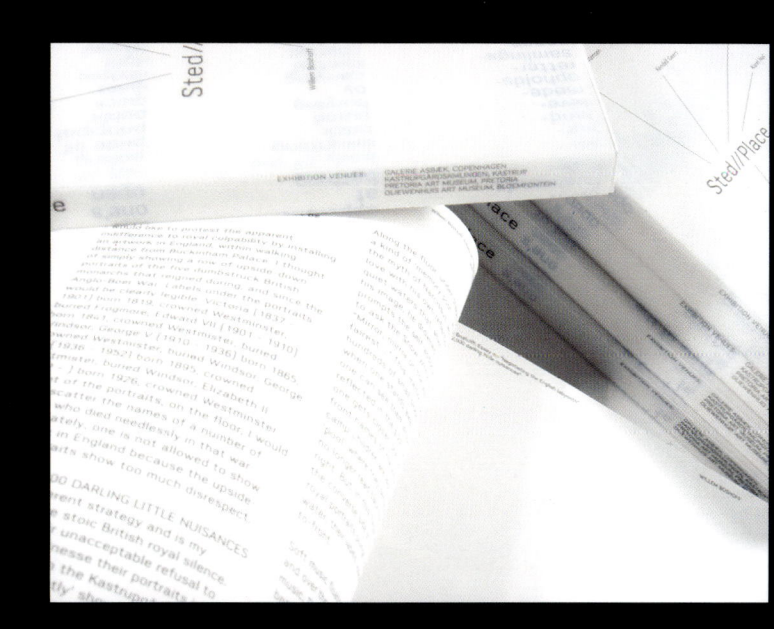

We strive for a "fusion" practice that moves well beyond a multidisciplinary approach. Integrated, project-specific teams focus on shared and mutually creative ways of working. Typically client teams take part in the process in forums such as roundtables and advisory groups that critique projects and the firm as a whole. EDAW supports powerful communications technology and an open firm culture to tear down old walls—between this and that office, this and that specialist, this and that time zone... and between our goals and yours.

Fusion is more than collaboration; it propels the search for the best idea.

Planners team with archaeologists, historians with engineers, designers with biologists. We listen, learn, debate. We harness the power of disagreement — push and pull, merge ideas, shape realities. This is the best of EDAW.

Another asset we share is a global store of experience. EDAW professionals on different coasts—and continents—regularly convene practice circles by videoconference to exchange ideas within their specialties, while in-house symposiums on interdisciplinary topics explore convergent trends among fields.

The U.S. Navy wanted to do the right thing with the vernal pools along the Pacific coast at Marine Corps Air Station Miramar, California. But were these puddles really irreplaceable homes to hundreds of fragile life forms? (They were.) What about military, economic and community uses for the land around them? The Navy turned to EDAW.

Tiny as they are, Miramar Air Station's vernal pools raise a major issue: the meeting of military mission on federal land with an ecological imperative to save fragile habitat.

The big job of designing Atlanta's Centennial Olympic Park proved even bigger when we realized it would become a regional economic catalyst, "Atlanta's waterfront," in the words of this non-waterfront city's mayor.

"When you need to deal with a million acres there's only one firm you call," says the chairman of the St. Joe Land Company. Today a wood products reserve spanning 14 counties, St. Joe's slice of Florida's panhandle is tomorrow's metropolitan region, an ecological treasure, and a magnet for recreation and tourism—all that and more.

Understanding it involved more than 20 [...] and creative disciplines, as well as pow[...] for collaborating, mapping and comm[...] (We had them.)

FROM A PUDDLE TO A MILLION [...]
FOLLOWING PAGES INTRODUCE REP[...]
EDAW PROJECTS AT EVERY SCA[...]
INDIVIDUAL STORY FULL OF [...]
CHALLENGE, AND OPPORTUNIT[...]
TO "SUPER REGIONAL AND B[...]

From Vernal Pool to Metropolis

EDAW

Gateway Science School Courtyard
St. Louis, Missouri
Client: St. Louis Public Schools

L 04

An award-winning educational landscape helps erase the memory of the Pruitt-Igoe public housing debacle

Two acres of science and math disguised as play. Where 33 public housing towers once stood in shambles, children in the inner city now learn about Missouri's natural ecosystems by playing tag in an Ozark forest or watching a mid- and tall-grass prairie change color during the year. A weather station and windmill beat tether-ball and four-square hands down.

Transforming a brownfields site into Olympic housing, an ecologically sustainable village—an Australian model in green

The "Green Olympics" have given way to a green community. From an athlete's village to a 5,000-resident neighborhood that features 850 solar-powered homes. Ninety percent of construction hard waste and sixty percent of soft waste are being recycled. Carbon-dioxide emissions are [...] being reduced by 2,000 tons a year. And, by the [...] it functions as a vibrant urban center.

Designing a Chinese city while m[...] environmental standards

The centerpiece of a 70 km² new town devel[...] with a future population of 600,000 residen[...] Lake's 513 hectares are designed to hous[...] 500 companies with eight waterfront [...] around a healthy lake. A large cen[...] waterfront promenade complemen[...]

Newington Olympic Village Plan and Landscape
Homebush Bay, New South Wales, Australia
Client: Mirvac Lend Lease Village Consortium/OCA

Jinji Lake Landscape Master Plan
Suzhou, China
Client: Suzhou Industrial Park Administrative Committee

+ Templin Brink Design

Page
177

Title of work
EDAW Capabilities Brochure

Type of work
Corporate brochure

Client
EDAW

Art Director
Gaby Brink

Designer
Gaby Brink, Marius Gedgaudas

Origin
California, USA

Year produced
2002

Description
EDAW is one of the world's leading landscape architectural firms. The corporate brochure was designed to illustrate their various practices through a simple message and appeal to their diverse client base. While understated and elegant, it reflects EDAW's thinking both conceptually and visually – showcasing a landscape architecture firm's work through tritone photography.

+ Mirko Ilic Corp

Page
178

Client
S.L.M

Origin
New York, USA

Title of work
B&W Zagreb

Art Director
Mirko Ilic

Year produced
2002

Type of work
Book

Designer
Mirko Ilic
Luka Mjeda (photography)

Description
The idea was to design a bilingual book with a limited budget, so the book jacket can be unfolded and used as a promotional poster. There was a smaller version of the book printed from the extra white paper in the printing process that was used as a promotional booklet.

LUKA MJEDA
C/B ZAGREB

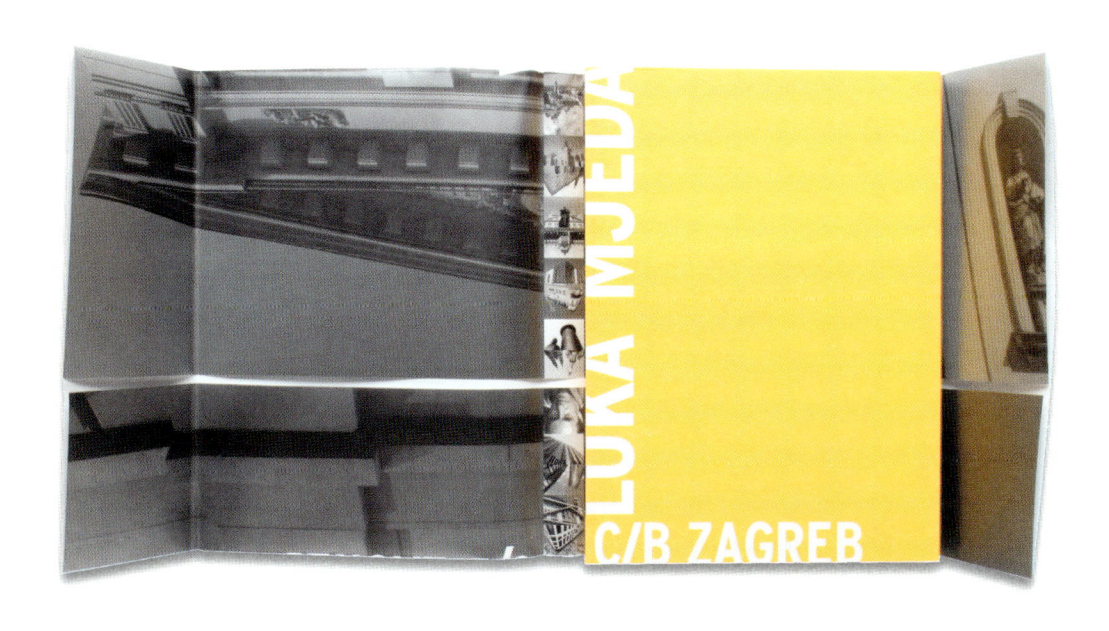

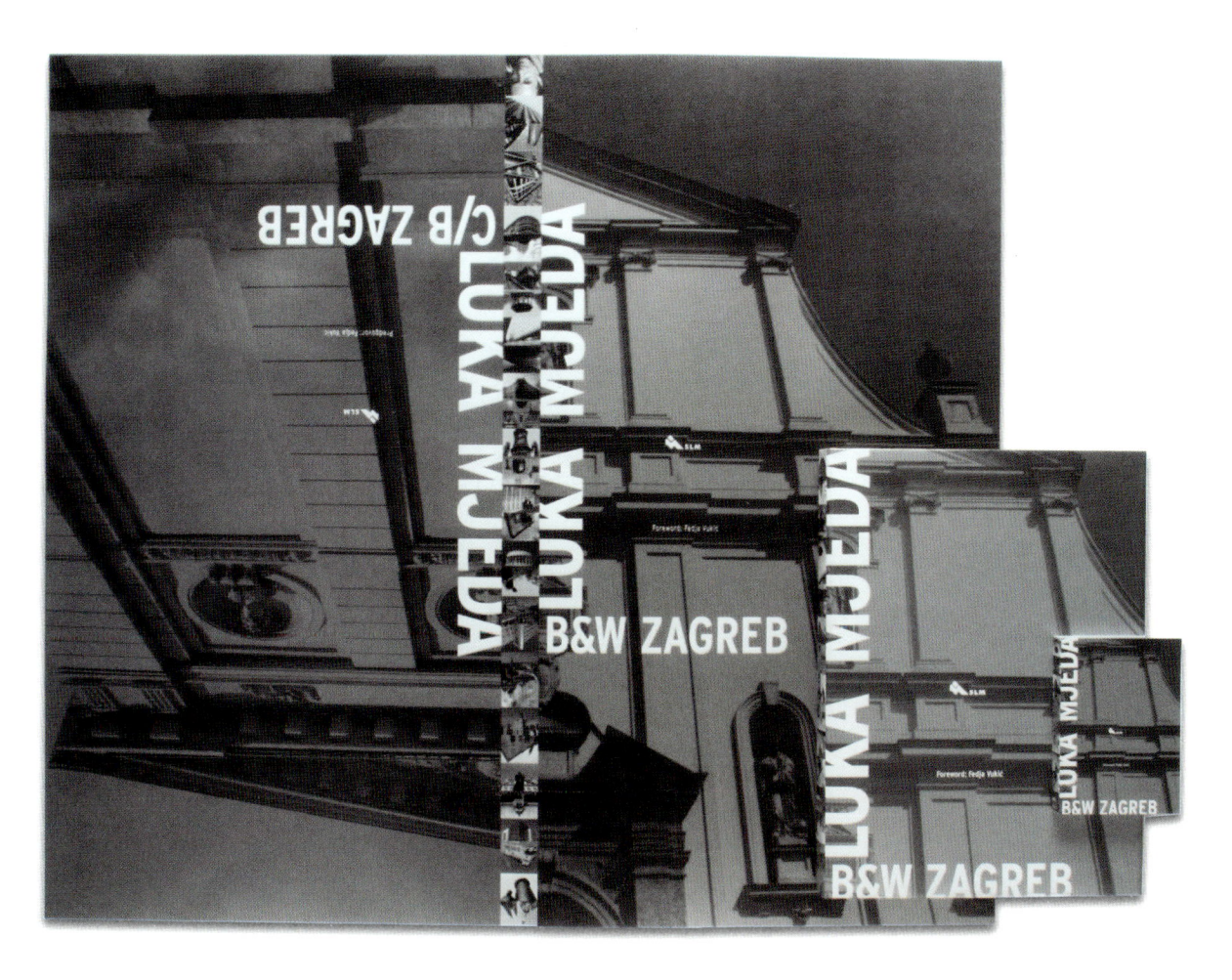

LUKA MJEDA
B&W ZAGREB

+ Form®

Page
180

Client
International School of Basel

Origin
London, UK

Title of work
International School of Basel Brochure

Art Director
Paula Benson
Paul West

Year produced
2003

Type of work
Brochure/prospectus

Designer
Paula Benson
Claire Warner
Paul West

Description
Modern, upbeat and colourful, this brochure evokes the school slogan 'Forty Nationalities, One Spirit'. Emphasis is placed on imagery by making use of photography by Kate Martin and copy that is open, friendly and reliable. A fluorescent yellow box designed as a self-sealing mailing device encloses the brochure, creating presence when arriving in the post and a 'coffee table' appeal.

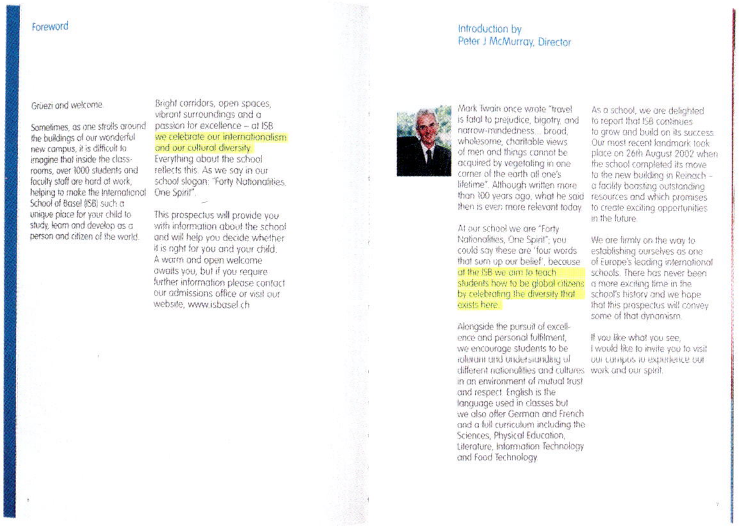

Foreword

Grüezi and welcome.

Sometimes, as one strolls around the buildings of our wonderful new campus, it is difficult to imagine that inside the classrooms, over 1000 students and faculty staff are hard at work, helping to make the International School of Basel (ISB) such a unique place for your child to study, learn and develop as a person and citizen of the world.

Bright corridors, open spaces, vibrant surroundings and a passion for excellence – at ISB **we celebrate our internationalism and our cultural diversity**. Everything about the school reflects this. As we say in our school slogan: "Forty Nationalities, One Spirit".

This prospectus will provide you with information about the school and will help you decide whether it is right for you and your child. A warm and open welcome awaits you, but if you require further information please contact our admissions office or visit our website, www.isbasel.ch

Introduction by
Peter J McMurray, Director

Mark Twain once wrote "travel is fatal to prejudice, bigotry, and narrow-mindedness... broad, wholesome, charitable views of men and things cannot be acquired by vegetating in one corner of the earth all one's lifetime". Although written more than 100 years ago, what he said then is even more relevant today.

At our school we are "Forty Nationalities, One Spirit"; you could say these are 'four words that sum up our belief', because **at the ISB we aim to teach students how to be global citizens by celebrating the diversity that exists here**.

Alongside the pursuit of excellence and personal fulfilment, we encourage students to be tolerant and understanding of different nationalities and cultures in an environment of mutual trust and respect. English is the language used in classes but we also offer German and French and a full curriculum including the Sciences, Physical Education, Literature, Information Technology and Food Technology.

As a school, we are delighted to report that ISB continues to grow and build on its success. Our most recent landmark took place on 26th August 2002 when the school completed its move to the new building in Reinach – a facility boasting outstanding resources and which promises to create exciting opportunities in the future.

We are firmly on the way to establishing ourselves as one of Europe's leading international schools. There has never been a more exciting time in the school's history and we hope that this prospectus will convey some of that dynamism.

If you like what you see, I would like to invite you to visit our campus to experience our work and our spirit.

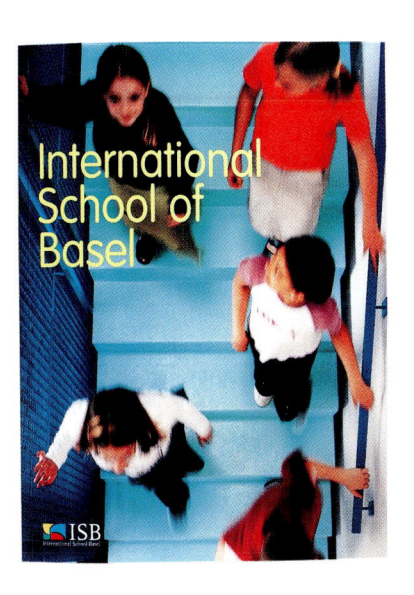

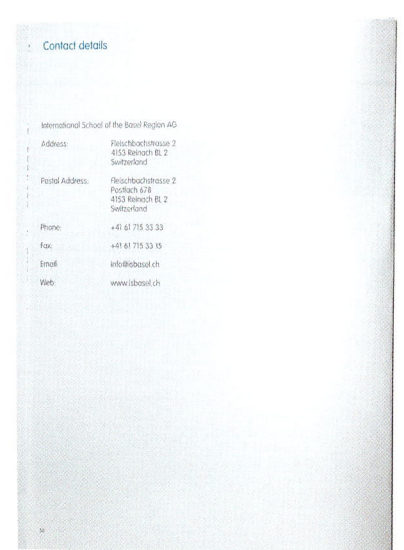

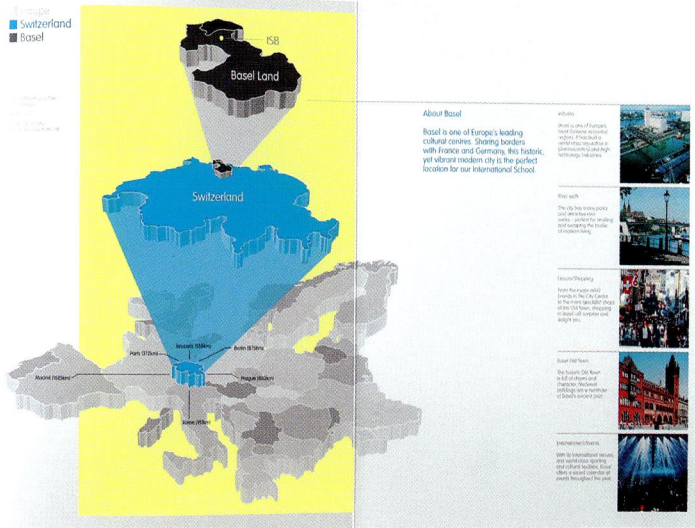

International School of Basel

Contact details

International School of the Basel Region AG

Address: Fleischbachstrasse 2
4153 Reinach BL 2
Switzerland

Postal Address: Fleischbachstrasse 2
Postfach 678
4153 Reinach BL 2
Switzerland

Phone: +41 61 715 33 33
Fax: +41 61 715 33 15
Email: info@isbasel.ch
Web: www.isbasel.ch

About Basel

Basel is one of Europe's leading cultural centres. Sharing borders with France and Germany, this historic, yet vibrant modern city is the perfect location for our international school.

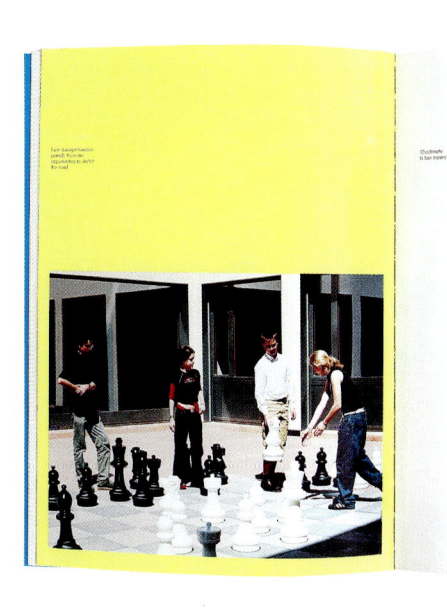

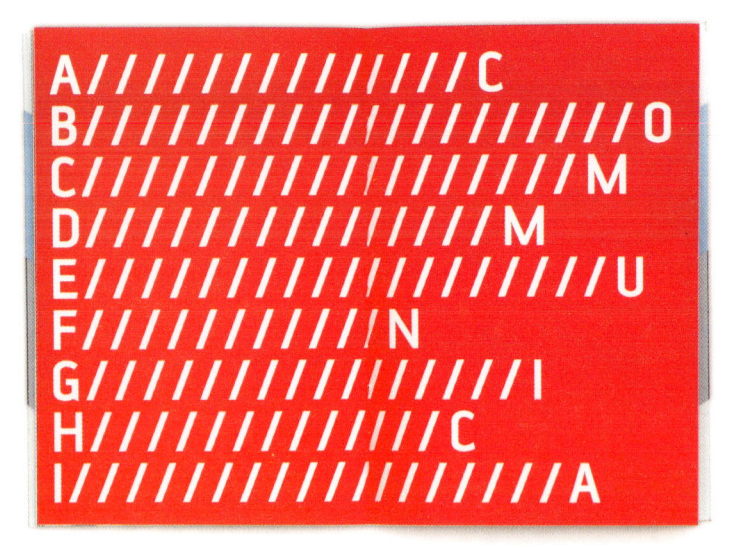

+ A2-Graphics/SW/HK

Page
182

Client
1508 A/S

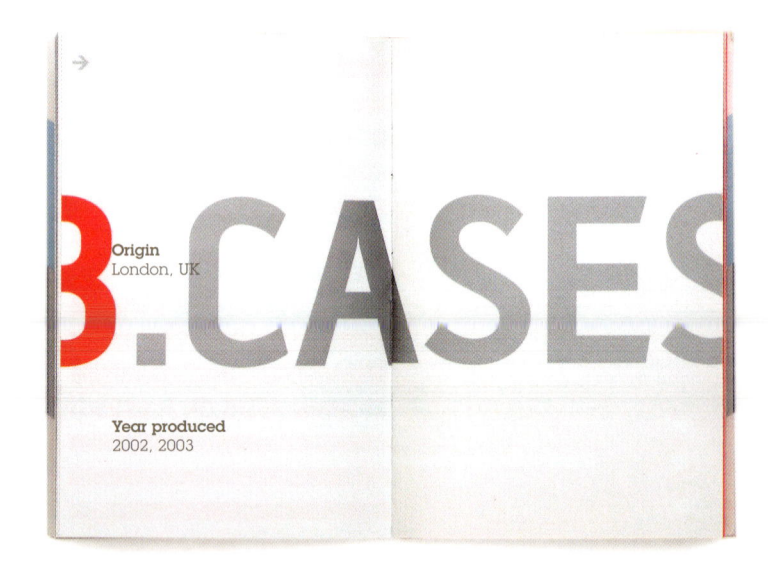

Title of work
1508 Self Promotion

Art Director
Scott Williams, Henrik Kubel

Type of work
Corporate brochure

Designer
Scott Williams, Henrik Kubel

Origin
London, UK

Year produced
2002, 2003

Description
A2-GRAPHICS/SW/HK was commissioned to create the name and a dynamic visual language for a company whose service is to advise and implement strategic communication and web design for the Internet. 1508's visual language is inspired by Buckminster Fuller's projection of the earth, a map created to achieve the most accurate visualisation of the earth in two-dimensions.
Fuller's projection has been used as a template to create a new representation of the five continents, which allows them to be arranged in numerous ways, enabling one location to connect and unite with another. This flexible identity can easily be shifted and changed across all applications. A principal typeface consisting of three weights, specially designed by A2-GRAPHICS/SW/HK, was employed throughout the project.

+ Envision +

Page
183

Type of work
Exhibition catalogue

Client
Royal College of Art (Architecture and Interiors), London, GB

Origin
Bühlertal, Germany

Year produced
1998

Description
The catalogue documents projects that explore the boundaries of architecture and virtual space, reflecting these concerns by the use of gridlines and a strong structural band across each spread. The bands' colour and position identify the chapters of the book. The vivid grid-based design and the bold use of a second colour add a layer to each spread, creating a format that is inviting and intricate, yet inexpensive. The cover juxtaposes an abstract image on the outside with a monochromatic shot of London on the inside and underscores the exhibition's theme: the threshold between real and virtual.

+ Envision+

Page
184

Title of work
Building On Our Foundations

Type of work
Corporate brochure

Client
Nestlé, Vevey, Switzerland

Art Director
Esther Mildenberger

Designer
Esther Mildenberger

Year produced
2001

Description
To celebrate the renovation of Nestlé's Swiss headquarters and to promote them as forward looking, active, and open, Envision+ was asked to produce a limited edition book. This permanent record of the headquarter's history and renewal, introduced international partners to qualities of the building and the dynamic life at Nestlé's center. The book is a visual exploration of the building in eight chapters, each with a different look and feel. Colours, different paper qualities, and Nestlé's brand values set in bold typography are used to pace the rhythm of the publication.

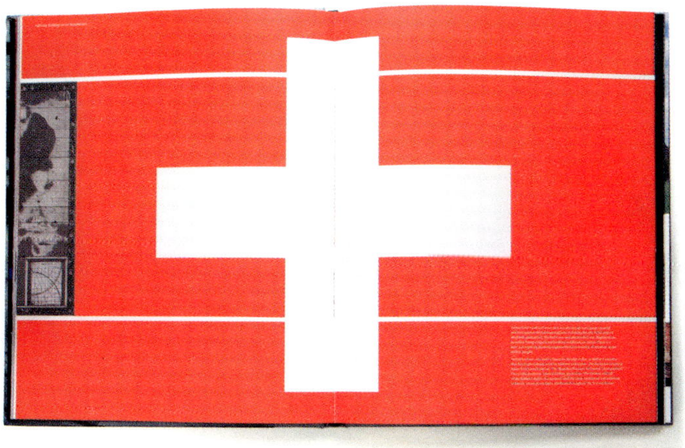

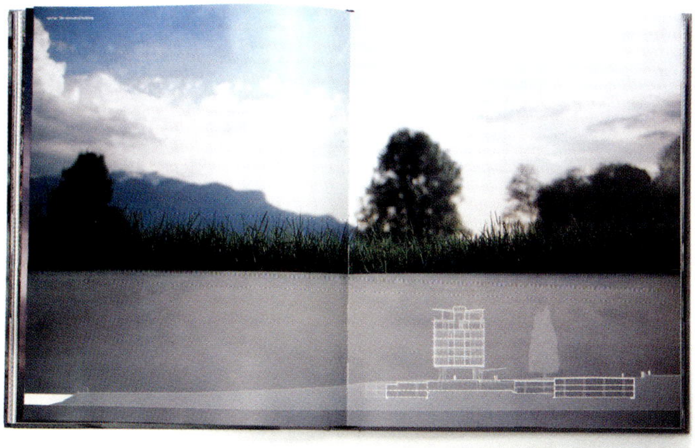

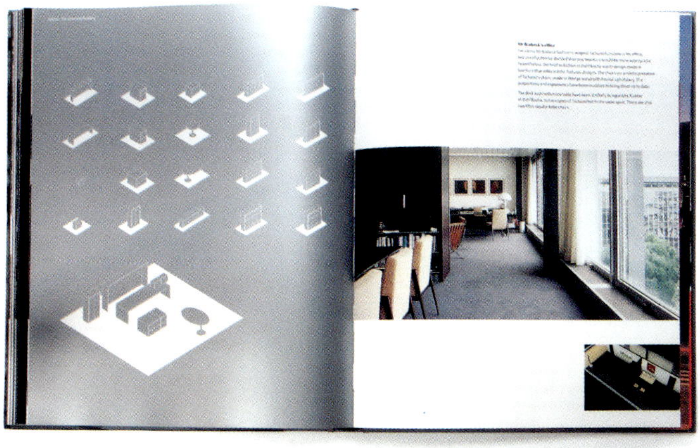

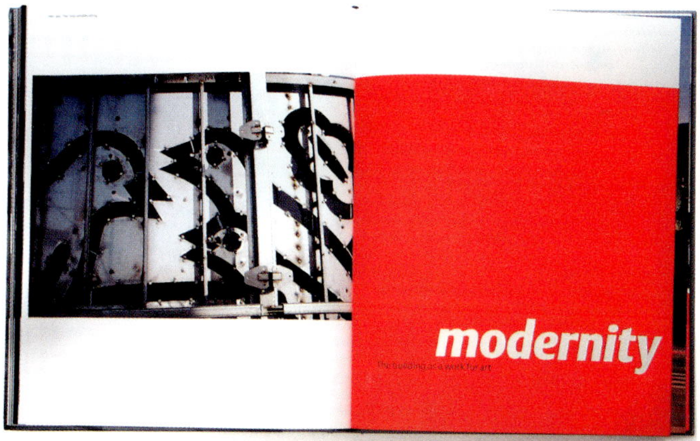
modernity

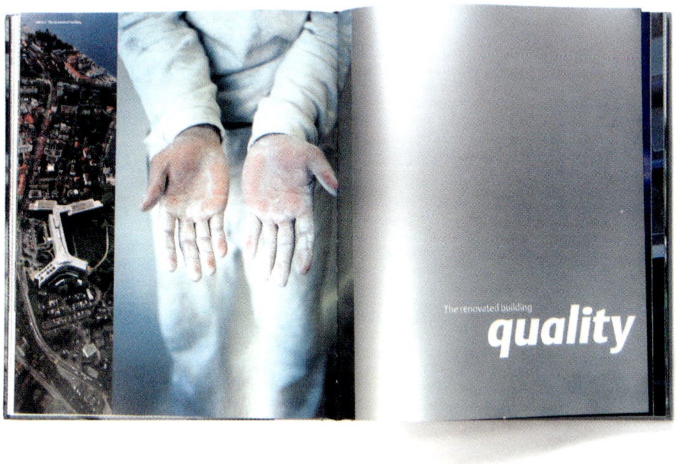
The renovated building
quality

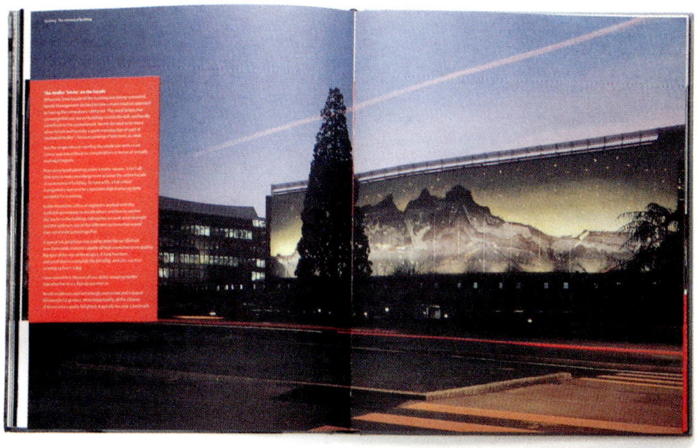

THE BRIDGE TO THE FUTURE IS CROSSED.

REAP THE BENEFITS

THEY SAY WE USE ABOUT 10% OF OUR BRAIN.

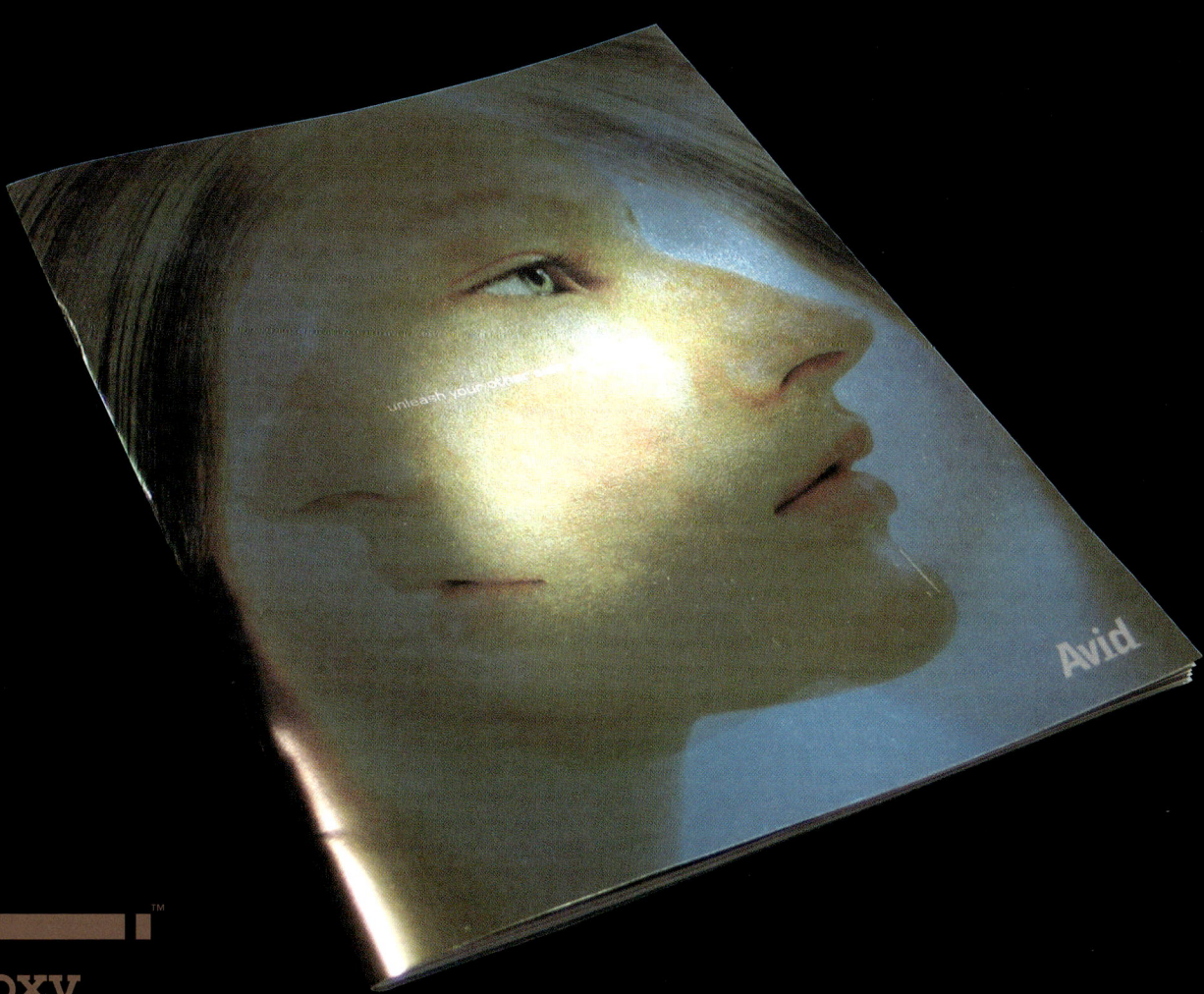

+ Époxy

Page
187

Title of work
Avid Magazine

Type of work
Promotional magazine

Client
Avid Technologies

Art Director
Daniel Fortin (creative director)
George Fok (creative director, art director)

Designer
George Fok, Patrick Pellerin

Origin
Québec, Canada

Year produced
2001

Description
Fashionable and avant-garde, this brochure serves as a styling piece for Avid's DS, the one-stop post-production unit. The theme of 'unleash your other side' emphasises the powerful features of DS, which provides the post-production artist with seamless creation possibilities.

+ Mlein Press

Page
188

Client
Mlein Press

Origin
Munich, Germany

Title of work
Zapf Dingbats Recycled

Art Director
Michael Moser, Heike Henig

Year produced
2003

Type of work
Book/series

Designer

Description

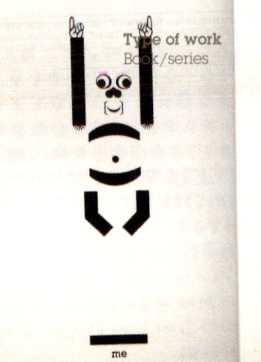

Pg.189 / Contributors

A2-Graphics/SW/HK
London based design studio A2-GRPAHICS/SW/HK was established in 2000 and is run by principal partners Scott Williams and Henrik Kubel, both graduates of the Royal College of Art. The duo works within the art, fashion and corporate world and specialise in publication, spatial design and development of bespoke type. Both partners are regularly invited to judge international design competitions, as well as being visiting lecturers in graphic design and typography at Chelsea College of Art & Design and Buckinghamshire Chilterns University College.

Page 63-65, 158-159, 163, 182

AdamsMorioka
AdamsMorioka, Inc. is a Beverly Hills based design and strategy firm founded by Sean Adams and Noreen Morioka in 1993. AdamsMorioka quickly gained an international reputation for leading the movement of simple, clear work in brand development. AdamsMorioka's manifesto is 'clarity, purity and resonance'.

page 84-85

Anthony Burrill
Anthony Burrill is a freelance designer who works for a range of clients in the advertising, music, publishing and art industries.

Page 112-113

Astrid Stavro
Lab Magazine is a visual creative platform that brings together interesting features and interviews from the fashion, graphics and illustration, music, animation and architecture industries. *Lab s* unique mixture inspires creativity by creatives and challenges readers to become contributors. By combining the directorial and exciting work developed by new and emerging talent from within the creative industry, *Lab* stands alone on a meritocracy of design, where what matters is not reputation as much as ability. The layout, typography and grid change every issue in order to reflect our experimental philosophy.

Page 30-31

Benjamin Güedel
Born in Bern, Switzerland in 1968, Benjamin Güedel studied graphic design from 1990 until 1994. He then became a self-employed illustrator and graphic designer, working in Berlin, Germany and Zurich, Switzerland ever since 1995.

Page 134

Big Active
Big Active is a London based creative studio that specialises in art direction and design, as well as the creative management of certain internationally recognised illustrators and photographers.

Page 25-27, 156-157

Bleed
The design agency Bleed was established in 2000. Bleed's distinctively global vision is redefining the visual language of today's branding culture. Bleed creates collaborative forums that encourage cross-disciplinary input into each project.

Page 130-133

Blokes
Blokes are Urs Lehni and Rafael Koch. Since graduating from art school in 1999, they have been working independently as designers and guest lecturers in Switzerland. Besides working for clients, they also develop their own projects like «vectorama.org», «Lego Font Creator», «CHIDO» or «Our Magazine».

Page 154

Boris Brumnjak
Boris Brumnjak was born in Berlin and studied at Lette-Verein Berlin, a professional school for graphic design, fashion and photography, from 1996 until 1999. He then worked in Berlin and Chicago. Since 2001 he has headed a workshop about typography. He now works in an unspectacular town called Wuppertal in Germany.

Page 135

Build
Build was founded by Michael C. Place, who was born in North Yorkshire, England in 1969 and studied at Newcastle College. He first worked in London with Trevor Jackson at Bite It! and then the Designers Republic (tDR) in Sheffield. His work includes record designs for Champion Records, Gee Street Records, R&S Records, Satoshi Tomiie, Warp Records and Sun Electric. He has produced the Wipeout series for PlayStation and the book *3D>2D Adventures In + Out of Architecture*. In 2001 he returned from traveling and started his own design company 'Build' in London. It specialises mainly in design for print.

Page 48-55

Büro International London
Büro International is a young network of designers and visual artists in London, Berlin and Copenhagen.

Page 92, 120-121

Chen Design Associates
Established in 1991, San Francisco-based Chen Design Associates provides strategic vision and creative content for clients in the arts and entertainment, education, healthcare, non-profit, publishing and technology sectors. The firm has developed highly effective and award-winning work through concept, writing, design, photography, illustration, annual reports, packaging, books, prints, and website projects. Clients include Apple Computer, Adobe Systems, California Pacific Medical Center, Chronicle Books, Joe Goode Performance Group, Mohawk Paper Mills, Philharmonia Baroque Orchestra, the Roberts Enterprise Development Fund, Rockport Publishers, Sequoia Hospital and various colleges of the University of California, Berkeley.

Page 90-91, 140

CHK Design
Christian Küsters holds a degree from the London College of Printing and Yale University. He established CHK Design, his own London-based company and launched Acme Fonts, a digital type foundry. Küsters teaches at Camberwell College of Arts and is an Art Director of Art Director of *Architectural Design* magazine. He has written for magazines such as *Eye*, *Baseline* and *Graphics International*. He is co-author with Emily King of *Restart: New Systems in Graphic Design* (Thames & Hudson, London, 2001). He curated and designed with Marcus Maurer 'Design Now – Graphics', an exhibition on contemporary graphic design for the Design Museum in London.

Page 36-41

Dainippon Type Organization
Established in 1993, Dainippon Type Organization is an experimental typography team. From the Japanese and English alphabet, they have deconstructed, shaped and formulated a fresh typography that hasn't lost an irresistible Japonesque feel.

Page 114-115

Deanne Cheuk
Deanne Cheuk has been labeled one of the top 50 creatives in the world by The Face magazine; 'a leader' by Flaunt Magazine; and 'the fashion world's darling of the moment' by the Canadian National Post. Her clients are as diverse as Tokion Magazine, Urban Outfitters, and Levi's Strauss. She regularly compiles the graphic 'zine of inspiration Neomu.

Page 8-15

Envision+
Envision+ is a design network of partners that are international in experience, thinking, and range. They are devoted to ideas and design that provoke thought, interaction, and smiles. Founded in 2001 by Brian Switzer and Esther Mildenberger, Envision+ specialises in branding, interaction design and editorial design. Their projects cross languages, borders and disciplines. They love complex problems, close exchange and results everyone is proud of. Last but not least, Envision+ clients include Ferrari, Nestlé, Birkhäuser, avedition, as well as other corporate and cultural institutions.

Page 66-69, 82-83, 116-119, 183-185

Époxy
Founded in 1992, Époxy is a cutting-edge creative shop specialising in the technological, cultural and branding sectors. Via its offices in Montreal and Paris, Époxy offers a full range of services, including: advertising, branding, 2D/3D graphic design, film/new media animation and interactive communications (mobile telephony, Internet, CD-ROM and DVD-ROM). The company's creative talent has been acknowledged repeatedly both at home and abroad. Époxy's wide-ranging client portfolio features such prestigious names as the Daniel Langlois Foundation, Dharma Resorts, Walt Disney, Eyewire/Getty Images, Interbrew, Labatt Breweries, Avid/Softimage and Sony C.A.I.

Page 80-81, 155, 186-187

e-Types
e-Types is a brand agency that designs corporate identities and advises companies and organisations on identity, brand positioning and brand strategy. e-Types was founded in 1997.

Page 164-175

Flink
Flink is a multi-disciplinary creative studio, based in Antwerp, Belgium. Their work crosses over vast disciplines, including: brand development, corporate identity, interactive media, packaging and print.

Flink has an open and flexible structure to allow organic growth: thinking with their hearts and minds has always been their greatest asset. Their ambition is to produce good work that speaks for itself.

Page 102-108

Pg.190 / Contributors

Form®

Form® is an award-winning graphic design consultancy based in London. Established by Paul West and Paula Benson in 1991, their background focused on creating campaigns for many high profile bands in the music industry, working as art directors and designers of record sleeves, logos, POS and merchandise. Over the years their client list has expanded dramatically and in addition to the music work, they now receive regular commissions for identity and branding; book, brochure and DVD packaging design; advertising campaigns; websites; and moving image projects.

To date, Form® clients have covered the areas of music, sport, fashion, furniture, architecture, interiors, events, TV, film, video, publishing, marketing and PR, and they welcome challenges from all areas where clients require an inspiring and creative approach – they don't like to be pigeonholed!

Page 180-181

Hyperkit

Hyperkit is a London-based graphic design practice founded in 2001 by Tim Balaam and Kate Sclater. Their skills and experience enable them to work on a project in its entirety – from devising the initial design concept, to producing the identity and printed material, and developing the website. This approach allows us to create a coherent visual presence across many different formats and media. The solutions come out of a process of combining personal interests and fascinations with commercial practice, allowing each to inform the other. Hyperkit believes in developing work that is engaging to the user and sympathetic to the subject and context.

Page 122-125

Jop van Bennekom

Jop van Bennekom is an editor, art director, author, designer and strategist, as well as a publisher. He was born in Scherpenzeel, Netherlands in 1970 and graduated with an M.A. from the Jan van Eyck Academy in Maastricht. After college he started to examine the meaning and possibilities of the media, resulting in the creation of his own magazine titled *RE-* (later on re-named *Re-Magazine*). Bennekom also briefly art directed at *Blvd.* magazine in 1998, but quit shortly afterwards to begin his own publishing. He designed the architecture magazine Forum, which won the Rotterdam Design Prize in 2001. That same year he launched his other internationally acclaimed gay magazine *BUTT*.

Page 16-24

Lippa Pearce

Lippa Pearce is a multi-disciplinary design consultancy based in London. Found in 1990, with Domenic Lippa and Harry Pearce as joint Design Directors and Principal Designers, Lippa Pearce has been featured in the D&AD Annual consecutively over the past 13 years. Their clients include Boots, Halfords, Marks & Spencer, Unilever, TDK and Linklaters, as well as Typographic Circle, Audley, Equazen *Nutraceuticals* and Geronimo Inns. Having worked together for 20 years as designers, Harry and Domenic have the philosophy that you have to be brave to stand up for what you believe in and ultimately want to design.

Page 86-89, 152-153

Lonne Wennekendonk

Lonne Wennekendonk, born in 1974, works as an independent designer for cultural and non-profit organisations. She works closely with copywriters, photographers and other designers. Moreover, she collaborates with her clients. For Lonne, collaboration is the way to achieve the best and most suitable product. She believes it's important to communicate directly with the decision-makers in each assignment. Before she starts working on an assignment, she meets and converses with the client. When these sessions go well, both parties inspire each other and Lonne gains the trust to do the job.

Her ideal assignment is one in which she is part of the editorial board and is able to decide on content: text, images, and editorial direction. Human stories are her inspiration.

Page 160-162

Martin Woodtli

Martin Woodtli is perhaps the most accomplished representative of the new design scene in Switzerland, where the joy of the design process (as opposed to monetary reward) seems to determine the direction of the studios. Swiss designers would rather work for small cultural projects to which they are often connected personally, than to fall into the trap of large advertising conglomerates. Woodtli does not subscribe to the silly adage circulated by many of his colleagues about the computer being just a tool; he sees it simply as a process. He can also actually think with the keyboard. His proficiency in various programs is such that he sketches with the keyboard as quickly and uninhibitedly as with pencil and paper.

Page 34-35

Meiré und Meiré

Mike Meiré (born in 1964) has been working as a designer and art director since 1983 and is the founder and Creative Director of the agency for brand coding Meiré and Meiré. In addition to editorial design, strategy, consulting, planning, public relations, campaign design, interior design, trade design and architecture, the agency develops and realises numerous international art and cultural projects.

Page 56-62

Milkxhake

Milkxhake is a new Hong Kong based design flavour founded by three designers in 2002 and specialising in graphic and interactive mixtures.

The founders started from a design project when studying in Digital Graphic Communication at Hong Kong Baptist University, tasting a cup of milkshake. Their name 'milkxhake' provides not only a cup of the drink, but also symbolises the spirit of 'mix' through their logo.

Page 126-127

Mirko Ilic Corp

Originally from Bosnia, Mirko Ilic moved to the United States in 1986. In the early 90's he was Art Director of the international edition of *Time* magazine and the *New York Times* 'Op-Ed Pages'. In 1995 he established Mirko Ilic Corp., a Graphic design studio and has since been awarded by the Society of Illustrators, Society of Publication Designers, Art Directors Club, *I.D.* magazine and the Society of Newspaper Design. He was Vice-President of the New York chapter of AIGA from 1994-1995 and taught design at Cooper Union as well as the Master's Degree in Illustration at the School of Visual Arts. He is co-author of the book *Genius Moves: 100 Icons of Graphic Design* together with Steven Heller.

Page 150-151, 178-179

Mlein Press

Mlein Press is a small publisher of typographic books, magazines and ideas that does it not for profit, but for fun and for making others smile - that is enough payment...

Page 188

Moiré

Moiré is composed of three creative forces: Bianca Brunner, born in 1974, who is a photographer/graphic designer now living in London, U.K.; Marc Kappeler, born in 1975, a graphic designer who lives in Zurich, Switzerland; and Markus Reichenbach, born in 1975, a typographer who currently lives in Berne, Switzerland.

Page 32-33

Nuno Martins

Nuno Martins was born in 1979 in Oporto, Portugal where he lives and works today. He graduated in Communication Design from Faculdade de Belas Artes do Porto (1998-2003) and studied at Willem de Kooning Academie – Hoogeschool in Rotterdam, Netherlands.

Page 128

Public

Public renders graphic design services in print and digital media, including: identity, collateral, publishing, packaging, and environmental design. Public is dedicated to delivering visually arresting, thought provoking visual communication that both challenges and entertains.

Page 76-79

RMAC

The RMAC Design Studio was founded in 1996 and is based in Lisbon, Portugal. Altogether about twelve people, the studio has a spontaneous and observant spirit in solving every challenge from the clients. The Studio works on graphic, industrial and interior design projects. They claim: 'No image lives forever. Work is always in progress. RM/Design is our life.'

Page 46-47, 146-149

Sagmeister Inc.

Born in 1962, Stefan Sagmeister is a native of Bregenz, Austria. He has a MFA in graphic design from the University of Applied Arts in Vienna and a master's degree from Pratt Institute in New York. Following stints at M&Co. in New York and Leo Burnett Hong Kong, where he was Creative Director, Sagmeister formed the New York based Sagmeister Inc. in 1993. He has designed graphics and packaging for Rolling Stones, David Byrne, Lou Reed, Aerosmith and Pat Metheny. His work has been nominated four times for the Grammies and has won most international design awards. He currently lives in New York.

Page 94-101

Segura Inc.

Founded by Carlos Segura in 1991, Segura Inc. is a multi-faceted design and communications firm that specialises in print, collateral and new media communications. Prior to establishing Segura, Carlos had worked as an art director for many advertising giants such as Young & Rubicam, Ketchum, HCM Marsteler and Bayer Bess Vanderwacker. Besides focusing on their best profession – graphic design, printed advertising, corporate identities and other new media – the company does whatever creative design through whatever medium is allowed, delivering messages with a distinctive sense of style and simplicity.

Page 44-45, 70-75

So+ba

Founded by Alex Sonderegger and Susanna Baer in 2001, So+ba is a dynamic creative design agency based in one of the most exciting of Asian metropolises: Tokyo, Japan.

Page 28-29, 136-137

Supershapes

Supershapes was born as a creative outlet of designer Patrick Sundqvist in 1999. However, through a metamorphosis of purpose, by 2002 Supershapes had grown into a multi-disciplinary design studio. The studio is firmly rooted in an investigative process, which strives to create appropriate work with purpose, beauty and function. At the core of this creative process are honesty, curiosity, craft consciousness and a sincere desire to communicate.

Page 141

Sweden Graphics

Sweden Graphics has been around since 1998 and claims to not have an official history. However, more important is how they see graphic design: Sweden believes that graphic design has finally started to gain its long needed audience after all these years of new media and I.T. bombardment. They believe the graphic design world, full of wonderful knowledge about typefaces, colour and compositions, has become an integrated part of the younger generation thanks to the Web. Sweden Graphics' innate understanding of this new graphic world will turn graphic design into a means of expression that is so powerful not because there are competent speakers, but competent listeners.

Page 109-111, 129

Templin Brink Design

Launched in 1998 by Joel Templin and Gaby Brink, Templin Brink Design has a vision of intimacy: intimacy of process, where clients are more involved in the creation of the work; intimacy of accountability, where clients know the principals of the firm are doing the work; and intimacy of result, where the work creates a deeper connection between the brand and its audience. Together Templin and Brink have developed an organic working process that inspires creative solutions. T.B.D. specialises in integrating brands across all media, providing clarity, consistency and stickiness at every touch point with the consumer.

Page 176-177

Teresa & David

Based in Stockholm, the design studio Teresa & David was established in 2001 by Teresa Holmberg, a native of the northern town of Uppsala who graduated from Beckmans College of Design, and design journalist David Castenfors, who was born in Stockholm. Teresa & David has broadly worked on graphic identity, motion graphics, book design, magazine and illustration. Variety is vitally important to them, not just to stimulate a high level of creativity, but also to prevent getting stuck into only one certain style. Their work philosophy is based on passion, fun, patience and dignity.

Page 42-43

viction:design workshop

Viction:design workshop was founded by Victor Cheung in 2001 in Hong Kong. Their workshop provides a broad range of design services to maximise the true potential of their clients, building sophisticated and innovative solutions that enable them to develop deeper and more personalised relationships with their customers.

Page 142-145

WIG-01

WIG-01 are two pixel punks who are passionate about creating graphic design and illustrations. WIG-01 will work for anyone who wants to separate himself from formulaic, mediocre design and who is prepared to take risks.

Page 138-139

Acknowledgements

We would like to thank all the designers and companies who made a significant contribution to the compilation of this book. Without them this project would not have been possible. I am also very grateful to many other people whose names do not appear on the credits but who made specific input and continuous support the whole time.

The interviews are greatly benefited from additional documents and conversations, kindly made available by Deanne Cheuk, Jop van Bennekom at *RE-Magazine*, Stefan Sagmeister at Sagmeister Inc. and Fanny Khoo at Flink.

Sarah Marusek, Iric Chun, CC Lau, Jeanie Wong and Agnes Wong offered many helps in the editing and interviews. We would like to thank Alex Chan, Hung, Rosena, Stanley Mu, Dominic Wong, Shaida Lai and all the producers for their invaluable assistance throughout. Its successful completion also owes a great deal to many professionals in the creative industry who have given us precious insights and comments.

Victionary

Future Editions

If you would like to contribute to the next edition of Victionary, please email us your details to submit@victionary.com